EDITING WITH UNDERSTANDING

★★★★★★★★★★★★★★★★★

Milton Hollstein
University of Utah

Larry Kurtz
University of Arizona

Editing with Understanding

A TEXTBOOK AND WORKBOOK

Macmillan Publishing Co., Inc.

New York

Collier Macmillan Publishers

London

Macmillan Publishing Co., Inc.
866 Third Avenue, New York, New York 10022

Collier Macmillan Canada, Ltd.

Library of Congress Cataloging in Publication Data

Hollstein, Milton Clifford.
    Editing with understanding.

    Includes index.
    1. Journalism.   I.   Kurtz, Larry, joint author.
II. Title.
PN4778.H58   070.4'1   80-14863
ISBN 0-02-356290-0

Printing: 1 2 3 4 5 6 7 8   Year: 1 2 3 4 5 6 7 8

PREFACE

Journalism courses offer an unusual opportunity to help students develop the ability to think critically. They allow not merely reading and discussion but *application* of knowledge and judgment. This is especially true in the editing course, which is by nature creative and critical.

A self-contained textbook-workbook allows students to apply the text discussions immediately and directly to identified problems. *Editing with Understanding* meets a need we have long felt, as teachers and newsmen, for a book that stresses editing as judgment rather than mere mechanics.

In the text matter we focus on concepts. Our hope is to speed learning by getting students rapidly through the most essential introductory matter and into discovery in the role of editorial decision maker. Our aim has been to provide exercise materials that are enjoyable, topical, and as realistic as possible.

Students who successfully complete this course will be self-starters as editors. They will recognize that a great deal of what is written for publication is wrongheaded and confusing. They will be better critics of their own work and therefore better reporters and writers. They will be more appreciative of stories that are clear, accurate, complete, and emphatic and less tolerant of those that are not.

We are grateful to the many media sources—newspapers of many kinds, news services, press agencies, syndicates, advertising offices—for the stories on which these exercises are based. Special thanks are due our own mentors and associates on the several papers and news service on which we have learned our craft, especially *The Salt Lake Tribune* and the Associated Press. Special thanks go to the *Deseret News* of Salt Lake City for permission to use a portion of a headline schedule and counter.

M. H.
L. K.

CONTENTS

★★★★★★★★★★★★★★★★★

PART I: THE NEWS FUNCTION

PART II: LANGUAGE

PART III: ACCURACY AND CREDIBILITY

Part I

★★★★★★★★★★★★★★★★

The News Function

1. INTRODUCTION

Editing. What is it? It's an art. The art of selecting and perfecting. A writer paints a picture with words; an editor sharpens the picture, bringing it into focus. The writer creates; the editor shapes.

Can you be an editor? Of course! But it takes time and thought, patience and practice. You can't become a good writer by reading about writing; you have to write. You can't become a good editor by reading about editing; you have to edit. That's why this textbook is also a workbook.

With few exceptions the stories in this book were written for newspapers and news services. They represent materials actually dealt with by editors, raw copy that had to be reshaped. The authors have taken liberties with some of this material, largely by inserting statements or errors against which editors should be on guard, to compress a comprehensive editing experience into one volume. Names and places are fictional in most stories.

Some of the articles contain more problems than are found in copy written by experienced reporters. They will give you an opportunity to make many editing decisions in a short time. Each editing exercise makes a learning point. And while this book is strongly oriented toward newspapers, the editing principles are applicable to all media work.

A major objective is simply to help you become a better writer. By working critically with the copy, that is, the written words of others, you will become a more thorough judge of your own work and more adept at revising your own material. Revision is an important part of all good writing, and for most writers it is the most painful. Your work in this course parallels that done on larger papers by a specialist called the copy editor. The copy editor works at the end of the assembly line in the copy flow that begins with the reporter or news

1

service report and ends in the delivery to the production department of the most competent literary product that can be created under deadline pressures.

On very large newspapers, copy desks specialize in departmental news. There's a sports desk, a world desk, and so on. This book, however, is organized to give you practice in handling a variety of stories, the kind of work that would be done on what is called the universal copy desk.

The copy editor works at the nerve center of production, where decisions constantly are being made about the character of the daily miracle called the newspaper. The copy editor is a key person. No expenditure for paper, ink, or machinery is nearly as important as that for the copy editor. He or she works with news about every facet of human behavior—with commentary, with columns and other fare that amuse and divert, with stories that help readers solve problems or promote projects that would fail if not brought to the attention of the readership. The material you deal with as a copy editor will help shape the values of those it reaches. Good editors believe in the hearts and minds of their readers—that if the press sheds light, the people can find the way.

Usually, the copy editor is the last person in the editorial office to read for content (as opposed to mere typographical errors) before the work appears on the page. The copy editor has the final responsibility for making certain the story is correct—in punctuation, spelling, grammar, rules of usage, organization and length, style and direction. Most important, the copy editor has the final responsibility for the story's accuracy.

The copy editor is a subeditor. Copy editors deal less with the problems of selection than with how material selected by others can be improved. Nonetheless, you will learn a great deal about media problems and practices by making some decisions about content, the kind that editors make hour in and hour out in every medium. You will judge the propriety of stories. Are the stories suitable for your audience in such matters as taste and fairness and objectivity? You will also judge them for completeness, which is a matter of knowing what your audience needs and expects to know.

Copy editing offers the skilled newcomer an entrance to newspaper work and provides opportunities to move into the managerial ranks through successively more important assignments involving not only more discretionary tasks but also supervisory functions.

If you were asked to identify the characteristics of a good newspaper, you'd probably focus on those things that characterize the work of a good editor. Let us suggest some. A good editor

- Respects writing and editing precision, showing respect for the strengths of language and an awareness of the pitfalls.
- Is willing to change old ways of doing things, adopting innovations and being alert to how the newspaper can better serve its readers.
- Understands the subjects a paper deals with, from local problems to international affairs.
- Sorts out the meaningful from the trivial.
- Gauges the needs and the psychology of readers; is aware of why they seek or shun the newspaper.
- Has the courage to tackle tough issues—socioeconomic and governmental problems even in once touchy fields, such as theology and race relations.

At the management level, one further strength characterizes good editors: the ability to develop a staff with these characteristics.

You've probably heard the term *gatekeeper*. A gatekeeper is a decision maker and a regulator. At the entrance to a closely guarded mansion, the gatekeeper will stop you if you lack the proper credentials for entry. You may be able to get past the gatekeeper with hard work, imagination, and argument. An editor is a gatekeeper too. Material that lacks the proper journalistic or literary credentials will not be admitted into the public domain by the conscientious editor. Sometimes persuasion will change an editor's mind, just as the gate-keeper to a mansion may be persuaded to admit an outsider who makes a convincing argument in lieu of showing credentials. An editor should be receptive to arguments, but the burden of persuasion must always rest upon the advocate. The editor promotes no causes, except the presentation of information as clearly and as fairly as it is possible for the human mind to present it.

As an editor, the more often you apply that standard, the more easily you will able to handle situations involving uncertainty—the initial report on an airplane crash or other tragedy, the translation of complex legal or medical terms into layman's language, or the tough decisions on when to go ahead with controversial information before all the facts are in. You'll be able to act with confidence, because you'll know what's required for your next step. You won't be fumbling in the hope that everything will work out all right.

Indeed, an ability to be quickly decisive is essential in an editor. Newspapers use only a small portion of the information available to them each day. There is no time for agonizing over whether to use or discard an item. Other copy is waiting to be judged.

You'll find a lot of guidelines in this book, the distilled thoughts of thousands of editors. Take them to heart. They've been forged by experience and they make good sense. Throughout this book the authors have dealt less with rules as such than with principles. During your professional career you'll be improvising on these guidelines as you grow and as your roles change. Guidelines should never become traps that stifle your creativity or that of the writers you help. But no creative person improvises without having mastered good models. The great musical composers improvised only after they were so grounded in composition that they felt justified in breaking with the past when their freedom of expression was at stake.

Do you want rules? Here are four:

- Make it accurate.
- Make it clear.
- Make it interesting.
- Make it useful to your readers.

Try it. If you succeed, you'll be an editor.

2. WHAT IS NEWS?

We all seem to know what news is when we see it or hear it, but we have trouble defining it. We are never likely to see a standard by which all material may be judged as news. News in a fan magazine differs strikingly from that in a business newspaper, just as the purposes and personalities of the publications differ.

At the extreme, everything is news to someone. Some argue, in justifying the pursuit and presentation of any and all information, regardless of taste, that, "It happened. There-fore, it's news." As an editor, you will sharpen your judgments as you deal with the material that crosses your desk. Most likely, you will adopt a more restrictive position than the one just cited, particularly as you become aware of the wide rivers of words trying to squeeze into the relatively narrow channels of dissemination available. You will find yourself judging stories against each other on such factors as importance, interest, timeliness, and length. You will find yourself in disagreement with other editors. Human interaction and time and space constraints are as much a part of what emerges as news as are factors more readily reduced to definition.

Pick up a dozen newspapers on any given day. Chances are you will find few duplications, except on events of such overriding interest that to ignore them would be to perform a disservice. News, then, is largely a matter of choice. At the same time, an editor should be aware of traditions, trends, conventional wisdoms, and realities on which decisions are made.

In this book you will be asked to judge whether some stories are worth using at all. Even for the subeditor, whose primary function is to check copy rather than to select, it is essential to know about the nature of news.

Consider these definitions:

- News is anything that's interesting, or should be.
- News is anything that varies from the reader's accustomed picture of the world.
- News is anything the editor decides is news.

There's a lot of leeway here. You may have heard the claim that journalists merely hold up a mirror to society. The argument goes, "We don't make the news, we just report it," and, "We have an obligation to mirror society, warts and all." Mirror-image definitions are handy in their simplicity. They also shift the onus for news judgments from journalists to society. However, many journalists reject the mirror-image idea on the grounds that society is not reflected on the front pages of newspapers or on the evening television news. Most of us are not involved in summit conferences, airplane crashes, fires, or gold buying.

In oversimplified terms, news has long been pervaded by the "man bites dog" theory—the emphasis on the unusual or the spectacular. If a dog bites a man, that isn't news. If a man bites a dog, it's front page. When 50,000 people leave a soccer stadium, it's not news. If one person tries to fight back in against the mob, that's news. Every Sunday, millions attend church. That's not news. But if in one congregation someone shoots an usher, that's news.

News also is much more. It's trends, patterns, personalities, explanations, and information with no foundation in events. In short, formal definitions are hopelessly passé in today's world. This is because of changes in audiences and their media preferences and habits; changes in media competition; the increasing complexity of events; and the changing sources of news.

Coverage of fixed geographical boundaries is giving way to coverage of psychological areas, and the "beats" of bygone days are being restructured or abolished. Some newspaper editors no longer believe in having a reporter visit the same offices day in and day out, collecting information and developing contacts. Instead, they ask reporters to take a more thoughtful approach—offering ideas, drawing up questions, studying records, and otherwise practicing news coverage by initiative instead of by reaction.

People who say newspapers concentrate on sensationalism because they have to fill up the white space between advertisements show little understanding of the industry. The same is true of those who say newspapers select certain stories "to sell papers."

First, there is far more material available to even the smallest daily newspaper than can possibly be printed in any given edition. In this world of 4 billion people, a typical newspaper wrestles with a glut of words that comes not only from its staff, but also from many outside sources: from volunteers who want to get their stories told; from public relations practitioners who want to enhance the image of a product, a company, or a point of view; and from the international news agencies, which pour a nonstop flow of words across the desks of editors who seldom have more than a few seconds to evaluate each item.

Second, newspapers no longer rely on street sales and extra editions. About three-quarters of a paper's revenue comes from advertising, most of the rest from home subscriptions. The newspaper essentially is sold before it ever reaches the reader. There is little head-to-head competition between newspapers in this era of consolidation.

Nothing has done more to alter conceptions of news than the proliferation of media. Few hamlets are too remote to receive a television or radio signal, to be included within the primary coverage area of both daily and weekly newspapers, or to have a newsstand.

No medium can be careless in its choice of content. Each must define its audience, its approach to that audience, and its form of presentation. While some audiences are defined geographically, as in the case of a community newspaper, others are defined demographically, according to the age, interest, occupation, sex, or other characteristics of the reader sought. Within geographical entities, publications must weigh their products against the competing influences of others.

The Audience

Each medium's conception of who reads or listens to what helps determine the selection of news. Despite criticism of newspaper standardization, for instance, some papers are uninhibited in their portrayal of life. Others are sober and conservative. Some are timid in approaching news sources and fear to give offense. Others are militant and crusading. Some major metropolitan papers try to be national in scope, serving as newspapers of record. Others concentrate on their immediate locale. Some are rigidly patterned. Others adapt to the changing lifestyles of their audiences. Some editors strive to make their papers as comprehensive as possible on the assumption that the newspaper alone is the medium of completeness. Others believe the newspaper is only one of so many media choices available to the reader that no publication can be all things to all people.

There are about 1,760 daily newspapers in the United States. The number has remained relatively constant over the past generation, although some newspapers die (predominantly competing newspapers in the major metropolitan centers), while others are born (largely in the suburbs and smaller communities). Additionally, 9,000 weekly newspapers, 12,000 industrial publications or house organs, 2,500 business papers and magazines, and 800 consumer magazines cater to specific tastes and needs.

In recent years a new area of psychological research has aimed to determine what readers seek from their daily newspaper, or to identify the psychological dispositions of readers. Some studies have concluded that readers look to a paper for a psychological lift, depending on it for the satisfaction of emotional needs. One such study found psychological proximity more important than geographical proximity in attracting reader interest.

Approach to Audience

Most publications attempt to emphasize the themes that appeal to a particular locality: the dominant local business, the primary personalities of the region, local projects of government and business. Most also develop success stories about local people. They are sometimes accused of boosterism and trivialization of the news, but no story is trivial to everyone.

Larger metropolitan papers go beyond the local scene in their in-depth reports, offering material not available in suburban papers of the area.

The Formula

Most newspapers, regardless of size, follow a fairly standardized pattern of presenting news. Increasingly, this pattern falls into departments. The major departments are local news (or area, county, city or metro news, as defined by the paper), sports, lifestyle (an increasingly popular substitute for what used to be called women's or society sections), entertainment, business, and comics. Within these broad designations, considerable improvisation is possible. Some papers reserve Page One for national and international news. Others give local copy first priority. Some have extensive business pages, complete with closing stock quotations. The formula is dictated by both the total audience and the specialized segments within it.

The serious student of the press, trying to fathom how it works and influences its readers, should recognize that news judgment nowadays is based on balances and compromises. These are dictated by the social and political atmosphere, the receptivity of the audience, the zeal and competence of the newsgatherers, the climate of openness and tolerance among newsmakers, and economic factors.

Economics often determines content. Advertising volume, which frequently claims up to 70 percent of the space, determines the size of the news hole. The financial soundness of the paper determines how much can be spent on staffing and on purchase of news service and syndicate material. Production methods dictate whether news breaking close to deadlines can be included or whether pages already made up can be made over to accommodate better copy.

The traditional indicators of news judgment are *proximity*, the nearness of an event to the audience both geographically and psychologically; *consequence*, or the effects of an event; *magnitude*, or the numbers involved, both in human and monetary terms; and *timeliness*, or recency. Journalists in the United States have been tuned to these indicators and react to them automatically. That these factors are in flux does not negate their importance. It does, however, suggest that some other, broader generalizations may better serve the student seeking to understand news.

1. *News is relative.* News judgments vary not only from place to place, time to time, and culture to culture but also from one publication to another in the same time and place.

News judgment is not the same from day to day within the same publication. It is dictated by what is in hand. Not all days offer the same news choices. Some days offer an incredible confluence of stories that, under prevailing conceptions of what makes news, cannot be ignored. Others don't offer the same choices of important or breaking stories. To some extent, this is a problem of format. Some of the judgments on what makes Page One are dictated by the need to leaven, or lighten, the page. Similarly, judgments of what goes into a television news broadcast are conditioned by the need to entertain and to pace the presentation.

A great deal of newspaper content is predictable, because events that must be covered are cyclical. There is a certainty that news of tax decisions, graduations, and such will appear on appointed dates. Planned news—anticipated news—may account for four-fifths of the content of any publication. Nonetheless, hard news or "breaking" news—unanticipated news—often will displace the planned story.

2. *News is event oriented.* For generations the telling of news has consisted principally in the telling of events. The press reports the big events, swarming over them and attempting to report every conceivable nuance. This has become increasingly true in the television age. Some critics deplore the media's concern for the episodic—the surface aspects of a situation. They argue that the media must get away from the idea that news involves only the present moment, since much news goes on for months or years. They are distressed by the thought that readers need to be titillated every day, regardless of the significance of the news. They call for reporting that shows the dynamism and continuity and interrelationships of human affairs.

There also is criticism of excessive attention to the pseudo-event—the demonstration, press conference, beauty contest, anniversary, or award staged or contrived to draw media attention. Sponsors of contrived events often are knowledgeable about deadlines and other media logistics. They recognize traditional news indicators and the realities of competition. Contrived events usually are easy to cover and thus provide the media with inexpensive sources of news. Contrived events frequently command space that would otherwise be given to more important material.

Critics complain of event-centered reporting of public affairs like presidential campaigns. They say such reporting leaves the American public confused despite the acres of newsprint devoted to the races. They call for less preoccupation with the horserace aspects, such as which candidate seems to have momentum, and for more attention to how candidates respond to the issues.

A historian and newspaperman, Allan Nevins, once observed that an event is merely "a force made momentarily visible," and that it is far more difficult to report the undercurrents. Walter Lippmann observed as early as the 1920s that the press was good at reporting the obvious but less than adequate in trying to put forces into focus.

Since the dawn of the atomic age and America's increased involvement in world affairs, press critics have been calling for objective interpretation of events. In 1947, a private committee of nonjournalists conducted an inquiry into the conditions necessary for the maintenance of a free and responsible press. It cited a need to put news "into a context that gives it meaning."

In the 1960s, the Associated Press and United Press International began to reshape their news packages to include more interpretive material. To make the point that news has changed, UPI once compared contemporary news coverage with the biggest stories for the year 1928, noting the growing complexity and interrelationships of big news events over the years. In 1928, the big story of the year was the electrocution of Ruth Snyder and Henry Judd Grey for the slaying of Mrs. Snyder's magazine-editor husband in New York. The second biggest story was Herbert Hoover's defeat of Al Smith for the Presidency. The murder of Arnold Rothstein, the New York gambler, made the top ten. So did the launching of a German liner, *Europa*, and Captain Malcolm Campbell's speed record on the Utah Salt Flats. These stories all were nicely contained, simple and concrete, generally unrelated to each other.

Contrast that with the top UPI stories of 50 years later: In 1978, UPI's top headline stories were the Guyana mass killings; the Middle East peace talks; the deaths of two popes and the election of a third; and the U.S. economy and the dollar's decline. The news service's most significant stories, reflecting editors' appreciation of the difference between headline value and importance, were the Middle East peace talks; the U.S. economy; California's Proposition 13; and the Guyana mass killings. These stories were much broader than the simpler, singular events of 1928, indicating the fashion in which editors see news nowadays not only as single events but as a series of complicated issues.

Similarly, UPI rated the ten most important news events of the 1970s largely on the basis of their long-term significance, in this order: the resignation of President Nixon, the energy crisis, the end of the Vietnam War, inflation and the decline of the dollar, war and peace in the Middle East, the Guyana deaths, United States–China relations, the nuclear accident at Three Mile Island, space exploration, and the ouster of the Shah of Iran. The Nixon resignation was of course not a single event but the culmination of a long investigation and had long-term ramifications.

The Associated Press once told its staffers and members that there are two kinds of news: "One is the raw event as it happens. The other is the news behind the news—the submerged dimension of why and how, the interplay of concealed force that casts up spot news as waves cast up foam. Both forms need to be covered fully. But in our intricate world, very often it is the second kind of news that is the real news, that deserves the big headlines. The meaning is the message." Recognize that news is more than random events. However, the specific event continues to dominate the headlines.

3. *News is personality oriented.* Names make news. The doings of people who influence or stimulate us make news. People are interested in people. We all cherish the humanized and personalized situation. Any story is more interesting if it deals with the human dimension—not processes or impersonal concepts, but people working with them. Our interest is not so much in the epidemic as in the little, white-haired doctor who worked around the clock to stem it. The personalized situation is the stock in trade of the news magazines,

which from their beginning have featured personalities on their covers and built their stories around people. Personalities always have commanded attention in fan magazines. More recently, they have been the focus of newer, general-interest magazines such as those sold in supermarkets.

It is a rare editor who does not recognize the magnetism of the people approach. At the same time, scientists, businessmen, and others concerned with processes complain that the essential point of their work often is obscured by accounts of interesting but insignificant incidents involving people. Another complaint is that journalism has developed a peep-show mentality by focusing on the foibles and private lives of the so-called beautiful people, the rich and famous.

4. *News reflects opportunity.* Often news selection and display depend simply on opportunity for coverage. Many areas of the world lie fallow, wanting for news coverage because it is uneconomical to cover them. Most news from abroad comes from areas of conflict—the Congo in the early 1960s, Vietnam in the late 1960s, Iran in the last few years, Afghanistan in 1980—because conflict demands the kind of attention that tranquility does not. Journalism responds to crises—to conflagrations. This is the so-called firehorse syndrome.

Censorship by governments and pressure from advertisers also affect opportunity. More often, opportunity is affected by the decision-makers in the news industry. How much do they demand? Are they willing to settle for the easy stories, the contrivances of special interest groups and the predictable products of news beats? Or do they allocate their resources of money and personnel in such a way as to create opportunities?

5. *News judgments help a public dialogue go on.* The role that any nation assigns to its press determines what will be reported and how. In the communist nations, what makes news is not events or personalities but processes. The press is not assigned the role of pleasing the people with trivia. This is because the party and government have determined that the press must propagandize for the aims of the society as determined by the ruling apparatus. Crimes are reported only when reporting them serves to make a particular point. What we would regard as major events, such as forest fires and airplane crashes, may not be reported to the public at all, even when these disasters involve many victims, and they are especially unlikely to be printed or aired when they reflect adversely on the regime. Access to newsmakers by the press is severely limited, and unpopular ideas are not aired.

On the other hand, in a democratic system, we believe that no one has a monopoly on good ideas. The truth is not something to be decided by one ideology, one person, or one clique. What is best for society emerges from a multitude of opinions expressed in an open marketplace of ideas.

Good news-gathering procedures and sound news judgments reflect this philosophy. Meetings of boards and commissions are reported in depth and ideas of dissenters are probed to reveal the clash of ideas. People of all kinds are interviewed, and political and social conflicts are investigated.

Ideally the media serve as a sounding board of opinion by giving this direct access to even unpopular ideas. When people in a democratic society feel their views can be represented in the press, there are few complaints about lack of access to media. In recent years some groups have complained, however, about lack of access. Some have demanded a legal right to have their ideas printed in the paper as well as broadcast on the public airwaves. Some groups have resorted to contrived or pseudo events, such as demonstrations, which they know will be reported under prevailing conceptions of what makes news.

6. *News judgments are contagious.* Despite what has been said about the individual personalities of the media, all of them take cues from others. Media directed at the same audience monitor each other carefully. Newspapers often complain that radio stations steal their news, either through rewriting or by "ripping and reading" from the wire services, which use newspapers heavily as source material. At the same time, newspapers monitor

television newscasts and radio broadcasts. On the national level, the *New York Times* is much more influential than its 800,000 circulation would suggest. It is monitored by the networks, the news services, and other major newspapers. How the *Times* plays the news is a factor in decisions by other papers. Critics often complain that excesses of media coverage stem from "pack journalism," that is, the process by which media gravitate toward stories developed by others. Editors at the *Washington Post*, the newspaper that broke the Watergate story, said they were appalled by the "shark frenzy" that emerged in other media after the *Post* first exposed the Nixon administration scandal. Other characteristics of news could be listed. These, however, encompass the broad base.

The problem for both the media and the audience is not a lack of information, but congestion. Increasingly, it is not a qualitative problem but a quantitative one: What does one need to hear or read to be informed? Many of the media's problems stem from reader impatience with the deluge of information. Viewers and readers more and more ask the media to move through to an ultimate answer. Writers and broadcasters increasingly predict events and forecast outcomes, instead of merely reporting and analyzing. When their predictions are wrong, their credibility sags.

Vermont Royster, in a bit of self-proclaimed heresy on the blessings of ignorance, said when he was a *Wall Street Journal* editor, "It's no disgrace for the housewife wrestling with diapers not to read the *New York Times* from cover to cover. In real life, there are as many worlds as there are inhabitants of it, and each man's world is very small indeed." Royster also suggested that some people need all the news they can get about the balance of payments, the shortage of water, and other subjects, but "there's no virtue in pounding ourselves with each of them every minute of the day." Some have suggested that there's little that absolutely must be printed or broadcast, that it is sufficient if enough of a sustained nature is carried about recurring problems to permit intelligent and concerned citizens to make informed decisions.

As an editor, as a gatekeeper for the flow of information, you have a difficult task in deciding what to emphasize and what to reject. At the very least, you must keep in mind the importance of constant reflection and not succumb to the lure of easy formulas.

3. WHERE NEWS COMES FROM

Where does news come from? Everywhere. Sources vary among media outlets. Some rely entirely on their own staffs. Others rely entirely on submissions from free-lance writers. In between is a vast array utilizing a combination of sources.

Because we are emphasizing newspapers, we will outline a variety of sources on which newspapers depend. The degree to which any newspaper relies on a given source depends on many factors, including the size of the paper, its location, the economic conditions of the community, and other variables. However, most newspapers obtain their material through these sources:

Staff Writers

All newspapers use staffers to cover events in the community and to write feature stories, editorials, columns, and other material. Some writers have specific assignments, or "beats," such as local government, politics, police, business, and one or more sports. Working with their editors, using their own imagination, and keeping track of events on the public agenda, they generate a constant flow of information to the public. Some writers have no regular beat but cover whatever is assigned to them. These are known as general assignment reporters. They report at an assigned time and do whatever is asked. They may cover a club meeting, a fire, and a speech all in the same day. The next day they may find themselves researching an in-depth report on city financing.

Still other writers seldom leave the office. These are known as rewrite people. Usually among the most skillful writers on the staff, they take notes from reporters in the field and turn the raw information into coherent stories. They also are asked to rewrite some stories turned in by reporters or to rewrite information provided by other sources, such as public relations people.

Depending on the size of the newspaper, there may be a single writer for each of the major sports beats—high school events, baseball, football, basketball, and so on, or a single person may be responsible for all sports. The same is true of editorials and columns. On very large papers there are specialists on seemingly every conceivable topic, from agriculture to zoos. These people develop expertise in their areas and seldom venture into others in their writing. They also develop story ideas on their own, based on current issues, community interests, or their personal leanings. Frequently, they get ideas from the contacts in the areas they cover or from the general public in the form of phone calls, letters, or casual conversations at social gatherings.

Obviously, it is an unscientific and imperfect system. Reporters tend to gravitate toward sources who will talk freely and frequently. Those who prefer to stay in the background may never have their stories told. This is particularly true in government and legislative action. Some talky officials and legislators are quoted almost daily. Others never are heard from. Still, a conscientious newspaper will do its best to inform its community of both interesting and important matters. It is likely that events or issues of serious concern will find their way into print eventually, even if not always in timely fashion.

Stringers

Many newspapers circulate across a wide geographical area, sometimes more than 100 miles from the main office. It would be a waste of money to send a reporter a great distance to cover a public meeting of marginal interest or a sports event of routine proportions, so newspapers make arrangements with residents in the given area to telephone information to the main office, where a rewrite person turns the material into a story.

Many stringers do not have newspaper experience but have been instructed on the type of information desired. They may be paid by the number of words that appear in print, by the number of stories they submit, by a flat retainer fee, or by any of a number of mutually agreeable financial arrangements. Stringers often are encouraged to mail in story ideas or, if they have previous newspaper experience, to submit stories on their own. Larger newspapers may station staff reporters in strategic outlying locations, providing them with a telephone or, in the case of the most advanced publications, an electronic writing device connected to the main office's computer.

Publicity Releases

Each day, the bulk of a newspaper's mail consists of publicity releases from a variety of business and governmental sources. These are known in the trade as *handouts*. Editors generally look on this material with a bittersweet attitude. On the one hand, it is a nuisance to go through a mountain of material on a given day to find only a few items of local interest and at the same time know that what is accepted amounts to free advertising for the source. On the other hand, such releases often provide useful background or timely information that otherwise would require much staff time to develop. The editor–public relations relationship is examined in the section on public relations in Part IV.

News Services

A major source of nonlocal news for most newspapers is one or both of the two major news services, The Associated Press and United Press International. These organizations, with offices in every major U.S. city and scores of foreign countries, feed newspapers with a never-ending flow of information, which arrives by teletype machine or, to an increasing degree, by computer-to-computer transmission.

The teletypewriter is known as the wire, and news delivered by it or directly into a computer at the newspaper office is still called wire news. Editors who work with this news are called the wire editors and the daily report of all the news is known simply as the wire. The term *telegraph editor*, a throwback to the early days of the century when news was received by dot–dash telegraphy, still can be heard in some newspaper shops.

Unless you are reading one of the few national newspapers that can afford to have its own reporters stationed in key cities worldwide, most of the national and world news you read in your newspaper will be bylined by Associated Press or by United Press International or carry the symbol (AP) or (UPI). AP and UPI, with headquarters in New York, rely on their own staffs and on the cooperation of newspapers and stringers to provide them with information, which they transmit simultaneously to their clients. A story under an (AP) or (UPI) logotype may have been prepared by a news service reporter, rewritten from a newspaper, or fashioned from the notes of a stringer or a broadcaster. The same holds true of stories from surrounding states.

Why would a newspaper permit a news service to rewrite its material? It comes down to a "you-scratch-my-back-and-I'll-scratch-yours" philosophy. At the basic level, if the community served by newspaper A is interested in a baseball game being played in the community served by newspaper B, it is in the interest of both papers that newspaper B provide the score and other information to the local news service outlets. That way, when the situation is reversed, newspaper B can rightfully expect the same kind of cooperation from newspaper A. It doesn't always work that way, but the sharing philosophy has operated for more than a century and tends to serve the nation's news media well.

The news services, which are responsible for what moves across their circuits, rewrite the information they receive from newspapers or other sources. They also develop a great deal of original copy. A discussion of news service work is provided in the chapter on the news services and wire copy in Part IV.

Syndicate Material

You've seen columns on home repairs, medicine, personal problems, wine, food, travel, and a number of other subjects. A number of these are distributed nationally through a syndicate that sells the same material to many newspapers. In the past the material was mailed to newspapers and, because of its professional quality, was seldom edited locally. More recently, some newspapers have begun to receive the material electronically. This information, also known as "canned" copy, usually is timeless, meaning that it can be published any time without losing its value. It is not usually pegged to an event of the moment, except in the case of political columns. Newspaper editors often find themselves deluged with "canned" offerings and easily could fill their pages with it if they chose to subscribe to a number of syndicated services.

Free-Lance Material

Some people earn a living the hard way—by submitting material to publications without knowing whether it will be accepted. Some are quite successful, but most who attempt it earn meager monetary rewards. Newspapers are cautious about accepting free-lance material, often because they do not know the reliability of the source, but now and then newspapers do buy free-lance material on specific subjects.

Tips

Even given the vast amount of material available from the sources already listed, newspapers have yet another source: the tip. Tips can come in the form of phone calls or letters, often anonymous, from members of the public or from business interests or govern-ment employees. Sometimes newspapers receive documents from unknown sources, a phe-nomenon known as getting news "over the transom." Some newspapers invite such tips and award cash prizes for the best tip of the week or month. Editors reason, with justification, that this is a busy world and that they may easily miss an event or issue of interest to the community at large.

Other Sources

There are other sources: books; scientific, scholarly, and trade publications; even neighbors and friends of people who write and edit news. Again, news literally comes from everywhere.

As mentioned earlier, the extent to which a given newspaper will rely on one source as opposed to others depends on many factors. To draw a hypothetical contrast covering both ends of the daily newspaper spectrum:

The Daily Clarion has a circulation of more than 100,000 in a metropolitan area. It has several "beat" reporters, each covering a specific area. It also has a staff of general assignment reporters. Its sports department has specialists. It employs a staff of three editorial writers. It has a drama and art critic, a political columnist, and several rewrite people. One editor is assigned exclusively to edit news service and syndicate copy. Another handles local copy. Roles are clearly defined and specialized. Editor A, concentrating on the material and the pages assigned, likely will not know what editor B is doing across the aisle until the newspaper comes off the press.

The Daily Bugle has a circulation of 3,000 in a rural area. It has only two editors—the managing editor and the sports editor. The managing editor reads all nonsports copy—news service, local, and syndicate—and knows where every story will be placed in the newspaper. Editorials also may be part of this editor's responsibility. Two reporters cover the local scene, carrying out both beat and general assignment responsibilities.

On both papers, the process of putting the product together is much more complex and involves more people than have been mentioned here. This overview, however, should be helpful to you when you visit a newspaper plant.

SELECTED READINGS

Boorstin, Daniel J. *The Image: A Guide to Pseudo-Events in America.* New York: Harper & Row, 1963. "About our arts of self-deception," particularly valuable on how news gathering and news making feed on contrived events. A widely quoted book for many years.

Commission on Freedom of the Press. *A Free and Responsible Press.* Chicago: University of Chicago Press, 1947. Recommendations on how the press must perform if it is to remain free. A historic inquiry important to anyone with an interest in press ethics and responsibility. Stresses the need to put news into a "context that gives it meaning."

Epstein, Edward Jay. *News from Nowhere.* New York: Random House, 1973. A study of network news operation. Valuable for understanding how news decisions are made in media generally.

Gans, Herbert J. *Deciding What's News.* New York: Pantheon Books, 1979. A sociologist's attempt to analyze how news is selected for presentation on the CBS Evening News and NBC Nightly News and at *Newsweek* and *Time.*

Lippmann, Walter. *Public Opinion.* New York: The Free Press, 1965. The great classic volume, originally published in the early 1920s. The late political pundit tells how decisions on public questions are made on the basis of myths and stereotypes, the "pictures in our heads," and discusses the limita-tions of the press in providing information to guide public policy.

Mills, Nicolaus. *The New Journalism: A Historical Anthology.* New York: McGraw-Hill, 1974. Several books in the 1970s looked into the New Journalism movement. This is an anthology of 40 articles on the press's "literary innovations as a response to pressures in American life."

Monaco, James. *Celebrity: The Media as Image Makers.* New York: Dell, 1978. How and why celebrities are made by the media.

Tuchman, Gaye. *Making News: A Study in the Construction of Reality.* New York: The Free Press, 1978. An attempt to learn about news as a "social construction of reality," with description and examples.

4. PREPARING NEWS COPY

In this course, we will do our editing with a pencil. Sometimes, rewriting on the typewriter or videoscreen is necessary to make copy clean and coherent. You will find it necessary to retype only two or three of the exercises in this book. You will have to rearrange some with scissors and paste and mark some quite heavily.

Make all the necessary marks, using the appropriate symbols. Give plenty of directions to the printer. Don't overedit or butcher the copy. Make only changes you find needed or desirable—no unnecessary marks. Make all your penciled editing marks firm and distinct. You should use a No. 2 soft pencil. Erase where necessary.

You may wish, or may be asked, to explain to the instructor any changes you make. Write out explanatory matter in the margin and draw a circle around it, just as you would write out instructions to the printer. You will find this necessary in some assignments where you might reject a story because of libel, poor taste, or incompleteness.

The major copy-editing symbols are indicated at the end of this section. Although some neophytes look on them as hieroglyphics, most of the symbols are little more than common-sense marks. When a word or phrase is to be deleted, it is simply lined out. When two words that have been run together in the typing are to be separated, a line is simply drawn between them. To insert a period, use a circled dot (or sometimes an x). Most of the relatively unusual marks just speed the process along.

Any marking system that makes clear to the printer what changes are needed is acceptable. Practices vary among publications. For example, some papers use a CQ ("correct as written") mark above words with varied spellings or words that might be challenged unless some indication is given that they have been checked. Other papers ask editors to draw a box around the word, and some even underline it, though this practice is risky because underlining also is used commonly to italicize. Some papers insist that double dashes (- -) be used to indicate the dash and that parallel dashes be used (=) for hyphens.

Copy editors sometimes borrow from proofreaders some marks, such as the delete or "dele" mark (℘) or the space mark (#). Proofreading is the marking of needed corrections in the proof, or the material after it has been set in type. It is not the same as copy editing. Proofreading marks have been developed to be used in tight space. Occasionally you will find these marks helpful in editing copy, but it is not necessary to use them consistently—for example, a deletion mark in addition to lining out is superfluous in copy editing. Superfluous proofreading marks simply mess up the copy and make typesetting more difficult. Keep your copy as clean as possible. Avoid lots of arrows showing how copy is to be rearranged. It's better to cut and paste or line out and rewrite.

Make sure every story has a slug line, a word or at most two clearly indicative of the story. (Avoid common slugs like "Fire," since they are not sufficiently indicative of any one story. Similarly, stories about the president of the United States rarely are slugged "President" but rather "President-Trip.")

The slug is written on the story by the reporter but may be changed by the makeup editor. The slug may not be changed by the copy editor even if it seems inappropriate. The reason is that the slug follows the story through the entire production process and the story slug on the proof is matched with layout dummy, or blueprint that tells where the story is to be placed in the paper. In some small shops, the slugline is written by the headline writer because that person also is laying out the paper. Also make sure every story has an end mark, usually the sharp (#). In some shops a -30- or a notation of the time the story is completed and submitted is used. All extraneous material should be lined out, including the name of the reporter where it appears on the copy. In some shops all pages or "takes" of a story are pasted together; in most, succeeding pages are numbered, either as "add 1/Nuclear," "add 2/Nuclear," or "page 2/Nuclear," "page 3/Nuclear," etc. At the bottom of each page the word *More* is used when more is to follow. In some exercises in this book the slugline, end marks, subsequent page numbers, and *More* have been deliberately excluded to give you practice in writing them in. All these marks should be circled.

COPYREADING SYMBOLS

PURPOSE	EXAMPLE
To mark beginning of paragraph	Two persons were
	baseball
To insert a word	The player
To insert a letter	Two persos were
To change a letter	The bay returned
To change a word	The ~~murderer~~ *accused* said that
To delete a word	The ~~handsome~~ bridegroom
To delete a letter	The Uhniversity of Michigan
To close up a space	News paper
To separate words	Mr. Jones replied
To transpose letters	Clalifornia
To capitalize a letter	Gov. jones
To change to lower case	Several Persons were
To indicate boldface	A later bulletin reported
To indicate italics	Other developments
To indicate abbreviation	(Senator) Jones declared
To indicate no abbreviation	He lived in (Calif.)
To indicate a figure	(Twenty-seven) times

PURPOSE	EXAMPLE
To transpose words	Salt/City\Lake
To write out a number	③ women testified
To indicate a period	Dr⊗Smith said
To restore copy marked out	She ~~later~~ *stet* said

EXERCISES

Edit the following paragraphs, using the appropriate symbols: The stories need no substantive changes but do require considerable marking.

FOR most acuet hart attakt victums, the special emergency aid they recieve imediately is all that stand s between them and death   And the cost for this, about fifty-nine dollars per case is a bargain by anyones standards

Hughes Aircraft took advantage this of provision to get a $12,000 refund on duties duties paid for raw materials that wnt into a dimond porthole on the pioneer venus II spacecraft when which fell to the survace of Venus last December.

Despite public concern that terrorists could steal Plutonium to make Atomic Weapons, the Nuclear Regulatory Commission publishes a virtual guidetobreaking into a plutonium plant.

Christopher Tolkien, son of the late British author

JRR Tolkien, hassigned with Caedmon, the New York-based produccer

of spoken word records and tapes, to record portions of
      father's
his tale sof Middle-earth and it's elves, The Silmarillion.

The paragraphs as edited, using the appropriate symbols:

FØR most acuet) hart attak victums, the special

emergency aid they recieve imediately is all that stand s

between them and death. And the cost for this, about

fifty-nine dollars) per case, is a bargain by anyones standards.

Hughes Aircraft took advantage this of provision to

get a $12,000 refund

on duties ~~duties~~ paid for raw materials that wnt into a

dimond porthole on the pioneer venus II spacecraft, ~~when~~

which fell to the surface of Venus last December.

Despite public concern that terrorists could steal

Plutonium to make Atomic Weapons, the Nuclear Regulatory

Commission publishes a virtual guide to breaking into a

plutonium plant.

Christopher Tolkien, son of the late British author

JRR. Tolkien, has signed with Caedmon, the New York-based producer

of spoken word records and tapes, to record portions of
      father's
his tale sof Middle-earth and it/s elves, "The Silmarillion."

5. ELECTRONIC EDITING

Media are deeply involved in technological changes. Print media have been supplemented and challenged by commercial, public, cable and pay television, films, computerized informational storage and retrieval systems, video cassettes, and even a call-up system in which pages of print can be displayed on the TV tube. Print itself has undergone a revolution in production. A corresponding revolution is taking place in the transmission of data over long distances through satellites, lasers, microwaves, and optical fibers. The lead time for translating technical innovations into commercially viable systems also is diminishing. It took 112 years for photography to be applied widely on a commercial basis, 35 for radio, 15 for television, and five for the transistor.

Newspapers have been involved in a revolution that is reshaping the face of the industry. You've seen pictures of newspaper editors. They're the ones with the green eyeshades, the suspenders, the scissors, pencils, and pastepots. They're the people sitting at those untidy desks piled high with unruly stacks of paper. Right? Not quite.

Times have changed, and they're still changing. If you look hard enough, you can still find a few of those old-style editors, but they're the exceptions to the rule. Today's editor sits in front of what looks like a keyboard-equipped television set. That's the scissors, pencils, pastepots, and paper—all in one neat package. Call it whatever you choose: VDT (video display terminal), CRT (cathode ray tube), terminal, tube, or scope. It will be years before the industry agrees on a term, so we'll use yet another: *videoscreen.*

Electronics has transformed the newspaper industry. Nowadays, newsrooms look a lot like insurance offices, banks, or travel agencies. If you want to be an editor, you'd better be ready to play with electronic keyboards. Don't worry. It isn't half as hard as it looks or sounds. It's just different. You'll learn enough from this book to get you started, no matter what type of equipment you encounter.

Keep this in mind: Some things won't change, regardless of technology. Editing skills are among them. Historic tools of the printing industry, such as the metal linecasting machine, have all but vanished. Today's techniques may be obsolete tomorrow. But the editor will always be essential. Remember that point as you read the following pages and familiarize yourself with the new electronics, the kind with which you're likely to work.

It's important that you understand the new electronics, because in the time it will take you to finish this course several more newspapers will have converted from old-style methods. Someday, all newspapers will be electronic. All reporters and editors will use videoscreens. It does not take long to master most electronic keyboards, particularly if you are a good typist. However, you're a step ahead if you can tell a prospective employer you've had experience with videoscreens.

If you have an opportunity to visit an electronic newsroom, do so. You are certain to learn something helpful simply by watching. Every newsroom has a slightly different method of operation, so it really doesn't matter which one you visit—just so it's electronic. Visit an electronic newspaper office even if the school where you are taking this course has its own video equipment. It will give you that much more perspective, and every little bit helps.

Videoscreens are quite new to an industry that before their arrival hadn't changed technologically in decades. In 1969, when man first landed on the moon, newspapers were being produced in this fashion: Reporters wrote their copy on typewriters and delivered it to editors. After changes had been penciled in and a headline written, a story would be placed in a pneumatic tube and sent to the backshop. There a linecasting operator would reproduce the story on a keyboard that transformed the typewritten word into raised metal type for the press, a line at a time. The metal type would be inked and a paper impression, or proof, made by placing a slip of paper over the type and applying pressure. A proofreader would check the copy for typographical errors, comparing it with the original. Any errors would be corrected by the preparation of as many new metal lines as necessary to replace the erroneous ones, and the proof process would be repeated for the corrected lines. The same process was used for headlines, which were set either by machine or by hand.

For stories received over teletypes of Associated Press or United Press International the process was similar, except that the metal version could be produced automatically through use of perforated paper that could be fed through the linecasting machines. The original copy still had to be read, edited, assigned a headline, and proofread—just as with locally produced copy. You can imagine how much time and manpower was involved in such an operation. Newspapers had operated in this fashion for decades, without significant change and with little variation among papers large and small. Basically, if you had seen one newspaper operation, you had seen them all. Eventually, however, newspaper owners determined that they could not forever edure the escalating costs of production under conventional methods. So began a revolution that started slowly, but grew with ever-quickening speed and in less than a generation has reshaped the face of the industry. The revolution took several forms, but all were motivated by a common desire to reduce production manpower and therefore costs.

The first dramatic change was implementation of so-called cold type, photographically based makeup that has replaced the traditional metal makeup in most papers. Perforated paper tape was important in early cold type operations. It was fed into phototypesetting machines, which automatically produced paper—instead of metal—versions of original copy. The metal linecasting machine and its operator were bypassed. Some newspapers hired typists to produce this paper tape. Others invested in machines that would read an entire page of copy instantly and spit out the appropriate paper tape. This latter system, commonly called the scanner technique, is being replaced, because of advancements in videoscreen technology.

The move away from traditional practices brought with it a transformation in the physical appearance of newspaper offices. Without the noise, heat, and dirt of the backshop, the newsroom and the composing room could be moved closer together. Instead of being separated by several floors, they could be adjacent.

Cold type cleared the way for implementation of the videoscreen, perhaps the most dramatic innovation in the modern history of printing because of the changes it has wrought to date and the potential it holds for the future. The videoscreen has eliminated a great many typesetting and proofreading jobs. Videoscreens can be connected directly to phototypesetting machines, eliminating the need for perforated tape. Local and news service copy can be stored in a computer and called up for electronic editing on the videoscreen. When the editing is complete, the pasteup copy can be produced immediately at the touch of a command button.

But that isn't the end of it. Some newspapers now are handling page makeup by videoscreen, thus eliminating the need for people in the composing room to paste up copy. A page may be prepared electronically, and at a single command a typesetting machine can produce a completed page. This is known as pagination—which at the start of the 1970s would have been considered science fiction by many newspaper executives. A day will come, perhaps before the end of the century, when some newspapers do away not only with pasting up the type on a page but also with making a printing plate from the pasteup. This will mean additional savings in labor and production personnel Everything will be done electronically and photographically through computerized systems. Someone once said that a day would come when a newspaper owner could turn out the product with one bright person and a computer. He may have been joking at the time, but the technology will be available for anyone who wants to prove it can be done.

The foregoing overview has been purposely superficial, simply to give you a quick grasp of changes which have taken place in the electronic age. It does not attempt to describe the many methods of videoscreen operation because every paper operates differently. More important to you is the effect electronics has had on the editing process.

Electronic technology has frightened a lot of students and professional people, just as major change has sent traumatic vibrations through other industries. However, various surveys indicate that few people, after working with electronic tools, want to return to type-writers, pencils, paste, and other paraphernalia of the old-style newsroom. Indeed, some former traditionalists are among the biggest boosters of electronic techniques. This is because they have experienced the efficiencies and time savings offered by modern methods. What are some of these? If you are a good typist, you will find the videoscreen much handier than a typewriter. The touch is lighter, enabling you to write faster. The videoscreen is nearly noiseless, thereby cutting down on thought-interrupting sound. When you reach the end of a line, your words will not pile up. Nor will your keyboard lock. Instead, a new line will start automatically. Think of how many arm and finger movements you'll save by never having to make a manual carriage return!

On a videoscreen, a little spot of light, known as a cursor, always shows you where you are on your electronic page. To start a page, you simply press a button, the screen goes blank, and the cursor moves back to the starting position. You have a fresh page with one simple stroke. The cursor also serves as your editing pencil and pastepot, but it is much more efficient that either. Let's say you want to switch your fourth and ninth paragraphs. Instead of cutting them out manually, interchanging them, and pasting them in place, you simply strike a couple of keys and it will be done automatically, at once. If you want to insert material, you press the "insert" button and type in the word, phrase, sentence, paragraph, or page; the videoscreen will automatically adjust all the other material so that it lines up neatly. If you want to delete material, you move the cursor to the proper spot, press a button, and the copy you want to eliminate will vanish instantly.

You'll also find the videoscreen helpful when the time comes to copyread. When you are scanning material on a typewritten page, it is easy to skip over errors. However, the cursor on a videoscreen literally forces your eye to pay attention to each character it touches—and it touches all of them. The Associated Press, a pioneer in the electronic technology of the newsroom, found that the number of errors in copy appearing in the daily news file fell dramatically after editors had used videoscreens for several months. Part of the reason surely was that the cursor was forcing editors to read the copy more closely, regardless of how quickly they went through it.

There is no benefit, of course, in speed for its own sake. News writing and editing are serious business, and one never should let the pressure of time force careless errors or haphazard treatment of material that goes into print. Still, the videoscreen brings us much closer than the typewriter to the ideal of imaginative writing and editing: being able to get thought onto page as efficiently as possible. It is hard to be creative or imaginative when your train of thought is constantly being interrupted by the need to make editing marks, to adjust margins, to start over, or to perform any of the myriad mechanical tasks which intervene between thought and page.

A section in this text stresses the importance of tightening copy. The videoscreen can help you practice this skill. Whether you're working with a typewriter or a videoscreen, you seldom wind up with complete sentences or paragraphs at the end of a page. You are left with lines that fall short. These are known in the trade as widow lines. With typewritten copy, it is difficult to eliminate widow lines. You'd have to count characters and spaces to make the lines come out even at the end. With some videoscreens, what appears on the screen will appear exactly the same when it is typeset. Therefore, you can practice eliminating widow lines and saving space. You can devise your own exercises simply by copying any source material onto the screen and knocking out short lines through rephrasing or editing. It's a terrific training exercise and you should use it frequently, even if your videoscreen does not produce the same version in type, line by line, as it does on the screen.

Like many people, you may become an instant fan of electronic technology. Do not forget, however, that there is truth in the old saying, "Garbage In, Garbage Out." The copy may look attractive on the screen, but if it is full of typographical errors when it emerges in slick-paper form, the chances are better than 99 percent that the fault was yours—not the computer's.

Until there is standardization of videoscreens in the industry, a text such as this can go only so far in preparing you for your first electronic job. Moreover, most schools either do not have access to videoscreens or don't have enough to go around. Thus we will approach the instruction of editing in the traditional fashion, with use of standard copy-editing symbols. If your class has access to videoscreens, your instructor may wish to program the exercises into the system's memory bank.

In any case, the new technology is to be welcomed as a tool that can help all of us— writers and editors—do our jobs more efficiently.

SELECTED READINGS

Gibson, Martin. *Editing in the Electronic Era.* Ames, Iowa: Iowa State University Press, 1979. A lively, solid textbook that emphasizes the role of the new electronic editing equipment.

Hattery, L., and G. Bush, eds. *Technological Change in Printing and Publishing.* Rochelle Park, N.Y.: Hayden, 1973. A collection of articles regarding new technology in printing and publishing.

Moghdam, Dineh. *Computers in Newspaper Publishing.* New York: Marcel Dekker, Inc., 1978. The on-line revolution. Describes major new types of electronic equipment in the newsroom.

6. STYLE

Every written work should be uniform and consistent in spelling, capitalization, abbreviation, and other usages. It is possible, for instance, to write $17.5 million as 17.5 million dollars or $17,500,000. The rules each publication adopts are known as the *style* of that publication.

As an editor, you must be a guardian of style. Readers will be aware of different forms of the same word in the paper, *canceled* and *cancelled*, *Colonel Smith* and *Col. Smith*, for example. The reader might well conclude the paper is sloppy. Good papers admonish every writer and editor that disdain for style rules or carelessness in following them betrays a lack of professionalism or of concern about quality. Writing is not a matter of rules. No compendium of rules can substitute for clear thought, getting the right information and conveying it clearly and forcefully to the reader. But the best story will suffer if its presentation violates style.

There are innumerable style guides, some with copious rules. The scholarly writer or publisher may, for example, obtain a standard guide published by the University of Chicago or the Modern Language Association. These cover style for scholarly works, including forms for bibliographies and references. Larger newspapers still publish their own style guides, many of more than 100 pages. Smaller newspapers commonly have relied on a set of tacitly understood rules and some general precepts (for instance, "we are a modified up-style newspaper"), but more and more commonly rely on the style book produced jointly by the two major U.S. news services, The Associated Press and United Press International. Still others follow the wire service rules except for improvisations to fit local needs or the paper's own personality. Some papers still use *Mr.* on second reference for all persons mentioned in a story as a mark of courtesy, although the *Mr.* has been abandoned by most papers and in the news services' style guide. Others go far to the opposite extreme and drop the honorific *Miss, Mrs.*, or even *Ms.* (as the wire services now do only in sports stories). Sometimes style quirks are insisted upon by the newspaper editor or proprietor to conform to personal idiosyncrasies, such as *thru, tho, cigaret,* and *fotograph,* all used consistently.

In 1960, an AP and UPI joint committee issued a basic stylebook, virtually identical in AP and UPI editions. This standardized style was developed because most papers were using teletypesetter (TTS) tape—automated tape fed directly into typesetting machines. For each publication to edit the stories to conform to its distinctive style would have elim- nated the advantage of the tape operation by requiring a great deal of manual typesetting. Early AP/UPI stylebooks were about 50 pages long and were organized by subject chapters, such as capitalization and abbreviation, with each rule of style numbered. A thorough over- haul of the earlier stylebooks—really an entirely new book—emerged from the news services in 1977, and was revised in 1980. It is an alphabetized book that includes not only style rules but also a great many diction and factual references that editors frequently have to check, such as preferred uses for religious and military titles and sports terms. This edition, containing about 5,000 entries, has been widely accepted in professional and academic circles.

The AP/UPI stylebook editors were told to set clear and simple rules and to rely on a chosen dictionary to resolve conflicts. Ideas for revisions came from editors nationwide and from three years of research into problems of usage and the voluminous criticisms news- papers face in their daily use of words. As their standard, the editors selected the *Webster's New World Dictionary of the English Language,* with *Webster's Third New International Dictionary* as a backup. The stylebook tells us (under "Word Selection") that any word listed in *Webster's New World Dictionary* may be used unless the style guide restricts its use. Is it proper to use *Muslim* or *Moslem,* both correct terms? The style guide tells that *Moslem* is preferred. No stylebook should be expected to be a compendium of grammar, though a few grammar problems are treated when they deal with distinctions between words such as *lie-lay* and *like-as.* The AP and UPI editions differ in format and in some supplementary content. The AP edition contains a libel manual and appendixes on libel law, photo cap- tions, and filing the wire.

Authorities differ. No style guide, however ambitious, can be totally exhaustive. Even the most diligent research is subject to error. Social conditions change and all style books, including the AP/UPI, are temporary in nature. The rules are not engraved in stone. Hence, the AP/UPI style guide already has been amended, and annual reviews of its precepts are made by the executives and editors. One critic, for example, objected to a stylebook entry that ruled residents of Hawaii should be called Hawaiians. "Hawaiians are a distinct racial group, and in a multi-racial society like Hawaii such distinctions are important," the critic said. The editors promised to review the criticism.

Editors sometimes are accused of following narrow conventions of usage, but style- book authors usually caution that they do not intend to discourage originality. One danger is that stylebooks may perpetuate outmoded rules or sometimes even spur-of-the-moment rulings that may have seemed sufficient and logical when set out. One newspaper, for example, insisted on *okeh* for *okay* or *O.K.* long after anyone could remember why. Some demand usages that are merely technically correct but of dubious merit. Some editors insist on the term *widow,* for example, rather than *wife* for a newly bereaved woman.

Pending revisions of the AP/UPI stylebook, editors sometimes will have to make arbitrary style decisions, though these ought not to become fetishes. During World War II, a copy desk editor asked a managing editor one day for a style decision on a new word, *superfortress*, coming into use to refer to a bomber. The snap decision: two words. So the paper continued to use the word as two in variance with most other papers' usages throughout the war. During the Vietnam war some papers used Vietnam as two words, some one, and some used the hyphen. The news services finally settled on *Vietnam*.

For the most part, guides take social custom into account. A good example in the current AP/UPI stylebook is the insistence throughout that sexist words and phrases be eliminated. *Fireman* becomes *firefighter*, and *mailman* becomes *letter carrier*. For example, "Copy should not express surprise that an attractive woman can be professionally accomplished, as in 'Mary Smith doesn't look the part, but she's an authority on . . .'"

Style changes slowly, and for good reason. Chaos would be the result if style rules were altered merely in the face of intensive pressure of the moment. Still another danger is that the editor will become so bogged down in editing to style as to miss other large problems of editing. Some authorities argue that there may be a high correlation between style craziness and poor editing in general. The forest may be obscured by the trees. Someday computers may be programmed to do the style editing job, freeing the editor for more discretionary editing tasks.

Transliterations—spelling words from another alphabet—pose particular problems as words from exotic languages come into common usage. Some news organizations in 1979 began to use the new official Chinese system for romanizing both Chinese place names and personal names, conforming to the Pinyin transliteration adopted in Peking. To avoid confusion, the old spelling was retained in parentheses, so it became Vice Premier *Den Kiaoping* (*Teng Hsiao-ping*). AP retained some well-known place names it said were deeply rooted in American usage—such as *China*, *Shanghai*, and *Tibet*, and the spellings of well-known deceased persons such as *Mao Tse-tung*. (Similar confusion sometimes surrounds pronunciations for broadcasters. During the Iranian turmoil in 1979-80, some broadcasters pronounced the Ayatollah Khomeini's name as "Ho-May-Nee," others as "Ko-May-Nee.")

Every editor must edit to style, knowing the style guide and conforming to it, even if in disagreement on particular points. However, style guides, like language usage itself, should be amended constantly.

For the exercises in this work, we will use the AP edition of the new AP/UPI stylebook, more and more a standard in the industry. Here are the major style rules as summarized by the news services themselves when the revised stylebook was introduced. Note here how style rules do change from one edition of a style manual to the next.[1]

Abbreviations

Dr., Gov., Lt. Gov., Mr., Mrs., Rep., the Rev., Sen. and some abbreviated military titles are allowed before a full name outside direct quotations. But if the titles appear before a name in direct quotations, all but *Dr., Mr.,* and *Mrs.* have to be spelled out. No abbreviations are allowed for *District Attorney, Professor, Superintendent,* and some other titles, because of the possibility of confusion.

Periods are dropped from a few abbreviations, such as mph and mpg, but retained if an abbreviation without periods spells a word (*c.o.d.*).

The old rules called for *Ft.* with an army post and *Fort* with a city name, *Mt.* with a mountain but *Mount* with a city name. In the new style it is *Fort* and *Mount* all the way.

---

[1] From the *AP Log*.

Capitalization

Most capitalization rules remain unchanged, but these have been modified: It is *Democratic Party* (capital P). Legislature falls in the pattern for *Senate* and *City Council*: The *Wisconsin Legislature*, the *state Legislature*, the *Legislature* (when the context allows no misunderstanding about legislature).

Courtesy Titles

First reference to a woman gives her first and last name. Second reference is *Mrs.*, *Miss*, or *Ms.* (for women who prefer *Ms.*) and a last name. On sports wires, second reference is last name only.

Metrics

Dozens of entries give formulas for metric conversions. Here are the rules:
- Use metric terms when they are the primary form in which the source of a story has provided statistics. Follow the metric units with equivalents in the terms more widely known in the United States. Or:
- Provide metric equivalents for traditional forms if a metric unit has become widely known. (An example would be the adoption of speedometers with kilometer markings.)

Numerals

Figures are used for all address numbers, ages (whether under 10 or over, animate object or inanimate), betting odds (5-3), dates, dimensions (5-feet-6), percentages, ratios (2-to-1), speeds, temperatures (except *zero*). One area where the old rule of "spell out one to nine, use figures for 10 and above" was retained was for distances ("He walked four miles.") and some series ("The couple has three sons and two daughters."). Numerals still must be spelled out if they start a sentence, with one exception: *1980* was a very good year.

Punctuation

Inc. no longer must be preceded by a comma: *J. C. Penney Co. Inc.* The same is true for *Ltd.*

Mother's Day and *Father's Day* have developed apostrophes.

Quotation marks are required around the titles of books that are primarily catalogs of reference material: almanacs, dictionaries, encyclopedias, gazetteers, etc.

Instead of using a dash to indicate 12 degrees below zero, either the words *minus 12* or *12 below zero* are required.

Dozens of entries indicate which prefixes and suffixes require hyphens. *Anti-* and *non-* are examples of prefixes nearly always requiring a hyphen. *Under-* and *over-* seldom do.

States, Provinces

The names of eight states are not to be abbreviated in datelines or text: *Alaska, Hawaii, Idaho, Iowa, Maine, Ohio, Texas, Utah.* The two-letter state abbreviations advocated by the U.S. Postal Service were rejected because of possible confusion.

Abbreviations for Canadian provinces are eliminated. *Montreal, Ottawa,*

Quebec, Toronto will stand alone in datelines, but all other cities are followed by the full name of the province.

Titles

A distinction is made between job descriptions, which are lower-case even when preceding a name, and formal titles, generally capitalized before a name but lower-case if following a name or set off by commas. Some examples; *astronaut John Glenn, swimmer Mark Spitz, Vice President Walter Mondale, Pope Paul VI.* Under the old rules, *pope* and *president* were capitalized even when standing alone; in the new style, they are lower-case.

An exception in the capitalization rule for formal titles involves a few cases where the title actually substitutes for a name (*Dalai Lama, Shah of Iran, Prince of Wales.*) These and a few others are capitalized in all references to the holder of the title.

Words

Percent is one word. *Employee* ends with two *e*'s. *Goodbye* has been given a final *e*. No change has been made in these often misspelled words: *embarrass, harass, judgment, permissible.*

EXERCISES

Edit the following sentences and the paragraphs on the following pages to conform to AP/UPI style.

1. The President will meet with his cabinet Monday morning.

2. Captain Robert Jones commanded Co. B, Fifth Btn., 395th Field Artillery.

3. Det. Frank Pierson of the vice squad took a swallow of coke and declared, "I worked at the Boston city hall, and I know you can't fight city hall."

4. The pitcher's record is now 6 and 5. The final score was 1 to 0. The team now leads the National League East.

5. Veterans' Day will be observed in ceremonies at 12 noon.

6. He called the nonaligned nations nondescript.

7. The DC10 is a jet liner favored for transport by the USAF.

8. The fireman took a drink of whisky.

9. He resided at 1024 West Twenty-fourth Street, Lincoln, Nebraska.

10. Jones was president of I. W. Jones Company, Incorporated, which
    manufactured machineguns.

11. As an office holder, the Governor okayed the idea of the Electoral
    college.

12. He decided to enter the New Hampshire Primary.

13. He was a member of the Catholic church.

14. She was a member of the P-TA.

15. Most Mid-Atlantic colleges are in mid-term.

16. The hitch-hiker was picked up at 6 A. M.

17. The gale-force winds bore down with speeds up to 70 m.p.h.

18. The F.B.I. said the boy was seven years old and lived on Lakeview
    Avenue.

19. She won the Pulitzer prize. The editor in chief also is a Pulitzer
    prize-winning author.

20. Representative David Jones, Republican of Virginia, is a PhD.

Meridian

Meridican Chemical Corporation reported Monday that net earnings for
the 2nd quarter declined 25 per cent on a sales gain of 10 per cent
from the same period last year.

Meridian's net earnings for the three months ended June 30 were
$20,020,000 or $.92 a share, compared with $26,800,00 or $1.24 a share
for the 2nd quarter.

J. Winston Clover, president, attributed the earnings decline to
the severe Winter and significant cutbacks in sales on the west coast
since Memorial day.

-30-

Teller

A twenty-one-year-old former bank teller was sentenced to 3 years'
probation Monday in District court on a charge of embezzling $7984
from Central bank last November 21st.

Robert Smythe Wilkinson pleaded guilty and made full restitution.
He was employed at the bank's branch at 2,495 Deutz Avenue.

#

(Meridian)

Meridian Chemical Corporation reported Monday that net earnings
for the 2nd quarter declined 25 per cent on a sales gain of 10 per cent
from the same period last year.

Meridian's net earnings for the three months ended June 30 were
$20,020,000 or $.92 a share, compared with $26,800,00 or $1.24 a share,
for the 2nd quarter last year

J. Winston Clover, president, attributed the earnings decline to the severe Winter and significant cutbacks in sales on the west coast since Memorial day.

-30-

Teller

A twenty-one-year-old former bank teller was sentenced to 3 years' probation Monday in District court on a charge of embezzling $7984 from Central bank last November 21st.

Robert Smythe Wilkinson pleaded guilty and made full restitution. He was employed at the bank's branch at 2/495 Deutz Avenue.

#

Strike

The full workforce of about two hundred was back on the job Friday at Quality Foods, Inc., processing plant here after a 2-day walkout.

The end of the wildcat strike that began Tuesday, June 3, came after a District Court injunction was handed down by Judge J. Robert Bullock. The judge scheduled Tuesday, June 19, for a hearing on his preliminary back-to-work order.

#

Driver

A man driving 50 mph on the law median strip on Twentieth St.

between Main and Oak was arrested Friday afternoon by City police

officers.

Lieutenant James R. Bonny said he saw the man driving on the lawn

and followed him to Oak Street, where he tried to arrest the man. A

scuffle took place, he said.

Booked into jail for investigation of reckless driving and

resisting arrest was Airman First Class Jimmy MacIver, thirty, Elgin

Air Force Base, Florida.

-30-

7. STORY STRUCTURE AND CONVENTIONS

Here are some news writing fundamentals to remember as you edit the stories in this chapter:

Objective writing. News writing is objective writing, generally impersonal and in the third person; that is, the author leaves the I, me, or we out of the story. Objectivity means that the writer's viewpoints stay out of the story. Some newspaper critics insist that no writer can totally divorce an account from a subjective appraisal dictated by personal experience and biases. Some see objectivity as a form of cowardice that fails to give the reader the full dimensions of the story or that substitutes facts for truth. The so-called New Journalists of the late 1960s and the activists of the 1970s supposedly pursued truth, but the goal was elusive and many New Journalists had an ax to grind.

Objectivity has served the American press well in the twentieth century. A *relative* objectivity most certainly is possible: The writer and editor attempt to tell the reader what needs to be known in a way that impartial observers would agree is fair and complete, not what a special pleader or propagandist would want to be known. This suggests that balance and perspective are needed—by getting both sides, by answering basic questions, and by digging for facts that do not lie on the surface. Shallow stories often result not from the pursuit of objectivity but rather from sloppy reporting. Opinion should be reserved for the editorial page, with columns clearly identified as analysis or interpretation. As an editor, you should be on guard for the writer's unintentional bias, often revealed in such phrases as *pointed out* and *warned* when *said* is all that may be fairly stated. When evaluative words like *torrential* are used, they should be supported by story detail. If they are not, delete them or change them.

Attribution and Authority. Closely tied to objectivity is the need for attribution. The reader must always know where the information was obtained. If the reporter's own observation or experience is reported, often as description, this is legitimate. Otherwise, individuals or documents are quoted, either directly or by paraphrase, but always identified for the reader. The verb *said* is almost always the most appropriate one to use for this purpose.

Leads.   The lead or first paragraph of any written work should serve three purposes: to introduce the subject, to interest the reader, and to convey the tone.

The five-W and H lead (Who, What, When, Where, Why, How).   This lead is still standard in American news writing. It serves adequately for most stories. It is well adapted to the skimming that characterizes newspaper reading and to concise relating of events. Reading the newspaper shouldn't be hard work, especially when readers have the option of watching television or listening to radio.

The traditional news lead has been much criticized for failing to put some stories into perspective. This is true especially of process-oriented stories and continuing stories. The newsmagazines, and to some extent broadcast newswriting, often precede the account of the immediate situation with a paragraph or so of background. Some stories are also best told or introduced by rhetorical devices such as anecdote, description, or question. In no case, however, should the lead "back into" the story, as the leads of some of the exercise stories in this chapter do. The major point should be clear from the outset. This means, for example, that an anecdote should be appropriate and meaningful and truly revealing of the point of the story. It also means that all major points of the story should be touched on in the lead, whatever its form.

In general, the latest significant factor or event is the lead. If two hikers are rescued from a peak, their rescue should be featured, not introduced later after the lead deals with their predicament. Tangential matter, no matter how interesting, has no place in the lead. In one of the following exercises you will have the opportunity to question a quite extraneous statement and relegate it to a subordinate position, where it belongs.

Help your writers by sharpening the focus of leads that are vague on first reading. You should not have to reread the lead to get the point. Leads of this sort are usually simply too long. Most leads should be no more than about 30 words long. Some effective ones are only 10 words long. Shorten the lead by eliminating detail that can be introduced later. Often, the less important of the 5W and H statements can be placed in the second or even later paragraphs. If you find it effective to report two actions or developments in the first paragraph, you can divide the lead into two sentences.

Body of story.   The inverted-pyramid story structure is still the standard. Most facts are told in diminishing order of importance, so that the story theoretically could be cut at any point and still make sense. Some, however, are best told chronologically after the main points are wrapped up in the lead and first few paragraphs following: for instance, a storm, a robbery, a major explosion.

An important point to remember in all stories: Support the lead with the first few paragraphs. This is true in complex stories, in which the lead may introduce several elements. Each major point introduced in the lead should be supported by some detail in the paragraphs immediately following. Then facts can be arranged in diminishing order of importance or chronologically. Speech reports usually are improved if the opening summary or quotation is immediately followed by a paragraph supporting it, before the speaker's other points are reported. Don't be afraid to reorganize a story.

Paragraphs.   Block paragraphing is used in most news stories. This means that short paragraphs, often of only a sentence each, are used for ease of reading and to keep the news columns clear of long, gray stretches of type. Some stories, especially extended analytical pieces, or long expository discussions, still adhere to more typical paragraphing of the sort you have learned in your English courses. This means that paragraphs are built around topic sentences, which are then fleshed out with detail. It also means that a new paragraph should grow naturally out of the preceding one. As a general consideration, however, you'll serve the reader well when you shorten paragraphs that go on for 100 words or more. Break them up with paragraph marks: ⌞⎯

EXERCISES

Bugged

Charging that Chief Robert Peck "bugged" a room where he was interviewing firefighters, City Commissioner Arnold J. Cortesi Friday told the department head to rezign or be fired.

"That's not ture," responded the 53-year-old veteral of nearly 2C years with the department--the last eight as chief. He has until Monday to quit the $36,800-a-year post or face commission action.

"I'll think about it..." Mr. Peck said of the ultimatum.

Mr. Cortesi said he's been investigating fire department operations for several weeks. He cautioned Chief Peck that he has the two votes needed for action..

The bugging charge was leveled only after Chief Peck said the commissioner's "time for a change" reasoning was unfair to him, the department and the public.

Commissioner Timothy Sheehan later acknowledged he was willing to fire the chief in mid-1977 but lacked needed support.

MORE...

First Add Bugging

John T. Walton, of the county firefighter's civil service commission said the group's by-laws permit Mr. Peck to return to the rank
he held before the appointment. Personnel records show he as a capatin.

Mr. Cortesi said he wants to fill the post from outside the
department because it's riddled with "cliques and dissention," the
commissioner declared.

"I'm asking Chief Peck to resign...according to the law..." Mr.
Cortesi told the session in his private office.

"The chief of the fire department may at any time be removed without cause..without trial...it's not necessary to state any cause for
removal.

"Monday I'll make it official in the commission meeting if he
refuses," Mr. Cortesi warned. "It's time for a change."

Chief Peck said he was caught off-guard.

"Playing politics with the fire department is bad policy," he
stated reminding commissioners that under his direction the operation
had gone from "nil" to one of the best in the country.

Calm but determined, Commissioner Cortesi told the session he'd
been discussing department operations with firefighters at the headquarters station as part of a continuing investigation.

The commissioner said he was warned later that an inter-com in
that room had been left open: "You got a report before I even left the
place," he told Mr. Peck.

Although he endorses the coming-up-through-the ranks concept, Mr. Cortesi said he feels outside leadership would help solve the problems.

During the interview he endorsed findings of a special committee that late last year concluded the department generally lacked written policies and procedures "which in turn result in arbitrary and incon-sisten operations decisions and personnel discipling..."

The report contended departmental priorities or a lack of them were found in the way firefighters were hired and used and money spent. "Morale is low" Mr. Cortesi said.

###

(Bugged)

~~Charging that Chief Robert Peck "bugged" a room where he was inter-~~ ~~viewing firefighters,~~ City Commissioner Arnold J. Cortesi Friday told *Fire Chief Robert Peck* ~~the department head~~ to resign or be fired.

~~"That's not ture," responded the~~ *Peck,* 53~~-year-old~~ *is a* veteran *n* of nearly 23 years with the department, *y* the last eight as chief. He has until Monday to quit the $36,800-a-year post or face commission action.

"I'll think about it..." ~~Mr.~~ Peck said ~~of the ultimatum.~~

~~Mr.~~ Cortesi said he's *has* been investigating fire department operations for several weeks. He ~~cautioned~~ *told* Chief Peck that he has the two votes needed ~~for action.~~

~~The bugging charge was leveled only after Chief Peck said the~~

~~commissioner's "time for a change" reasoning was unfair to him, the~~

~~department and the public.~~

Commissioner Timothy Sheehan ~~later acknowledged~~ *said* he was willing to fire the chief in mid-1977 but lacked needed support.

(MORE...)

(First Add Bugg~~ing~~ *ed*)

John T. Walton, of the county firefighter's civil service commission, said ~~the group's~~ by-laws permit ~~Mr.~~ Peck to return to the rank he held before the appointment. ~~Personnel records show~~ he ~~as~~ *was* a cap(a)tin.

~~Mr.~~ Cortesi said he wants to fill the post from outside *because* the department ~~because it's~~ *is* riddled with "cliques and dissenion," ~~the commissioner declared.~~

"I'm asking Chief Peck to resign according to the law, ..." Mr. Cortesi ~~told the session in his private office.~~ *said* (x)

"The chief of the fire department may at any time be removed without cause, without trial. It's not necessary to state any cause for removal.

"Monday I'll make it official in the commission meeting if he refuses," ~~Mr.~~ Cortesi ~~warned~~ *said.* "It's time for a change."

~~Chief~~ Peck said he was caught off-guard.

"Playing politics with the fire department is bad policy," he *said. He told* ~~stated reminding~~ commissioners that under his direction the operation had gone from "nil" to one of the best in the country.

~~Calm but determined,~~ Commissioner Cortesi ~~told the session~~ *said* he'~~d~~ *had*
been discussing department operations with firefighters at the headquarters station as part of a continuing investigation.

The commissioner said he was warned later that an inter-com in
that room had been left open: "You got a report before I even left the
place," he told ~~Mr.~~ Peck.

~~Although he endorses the coming-up-through-the ranks concept,~~
~~Mr.~~ Cortesi said he ~~feels~~ *felt* outside leadership would help solve the
problems.

During the interview he endorsed findings of a special committee
that late last year concluded the department generally lacked written
policies and procedures, "which in turn results in arbitrary and incon-
sistent operations decisions and personnel discipline..."

The report contended department priorities, or a lack of them,
were found in the way firefighters were hired and used and money spent.
"Morale is low," ~~Mr.~~ Cortesi said.

###

Protest

Riverview -- A petition signed by Riverview area farmers and property owners was presented to the City Council Thursday.

The petition, containing about 200 signatures, questioned the legal-
ity of planting trees along 10th street and the interstate highway
access road.

It was brought out in the petition that a group of farmers paid $90,000, plus interest, to provide an intricate drainage system for 3,000 acres in the central area, and that the drainage system "must work."

The farmers argued against the planting of trees specifically for the reason that roots damage and plug drains. Poor crops in shaded areas was another argument presented by the farmers.

John T. Young, councilmen in charge of the Shade Tree Commission, said the tree-lined highway would add aesthetic value to the city. He added a positive feeling in favor of the planting of trees was indicated in a poll he took a few weeks ago.

A vote was taken on the matter with three councilmen voting in favor of planting reees while two voted against it.

Councilmen Steven Williams, who initially voted against the project, did so agai n and questioned the illegality. He added a positive feeling in favor of the planting of trees was indicated in a poll he took a few weeks ago.

A vote was taken on the matter with three councilmen voting in favor of planting trees while two voted against it.

Councilmen Steven Williams who initially voted against the project, did so again and pointed out the illegality of the city planting on state right of way.

Mayor Arthur Tookey said since the money is under the control of the Shade Tree Commission, "It is their business where they spend it."

W. R. Roseberry, a proponent of the petition, said the farmers would take the matter to court.

Grammar

Those who finished the course definately learned skills in dia-
gramming and sentence structure, James Karbakas, central High School
principal, said of the Basic English Grammer course which he permitted
Deborah Heinz to try out in the phase 1 English classes the last
semester. Mr. Karbakas said the school are considering the possibility
of including the class in the school curriculum. Perhaps as a short
five-week course.

Mrs. Heinz compiled the course from Hoenshels Grammer of 1897
vintage, updating thematerial as needed. She taught the course under
supervision of Mrs. Ramona Nix head of the English department.

The first section of instant English, as Mrs. Heinz calls her
course, was covered during this school year. Mrs. Nix slaid students
who took the class felt it was well worth their time and are considering taking the English experiment second phase on their own should the
school fail to include the course next year.

Mrs. Heinz has authored two books on local history and numerous
short articles for magazines and news papers besides the "Instant
English" course.

Edit this story for a Monday evening paper.

In an interview Friday, University President James Rutherford
Maxwell discussed reports that he was being considered for a presidential
position at the Fowler University.

Maxwell discounted the rumors by stating he was not looking for another position.

He explained that Fowler university was a five-campus system and a very distinguished school. However, hesaid, "I am not sure what it is they are looking for. It's something I'll have to contend with over the weekend.

Sunday, Maxwell issued a telegram to the officials at Fowler University stating, "I'm honored to learn of the recommendation that I be considered for the presidency. I prefer my name be withdrawn from consideration for the position."

Maxwell was unavailable for comment Monday about his decision. However, Director of Public Relations Robert Harper said no comments cojld be made regarding the decision while the search process is going on. "There are proprieties to be observed in these situations," Harper declaimed.

Bomb

A homemdee bomb was found this morning on tbe roof of the vogue Theater, 402 1st Street. Alonzo Hamilton, manager of the theater, reported finding bomb the about 9:00 a.M.

This was the second bomb found at the Theater in the past two weeks. The first Bomb exploded at the theater on August 1 about 6:00 p.m. No movie was showing at that time and no resulted damage from the bomb.

Lieutenant Mike Amos, investigating Officer for the policee Department, said "the bomb was clumsily made from a bleach pastic

2/Bomb

bottle filled with a flammable liquid, possibly gasoline: Two sticks
of dynamite with a fireing cap and fuse was taped to the bottle.

Hamilton thinks the fuse was litt but went out when the bomb
thrown was onto the roof. Hamilton discovered the Bomb when he was on
the roof to examine an Air Vent, He said the bomb could have been there
for a day or two.

Police Chief Henry Merrill is preparing the bomb for shipement to
Washington D.C., where it will be examined by the FBI. Nothing has yet
been heard on the FBI analyses of the first bomb. Merrill hopes the
FBI might be able to tell if both bombs were from the same source.

Shortly after finding the first bomb, Hamilton received an anon-
nymous phone call warning that "this is only a sample of what's going
to happen" if the movie then playing was showed one more time.

The Theatre has been runing an adult film festival for the past
two weeks. The movies showing at the time of the phone call Up in
Sally's Room and Stewardess Party. This week Veronica's Hot Pants and
Coeds Confidential are showing.

A bomb scare also sent 400 employes at the federal Building home
from work early afternoon yesterday. Mrs. Helen Crow a secretary for
the United States Forest Service, received an anomynous call in which
a male voice warned that there was a bomb planted in the building.

Employees were sent home about 3:00 P.M., but an office by office
search of the building nothing revealed;

The Police chief said the "entire police squad" will continue the bomb investigations. The FBI may be involved ind the Federal Building investigation.

Crab Boats

Fierce winds and torrential rains pounded Buckeye Bay into a savage whipping mass of liquid fury Monday afternoon and before the gale had subsided, two crab boats were smashed along the bays rocky shore line.

Two 30-foot crab boats, the "Sea Wolf" owned by Wilbur Parker and "Sally Mae" owned by Dan Vegas, failed to withstand the ocean's furious lashes and were crushed against the rocks.

Nine trollers were in the bay at the time of the storm and only seven remained when the gale ended.

The "Sea Wolf" was ripped from its mooring and throw like a toy into the rocky edge of the bay. Its cabin was wedged between two piers at the docks where it had been tossed by the storm's 20-foot breakers. The engines and metal parts of the craft were grotesquely twisted around rocks along the bay's bed.

As thevelocity of the storm grew, "Sally Mae" which was riding out the some 500 feet from the dock's end, began to take in water. Dan "Sonny" Vegas, fisherman owner of the boat, took a 14-foot skiff into the rampaging waters in an attempt to salvage the craft. He barely escaped with his life when the craft sunk, sucking him into the icy waters. A fellow fisherman, Elmer Shipstad, had acted on a hunch and

2/crab boats

followed him to the sinking craft. Vegas was clinging to the over-
turned skiff when Shipstad reached him.

This is Vegas' own story of the ordeal which almost cost him his
life:

"I was sick in bed when the gale hit Monday afternoon and I
immediately got up and went to the dock. It was near dusk when the
"Sea Wolf" broke from its mooring and was being swept into the rocks
of the bay. We were trying to save it when someone shouted that my
boat was sitting low in the water.

"I boarded one of the skiffs, the 14-foot rowboat, and headed
toward "Sally Mae." When I reached her I climbed aboard and saw that
she was half full of water. About that time it began to sink and I
dove on the skiff alongside. When the crab boat went down it sucked
the skiff and myself underneath with it.

"When the skiff and I submerged, which was a matter of seconds,
long ones; the rowboat had flipped over and I was clinging to the side.
Elmer Shipman, who had followed me out, drug me aboard his skiff and
we fought 20-foot breakers back to the dock.

"I had been out before in that type weather, but I'll never go
again."

In a matter of hours, the wreckage of "Sally Mae" had been churned
from beneath the murky waters and lay strewn along the splintered
debris of the "Sea Wolf." When the upset bay had settled once more,
salvage operations for parts of the two crafts were begun as the seven
remaining boats bobbled contentedly in the mouth of the calmed bay.

ARS

The big news at the District convention of the ARS held at the Symphone Park Saturday was the announcement by Dr. Steven Hobbs, president of plans for a $2,000,000 new home for the nation wide organization to be build at Shreveport, La. This is planned for the ARS through the American Rose Foundation.

The search for a site for the project began four years ago and the American Rose Society was presented 120 acres of heavily wooded land in Shreveport valued at $250,000 for the American Rose Center. The development will include an administration building, visitors, educational and research centers along with numerous gardens including an international rose garden.

Shreveport has magnificent roses. Dr. Hobbs said, and the Center is certain to attract thousands of visitors. Walter W. Smith, Dallas, Texas, head of the committee for financing the project mentioned the importance of the research being done by the American Rose Society and that $600,000 has already been raised toward the building development.

Milo Ekblad, Eureka, Colorado, spoke on the common needs of man such as air, water and the uncommon needs which include adventure, excitement and quiet in order to have a balanced life. Mrs. Ekblad gave a traveloge on roses showing slides of bloom in gardens in the different parts of the nation. Norman Page gave a talk on the care of exhibition of roses. Mrs. Diane Coleman presented a demonstration of youth projects. A tour of local rose gardens followed.

A breakfast at 7:45 a.m. is scheduled Sunday at the Roadway Inn with a visit to the Jackson Rose Gardens, 2374 w1st Street, to follow.

2/ARS

Luncheon at 12:30 p.m. at the Rodeway Innn will be presided over by
G. E. O'Donnell.

Concluding the meeting will be a rose show at Central Park. It will
be open to the public from 1 p.m. to 5 p.m.

Friday evening delegates and members of the American Rose Society
were entertained at supper at the home of Miss Thelma Lockhart, convention chairman. Mary McGillicuddy Moulton presented organ music.
Chloe McVey, district director ARS, Denver, presided over the convention.

Crash

Lights from an on-coming car on the other sideof the divided highway reflected on wet pavement and caused a county motorist to swerve to
his right "to avoid" a grinding crash where he struck a guard rail
driving it through the front of the vehicle and missing him by inches.

James Pilot, 61, 9201 Tri-county Boulevard, was uninjured although
the guard rail tore through the windshield and the top of the car
withing inches of his head.

Deputy Sherrif Don Montoya said Mr. Pilot was southbound on
Seventh St. at 46th Avenue about 7:13 P.M. when in the rain when the
reflection made it appear a car was coming south in his lane of traffic.
Mr. Pilot was unconscious of the guard rail. He swerved to the right
and struck the guard rail about 4650 South, Deputy Montoya said.

Passing through the grill and radiater, the motor was then struck by the guardrail. It glanced upwards through the hood and then crashed through the windshield, deputy Montoya said.

Slaughter

Commercial slaughter plants in the state turned out more pork, about the same veal and less beef and lamb during August than the same month a year ago.

Nationally, red meat processing during the month was up 2 per cent from August, a year ago.

The state's processing of 17.5 million pounds during the month represented a 1 per cent decrease in beef, a 28 per cent reduction in lamb and a 300 per cent increase in pork.

The State Crop and Livestock Reporting Service also

noted that the livestock slaughter in the state in August was about 25 per cent more active than the this month last that month last year.

Ad Agency

It was announced by Mr. Leonard J. Marswell, President of Marswell Advertising Agency that Mr. George Butters, a veteran of the advertising business, has joined him as a partner. Marswell Advertising Agency, one of the oldest and reputible advertising companies in the area, will change its name to Marswell and Butters Advertising Agency. Their offices are located in the new Life Security Building at 2792 Industry Boulevard. Mr. George Butters brings to the agency a wealth of experience and creative advertising ability, states Mr. Marswell. Before returning to his native city, Mr. Butters was associated with such well-known adrevtising agencies as J. Walter Thompson Co., Smock-Wadell, and his own, Butters and Bredwell, a Denver agency. As Vice-President and co-owner of Butters and Bredwell, Mr. Butters acted as Senior Account Supervisor on all consumer and package good accounts. Then he took up residence in Los Angeles as Advertising Manager for the Albers Milling Division of the Carnation Company. While with Carnation, the ex-Navy Lt. Commander was responsible for national advertising, sales promotion, marketing, research and planning for 14 cereal products plus the Friskie line of dog and cat foods. In 1956, he moved to Star-Kissed Foods where he was responsible for the national advertising and sales promotion for Star-Kissed Tuna, Star-Kissed Frozen Foods and Nine Lives Pet Food. J. Walter Thompson was the next stop where, Butters was engaged as Account Supervisor of consumer products along with acting as marketing director on all region accounts. Libby, McNeill & Libby, Safeway Stores, Seven-Up Bottling Company, Standard Brands, Levar Bros., Alberto-Culver, Ford Motor Company and the Blue Chip Stamp Co. numbered among his accounts. Butters was Vice-President and Merchandising Director at Smock-Wadell Advertising in Los Angeles where he was involved with the Union Oil Company and Ralston Purina products. It was only recently that he decided to return to his native city, and it was even more recently that he married the former Rhoda Ryder Poncelli. The couple now reside in the Arlington Hills area with Kristi and Pat, two of his daughters, and Rhoda's daughter, Alyce. He is a member of the united Methodist Church and loves to hunt and fish.

Snow

YELLOWSTONE NATIONAL
PARK, Wyo. - officials said Wednesday Yellowstone National Park will open for winter snowmobiling beginning Friday. Officials said the unusually late start was due to lack of early winter snow in the park. officials said snowmobiling in the park may be discontinued at any time if the snow pack becomes too shallow to prevent damage to roads. Officials said only unplowed roads that normally are open to the public during summer months will be open to snowmobiles. The machines are not permitted off the established roadways nor on plowed roads open to wheeled vehicles.

Part II

★★★★★★★★★★★★★★★★

Language

★★★★★★★★★★★★★★★★

8. WRITING AND LANGUAGE: THE EDITOR'S ROLE

The editor's work is more critical than creative. The editor cannot think for the writer, but the editor can help the writer reach the audience. It is a rare writer indeed whose work will not be improved by the intercession of a fresh eye, if only because the writer is so close to the work that full detachment is impossible. Many great writers would have created nothing memorable without the assistance of an editor. A good copy editor can help make news writing what has been called literature under pressure. At the very least, an editor can make sure, at the end of the news flow process, that copy will be correct, tight, and complete.

There was an excellent writer–editor relationship between Athenodorus, the tutor, and Claudius, the aspiring historian who was to become Rome's fourth emperor, as expressed in Robert Graves's *I, Claudius:*

> Well, said Athenodorus . . . suppose you were to sit down and take your tablets and write me a letter, a short account of all that you saw on Mars Field; as if I had been five years absent from Rome and you were sending me a letter across the sea. . . . So I gladly scribbled away on the wax, and we read the letter through for faults of spelling and composition. I was forced to admit that I had told both too little and too much, and had also put my facts in the wrong order . . . and I need not have mentioned that the cavalry had horses: people took that for granted. And I had twice put in the incident of Augustus's charger stumbling: Once was enough if the horse only stumbled once. And what Posthumous had told me . . . about the religious practices of the Jews, was interesting but did not belong here because the recruits were Italians, not Jews. . . . On the other hand I had not mentioned several things that he would have

47

been interested to hear—how many recruits there were in the parade, how far advanced their training was. . . . Athenodorus . . . never let any careless, irrelevant, or inexact phrase of mine pass without comment."

—Robert Graves, *I, Claudius* (New York:
Vintage Books, 1941 and 1961), pp. 63, 64.

Here is an admirable statement of how the editor can help the writer. First, the matter must be correct in spelling and on other mechanical points. It should avoid careless repetition or belaboring of the obvious. It may not stray off by introducing tangential matter. And it must not leave any essential questions unanswered.

Journalistic writing is sometimes characterized as "journalese," or hackneyed writing. Journalists have argued against this characterization, but the criticism has merit, if only because the media are under time pressure. News writing also tends to be burdened with conventions, some of them archaic, when good writing is far less a matter of rules than of good information, clear thought, and precise expression. If this is true even of practiced writers, consider that a great deal of copy the editor works with comes from amateurs.

What emerges from the editor's hands should be writing correct on the general to informal plane—the kind of English used by educated persons in everyday written discourse. Such writing is not highly formal but it should be both correct and precise. News writing is more colloquial and more permissive than many other forms of writing because it aims at a general audience, but the best news writing is just good writing. It has the same ingredients of clarity, simplicity, brevity, honesty, vitality, and rhythm found in every other kind of good writing. Every editor should help the writer make the best choice of word and syntax.

Joseph Pulitzer told his writers: "Put it before them briefly so that they will read it, clearly so they will understand it, forcibly so they will appreciate it, picturesquely so they will remember it, and above all, accurately so they will be guided by its light."

Respect the author's style. Sometimes less is more in editing. Although only the straight presentation of facts is needed in stories of great interest or drama, other stories may require the writer's flair and technique to make them interesting. The editor's challenge is to balance standards and style. When a writer strays from accepted standards the copy should be changed. And when a writer's style degenerates into overwriting, the editor has an obligation to help tone it down.

All through this book you will deal with language problems often encountered in newspaper copy: incorrect grammar, misuse of words, overwriting, unemphatic writing (especially cliché-filled writing), unclear writing, and ponderous writing.

9. MAKING IT GRAMMATICALLY CORRECT

Beginners who write clear sentences are at a great premium. Managing editors and others find that young people fresh out of school generally are weak in English composition. If you are deficient in basic writing skills, begin to correct them now. How? By reading good writing models and by plenty of practice in writing and editing. By rewriting your own work several times. Books on writing can be of some help and a good grammar text, such as the *Harbrace College Handbook*, cited in the Selected Readings at the end of Part I, will be useful.

Many grammarians adhere to rigid rules, which they cite even when the rules are not supported by custom, convenience, or understanding. Others say that anything goes. Both err. The simplest approach to language would be to rely on hard-and-fast rules. Next easiest would be the opposite: to eliminate rules. Language is constantly changing. Grammar also rests on logic. When you write and edit according to accepted principles of grammar, your chances of writing logically, clearly, and powerfully are enhanced. The monumental *A Dictionary of Modern English Usage*, cited at the end of this chapter, says:

> What grammarians say should be has perhaps less influence on what shall be than even the more modest of them realize; usage evolves itself little disturbed by their likes and dislikes. And yet the temptation to show how better use might have been made of the material . . . is sometimes irresistible.

It is on this basis that some newspapers insist on more formal grammar than others. Some are keen on the distinction between *that* and *which* and on the formal use of sequence of tenses ("he said he was going" rather than "he said he is going"). Others require special grammatical constructions that become fetishes. One, for instance, insists that an auxiliary and its verb ("was going") never be split ("always was going"). Our style guide says, "Occasionally a split is not awkward and is necessary to convey meaning." (See the "Verbs" entry.)

The purpose of this chapter is first to alert you to any difficulties you may have in understanding grammatical principles, and second to give you practice in correcting some of the grammar problems often found in news copy. The problems discussed here include a majority of those the copy editor will be called on to correct. Your AP/UPI style guide will be of help. Pay special attention to the distinctions drawn between words that look or sound alike.

The following brief discussions of some major grammatical principles will help you in editing the exercises at the end of this chapter.

Sentence Faults

If you follow the advice you've had in your news writing courses about writing short sentences, you'll have few problems in writing sentences that are grammatically correct, clear, and effective. News writing demands short sentences for power and easy understanding on first reading. Sentences often are obscure when they are long and convoluted:

> Some old-timers adamantly declare that Dingle, which resting at 6,000 feet elevation sometimes has three feet of crusted snow in May and this year had, to everyone's consternation, strawberries unfrozen on vines in mid-October, was at onset called Cottonwood.

Here is a simple rewrite merely to shorten the sentence and straighten out the twistings:

> Some old-timers adamantly declare that Dingle was at onset called Cottonwood.
> The town rests at 6,000 feet elevation. Sometimes it has three feet of crusted snow in May. This year it had strawberries unfrozen on vines in mid-October. This consternated everyone.

A better rewrite, to straighten out the sentence tangle, improve the relationship of ideas, and get rid of the self-conscious words:

> Some old-timers firmly declare that Dingle was at first called Cottonwood.
> Because the town rests at 6,000 feet elevation, it sometimes has three

feet of crusted snow in May. In mid-October this year, however, strawberries were still unfrozen on their vines. This unusual situation surprised everyone.

Note that the writer introduced many extraneous ideas between the two parts of the main idea. This idea should even be a separate paragraph because it does not cohere naturally to any of the other ideas introduced. If we could think for the writer, we probably would be able to provide a transition between the idea in the first paragraph and those that follow in the second. Remember that by definition a sentence is one idea. The following rule is excellent advice to writers and editors on how to end a long sentence: Don't use more words; put in a period instead.

A word of caution here: Sentences that are so short as to be choppy often fail, because the relationship of the idea in one sentence to the idea in the next is not clearly conveyed. In the following example, the writer has lost his way by not giving proper emphasis to the ideas:

Every industry has had a major change in the last 25 years. There are few exceptions. One was the radio. It has changed many times. Its changes are due to inventions.

Here is the paragraph rewritten in sentences long enough to put the important statements in the main clauses and the supporting statements in clearly subordinate parts of the sentence to show the relative importance:

With few exceptions, every industry has had a major change in the past 25 years. One such industry is radio broadcasting, which has changed many times due to inventions.

Avoid "stringy sentences," that is, those sentences in which ideas are simply strung together. The "and which" construction is a dead giveaway that the sentence is carrying too many thoughts or that the relationships between the thoughts are not precise:

Original	*Rewrite*
The plant was set up specifically to handle potatoes, which account for approximately 50 percent of its production and which are somewhat more difficult to process than the other two species.	The plant was set up specifically to handle potatoes. Although potatoes are more difficult to process, they account for approximately 50 percent of production.

or

The plant was set up specifically to handle potatoes, which are more difficult to process than the other two species. Potatoes account for approximately 50 percent of production.

Long sentences can be used with good effect when there is a natural progression of ideas in the clauses. They can be effectively balanced by shorter sentences, as in James Reston's touching description of Jacqueline Kennedy at President Kennedy's bier:

> Out of the crowd she stepped under the vaulted ceiling of the vast rotunda, a trim and hale figure in funeral black with the golden Caroline on her hand, and kneeled ever so slowly before her husband's flag-draped coffin, and stretched out her hand and touched the flag and kissed the coffin and then rose as gracefully as a young girl and walked away. At least that was the way the people in Washington saw it through their tears.

Two faults commonly arise even in short sentences—the fragmentary sentence and the comma fault.

Fragmentary Sentences

The fragmentary sentence is sometimes called a sham sentence or a period fault. It is only a part of a sentence, usually because it begins with a subordinate word like a preposition, because it lacks a verb, or because it has a participle or "verbal" in place of a full verb. A fragmentary sentence is corrected by joining it by a comma or conjunction to another sentence of which it is logically a part.

Wrong: The man was arraigned in Justice of Peace Court. The City Court being closed for the holiday.

Right: The man was arraigned in Justice of Peace Court because the City Court was closed for the holiday.

Wrong: The council voted a record budget last night. Because the city tax base has grown.

Right: The council voted a record budget last night because the city tax base has grown.

If sentence elements are grouped logically, the problem of sentence fragments can easily be overcome:

Wrong: They walked across the plains; to establish a new colony; to think, to feel, to live, as they wished.

Right: They walked across the plains to establish a colony of their own. It would allow them to think, to feel, to live as they wished.

Comma Faults in Run-On Sentences

A similar problem is the comma fault. A comma may not be used to splice together two independent clauses that can stand alone as separate sentences. Either a semicolon is used, when the thoughts are very closely related or, more commonly, a conjunction is used that clearly indicates the relationship of the two ideas.

Wrong: The plane crashed in a wooded area, it had run out of fuel.
Right: The plane crashed in a wooded area because it had run out of fuel.

Less serious comma faults arise when a conjunctive adverb, rather than a full coordinating conjunction, is used to link the two sentences.

Wrong: He did well on the test, therefore he passed the course.
Right: He did well on the test. Therefore, he passed the course.
             He did well on the test; therefore, he passed the course.

Agreement of Subject and Verb

A verb must agree with its subject in number (singular or plural). Disagreement between subject and verb is usually caused by carelessness. Misunderstanding of correct usage usually occurs in the following instances:

1. *Collective nouns.* In American (as opposed to British) usage, nouns that stand for a group or collectivity take a singular verb: *government is* (not *are*), *the student body* (two words, please) *is* (not *are*); *the team is* (not *are*).
2. *Plural subjects with singular meaning.* The verb here is singular: *Three months is* (not *are*) *required for the internship.*
3. *Different number in subject and complement.* The verb always agrees with the subject, not the words that complete the thought after the verb: *The most difficult part of the trek was* (not *were*) *the last 20 miles over the mountains.*

Misrelated Modifiers

Every word or phrase that modifies or qualifies the meaning of another should be placed in the sentence so that the connection is immediately clear. Usually this means the related words or phrases come together:

Wrong: Jones came to San Francisco after his wife left him to work in the shipyards.
Right: Jones came to San Francisco to work in the shipyards after his wife left him.

Dangling Modifiers

Long introductory phrases should be used sparingly. Often they are used incorrectly. The introductory phrase "dangles" when the main clause does not have the same grammatical subject. The specific kind of initial phrase here is a participle. The meaning of a participial phrase is dependent on what follows it. It is the most common kind of dangling construction, but other phrases with no subject follow the same rule:

Wrong: Upon surveying the dam, several cracks appeared.
Right: Upon surveying the dam, the engineers found several cracks.
Wrong: To survey the dam, the instruments must be sophisticated.
Right: To survey the dam, the engineers must use sophisticated instruments.

Most of the problems associated with the use of participial phrases to begin sentences can be resolved by moving the phrase to follow the word it refers to or making a separate sentence of it.

Wrong: Held in conjunction with the Forest Products Research Society, the agenda. . .
Right: The meeting was held in conjunction with the Forest Products Research Society. The agenda . . .
Wrong: Presently the plant manager, George Vasiliou's 15 years experience . . .
Right: George Vasiliou is now the plant manager. His 15 years' experience . . .

or	The 15 years' experience of George Vasiliou, now the plant manager . . .
Wrong:	When asked to prosecute, investigation of the case resulted in . . .
Right:	The ———— Office was asked to prosecute. Investigation of the case resulted in . . .

Reference of Pronouns

The meaning of many pronouns depends on the nouns they refer to, the antecedents. When encountering pronouns like *this*, *these*, *that*, *them*, *which*, and *it*, make certain the noun related to the word is clear and agrees with it.

Wrong:	At one debate society meeting, *they* debated the question of . . .
Right:	At one meeting, the society debated the question of . . .
Wrong:	The class was boring, and *they* all wished it was over.
Right:	The students found the class boring, and all wished it was over.
Wrong:	He studies newspapers, intending to make *it* his career.
Right:	He studies newspapers, hoping to make news-editorial journalism his career.
Wrong:	He failed to study, *which* caused him to flunk.
Right:	Because he failed to study, he flunked.
Wrong:	Prof. Jones knew a lot about journalism and how to apply *it* in his lectures.
Right:	Prof. Jones knew a lot about journalism and how to apply his knowledge and background to his lectures.
Wrong:	A journalism student has a hard life. Many of *them* fail to graduate.
Right:	Journalism students have a hard life. Many of them fail to graduate.

Everyone and *everybody* are singular, not plural, and take a singular relative pronoun *his*, which is accepted for both genders. To avoid seemingly sexist constructions, more and more writers are going to *everyone/their*, which is not yet accepted as correct. It's better to recast the sentence if the *his* would be offensive.

Wrong:	Everyone should do their job.
Right:	Everyone should do his job.
Alternate:	Everyone should do the assigned job.

Case in Pronouns

Some problems in using pronouns arise from confusion as to the case, the way the relationship of nouns to pronouns is indicated. Pronouns in the *nominative*, or *subjective*, *case* are *I*, *he*, *she*, *we*, *they*, and *who*. Their corresponding forms in the *accusative* or *objective case* are used when the pronoun is a direct or indirect object or the object of a preposition. Most problems you'll have to straighten out occur when the object of the preposition is written in the nominative rather than the correct accusative case:

Wrong:	The instructor came between he and I.
Right:	The instructor came between him and me.

Before attempting the exercises, each of which contains one or more of the grammar problems listed above, correct the following sentences and in the space provided identify the fault.

EXERCISES

Correct the following sentences and name the grammar or punctuation error(s):

1. This year the class is studying emotional disturbances of children. Not just extreme cases.

    _____

2. He thanked everyone for their help.

    _____

3. They believe they will reach their goal for the library of $500.

    _____

4. His duties are to run the internal operations and entails supervision over 50 employees.

    _____

5. He has been employed for about two years and has been able to make pay increases. This has provided an incentive to produce.

    _____

6. Winters on the Mesabi range were always so bitter that great enjoyment was found in indoor hobbies.

    _____

7. Seeing the guard rail, the car swerved to the left.

    _____

8. Once the course is begun, the class works very hard.

    _____

9. The congressman has been educated in law and government and knows how to apply them to the best interests of the people.

    _____

10. After a period of moving from city to city myself and my family settled in Elm City.

_____

11. He referred to the many different localities in which he lived; made new friends; went to different schools, and adjusted to that particular city's way of life.

_____

_____

12. There was a television set, coffee table and chair taken.

_____

13. As a prior sales manager for a large department store, his week ends now are spent in part time selling.

_____

14. The children arrive at school looking like they've already spent the day there.

_____

15. He had worked on his high school paper, therefore he was pleased to find he already knew the fundamentals.

_____

Dog

Riverview County Sheriff's Sgt. Dee Connors said Friday Laboratory tests confirm that an impounded dog dilled a Riverview boy earlier this week.

Blood found on the coat of the Siberian Husky was definately that of a human, Sgt. Connors said.

The dog was im pounded Tuesday night at the Bar T Ranch where the body of Jerry Elson, son of Mr. and Mrs. Jacob Elson, ranch co-owners, was found maulled to death by his brother.

Sgt. Connors said the year old lifestock dog. owned by ranch foreman Rupert McGee, would be put to death, but he did not know exactly when.

The boy apparently provoked thedog when he came between he and a female dog in heat, according to Sgt. Connors.

(Dog)

~~Riverview County Sheriff's Sgt. Dee Connors said Friday~~ Laboratory tests confirm that a~~n impounded~~ dog killed a Riverview boy earlier this week.

Blood found on the coat of the Siberian Husky was ~~definately that of a~~ human, *said Dee* Sgt. Connors ~~said.~~ *of the sheriff's office.*

The dog was im pounded Tuesday night at the Bar T Ranch, where ~~the body of~~ Jerry Elson, son of Mr. and Mrs. Jacob Elson, ranch co-owners, was found maulled to death, ~~by his brother.~~

~~Sgt.~~ Connors said the year-old lifestock dog, owned by ranch foreman Rupert McGee, would be put to death, ~~but he did not know exactly when.~~

The boy apparently provoked the dog when he came between ~~he~~ *it* and a ~~female~~ dog in heat, according to ~~Sgt.~~ Connors.

Central

A new system for detecting fires in city scholls is currently being installed at Central High.

The detection system is sensitive enough to pick up smoke, fumes and heat almost immediately.

The system now being installed at Central High is plugged into a master box at Fire Department headquarters and will eventually eliminate manuel systems, according to Fire Marshall Michael Ringman.

There has been trouble at Central in recent weeks in regards to false drops, says Ringman, because the manuel alarms are easy to locate and the students enjoy getting out of school.

With the installation of new detector heads, once an alarm goes off the Fire Department knows its for real and won't be botherdd with false alarms, points out Marshall Ringman.

The system at Central will be sensitive enough to pick up smoke, fumes and heat, but not sensitive enough to pick up every little thing/

Last week, says Ringman, the detector system went off because of fumes emitted from a snowblower brought into the halls by a janitor. The system is being fixed to prevent this, Ringman added.

The system workers have been installing the detector heasds for two weeks now and should be finished shortly.

Sometimes the heads get knocked out by vandals, so "we'll put them in more difficult places this time," says the Marshall.

If the system proves successful Marshall Ringman has hopes of installing them in every high scchool, thus eliminating the manuel alarms altogether. "It sure would be easier on us," says Ringman.

#

Airport

Local airport plans along with aviation and its affect upon the community was the program presented to the Chamber of Commerce by Martin Emple, Vice President and General Manager of Sky High Air Lines.

Beginning with films showing the adequate results an adequate airport has had on several communities, the group heard of the plans in progress at the Arport.

In sight for Sky High air lines is a new taxi way, a maintainance center and a new large all weather aircraft. They do not now have such a plane.

Mr. Emple said they hoped soon to be able to fly in all weather outside condition and to add a 2nd flight daily to Salt Lake City, with a flight to Las Vegas in between. He also discussed time and costs, its importance to running the commutor service, there importance to the community, freight, air ambulence service and the flight schedules of the National parks.

The group also heard about a new bod bond election the city council has scheduled for Pebru r y 20 in an effort to raise funds for the improvement of the city water system。

Plans call for the drilling of an additional well and additional water mains that will be used to distribute the water supply to the systems customers, the mayor said.

Storm

Many city and county residents found themselves on skid row early Monday when a snow storm hit an area limited largely to the northern county. Beginning near 7 a.m., and after an overnight low of 17 degrees, city streets and highways were turned to ice.

Hitting just as the morning traffic rush began, many cars went skidding and spinning along roads, particularly in hilly areas of the city.

The problems caused by the morning storm were repeated Monday just after 7:30 p.m. when a light snow began. Coating streets and causing numerous accidents. Cars trying to make their way up hills on the east and north benches of the city were again stalled。

There was also ground blizzard conditions north of city in the Elk County. Police officials said that during the morning storm 52 accidents were reported on the east side alone. The Highway Patrol also reported a large number and all three law units said there were probably many more that were not reported.

The storm caught road maintenance crews unaware, but the cleanup department said crews were sent out as soon as they reported to work。

Ray Johnson, County highways administrator, said the storm, "kicked us

right in the pants. I don't want to see another one of these." He
said he immediately diverted men coming on the job to clearing and
sanding streets.

Almost all the rest of the state was clear and dry until near 6 p.m.
when an equally limited and just as vicious snow hit Juniper County,
turning the streets and highways there to glass.

Burned

    Two county firemen suffered first degree burns on their necks and
backs when a piece of burning panelling fell on them while fighting a
house fire.

    Sam Bennion and Don Webster were released after treatment at
General Hospital.

    Battalion Chief Albert Morris said the two men had entered adjacent
rooms and were fighting a fire ahead of them when the pieces of panelling
dropped off the wall.

    The fire occurred at the home of Robert Paulsen, 9234 Lakeside Drive
at 2:54 p.m. causing $9,000 damage.

    Cause of the blaze is still under investigation.

Traffic

    The City Traffic Advisory Council Friday said it will send a letter
to city council opposing the painting of "zebra" stripe crosswalks.

    The group noted they have received reports of senior citizens
slipping on the painted surface -- especially when they are wet.

Salvation

The Salvation Army of the City Command will be serving their annual Christmas turkey dinner for local families and unattached singles at the First Presbyterian Church from noon to 2 p.m. Christmas Day.

A pick up service consisting of one 20-passenger bus and three VW buses will run every 10 to 15 minutes along a route posted on charts placed in most of the hotels and motels where people needing this service will be staying.

The annual dinner is one of the traditional services that the Salvation Army renders to the area at Christmastime.

Abduct

CELERYVILLE, Elk County -- A 20-year-old service station attendant was abducted at gun point Friday at 1:30 A. M. and released unharmed on State Highway 31 about 10 miles north of here after a robbery in which $100 was taken.

The victim, James Woods, was alone at Roberts 66 Service, when three men and a girl in their twenties drove in to be serviced. Then one of the men pulled a pistol, rifled the cash register and forced Mr. Wood face down into the back seat.

Starting back on foot, a passing motorist picked Mr. Woods up and took him to the Celeryville Highway Patrol station.

Trooper Rodney Simons said raod blocks were set up on all major roads but the holdup car was not located.

10. USING WORDS CORRECTLY

When Witness A says "the contract cost $2 million" and Witness B says "the contract cost $1 million," which of the following is correct?

Witness "B" disputed the statement of Witness A.

Witness "B" refuted the statement of Witness A.

Dispute means to challenge. *Refute* means to prove erroneous. Therefore, since law is inexact, relative, and not a science, the choice almost always is *dispute* rather than *refute*. Yet *refute* is probably used as often as is *dispute*. Why? Because here, as so often, editors are not aware of important distinctions.

Does it matter whether you call a person an "accused murderer" or one "accused of murder"? Yes. The first implies that the person is indeed a murderer who at this point has only been accused. The second states the case precisely. Editors should be cautious in using labels. *Convicted murderer* is a common label, but it is just as inappropriate as *accused murderer*. The label is handier than the more precise *convicted of murder*, which may pose a greater challenge in phraseology. But a good editor will never shrink from the task of seeking precision.

Most of the diction problems you will encounter as an editor are covered by entries in your stylebook. As a start in using the style entries to resolve questions about word distinctions, test yourself on the exercises on the following pages.

EXERCISES

Cross out the incorrect word.

1. The air base said 50 FLIERS/FLYERS would take part in the show.

2. Some 500 FLIERS/FLYERS were distributed by the committee.

3. The accountant said the money would be DISBURSED/DISPERSED.

4. The people were charged with failure to DISBURSE/DISPERSE.

5. The petition was not expected to have any AFFECT/EFFECT.

6. The petition was not expected to AFFECT/EFFECT the outcome.

7. Gen. Williams said he was ADVERSE/AVERSE to the plan.

8. The weather was ADVERSE/AVERSE.

9. The crowd was estimated at MORE THAN/OVER 50,000.

10. An important PRINCIPAL/PRINCIPLE of law was involved.

11. The PRINCIPAL/PRINCIPLE said school would start Aug. 15.

12. The sacks will LAY/LIE there until somebody finds them.

13. He said he would LAY/LIE the paper on the doorstep.

14. She walked TOWARD/TOWARDS the airplane.

15. AFTERWARD/AFTERWARDS, they went to the store.

16. IT'S/ITS a sin to tell a lie.

17. IT'S/ITS fender was damaged.

18. He made an ALLUSION/ILLUSION to a famous quotation.

19. She said she was under no ALLUSION/ILLUSION about the outcome.

20. The speaker said: "I INFER/IMPLY from what you say . . ."

21. He asked: "Do you mean to INFER/IMPLY that I'm wrong?"

22. Smith, to WHO/WHOM the book had been sold, wanted a refund.

23. Allen, WHO/WHOM was seen in the alley, was arrested.

24. WHO'S/WHOSE lantern is this?

25. WHO'S/WHOSE knocking at my door?

26. FEWER/LESS people were on the street today.

27. I have FEWER/LESS money than you have.

28. "I need a lawyer," she said, "I'm hiring COUNCIL/COUNSEL."

29. The matter will be considered by the City COUNCIL/COUNSEL.

30. "I'm giving you a COMPLEMENT/COMPLIMENT for that work," he said.

31. The highs and lows COMPLEMENT/COMPLIMENT each other nicely.

32. She said she would be DISCRETE/DISCREET with the information.

33. The numbers are DISCRETE/DISCREET.

34. The show got UNDERWAY/UNDER WAY.

35. He liked to FLAUNT/FLOUT his wealth by buying expensive cars.

Distinguish between the following terms. Use the AP/UPI Stylebook.

1. Complacent

   Complaisant

2. Celebrant

   Celebrator

3. Further

   Farther

4. Fewer

   Less

5. Filly

   Mare

6. Flaunt

   Flout

7. Imply

   Infer

8. It's

   Its

9. Irregardless

   Regardless

10. Mailman

    Letter carrier

11. Majority

    Plurality

12. Noisome

    Noisy

13. Pretense

    Pretext

14. Raised

    Reared

15. Restaurateur

    Restauranteur

16. Over

    More than

17. Affect

    Effect

18. Principal

    Principle

19. Burglary

    Robbery

20. Stanch

    Staunch

For each of these give a simpler, "talky" word:

1. Purchased

2. Employ

3. Utilize

4. Attempt

5. Interrogate

6. Partake

7. Monumental

8. Terminate

9. Witness

10. Reside

11. Procure

12. Proceed

13. Contribute

11. SPELLING IT RIGHT

Bias, lack of balance, incompleteness, and other nuances are frequently difficult to detect, but misspellings are obvious. A good editor must be a good speller and have a dictionary handy. The slightest shiver of doubt should be followed by an immediate ruffling of pages, be they in a bulky, comprehensive reference mounted on a swivel stand or in a pocket-sized listing of frequently fumbled words.

A single misspelled word can destroy the image of an entire article, because the carelessness that permitted the misspelling reflects on the quality of the copy as a whole. Consider this sentence: "The teacher said she objected in principal to the spending of $1 million on a football stadium." The proper word is *principle*. But if the writer or editor doesn't know the difference, the reader may wonder as well whether the $1 million figure was correct.

An editorial page editor made the same point in commenting on other writing, in this case on the spelling in a letter submitted by a reader. Of 166 words, nine were misspelled. The editor said, "The letter was obviously the work of an intelligent, informed, and concerned person. However, the five percent misspelling rate so distracts from the effectiveness of the letter that the message is wasted, as was the author's effort in composing it. Bad typing doesn't account for *truly* spelled *truely*, or *inevitable* showing up as *inevible* or *terrific* being corrupted into *terific*."

Don't suppose for a moment that the subject-matter experts on your own newspaper staff will spell expertly even when using words common in their own fields: The medical writer may spell *hemorrhage* as *hemmorage*, the environmental writer may spell *carcinogen* as *carcinogan*, and the business writer may spell *demonetization* as *demonitization*.

Correcting spelling errors once an edition has gone to press or a story has moved on the news wires is cumbersome and expensive. When a copy editor has written a headline about a "tenative" agreement or talked of "hoards" of refugees fleeing, there's no recourse but to remake the page and get the correct spelling on the press as quickly as possible. (Television graphics also are prone to misspellings, and they should be checked carefully before they get on the air.) The news services send fast corrections of misspellings that appear on the wires. Sometimes they will send a writethrough of an entire story in order to make certain the correct spelling is used.

There is only one secret to becoming a good speller: hard work. Chances are that if you liked to read and write in elementary school you're a pretty good speller. That's because you enjoyed exposure to words and learned to recognize them visually or developed a knack for the various sound combinations that can be spelled in several ways. If you aren't a particularly good speller but want to be an editor, you have work to do.

Notice the spelling of words as you read them and as you write them. When you check a word in a dictionary, analyze why you may have spelled it incorrectly, particularly when you repeat mistakes. Be alert to confusions caused by similarity of sound, such as *principal* and *principle;* confusions caused by similar appearance, as in *angel, angle;* words you may misspell because they are so often mispronounced, as in *February (Febuary)* and *nuclear (nuculer);* and failure to think of a word by syllables, as in the frequently misspelled *laboratory.*

There are few universal rules in spelling. Nursery-rhyme phrases like the following probably have served good spellers as well as have formal axioms:

- *I* before *e*—except after *c* or when sounding like *a* as in *neighbor* and *weigh* (*achieve, believe, conceive, reign*).
- *Y* becomes *i* when *e-s* stops by (*money, monies; tummy, tummies; funny, funnies; biography, biographies*).
- When two vowels go walking, the first does the talking (*ear, spear, nail*).
- A long vowel in a short word means there's an *e* that isn't heard (*tote, make, trite, bugle*).
- The silent *e* steals away when *i-n-g* comes to stay (*wake, waking; choke, choking; race, racing; taste, tasting*).

Of course, there are exceptions to these. For instance, the first two examples in the first rule violate the third rule. The user of such rules faces a dilemma in words that may be pronounced more than one way, such as neither (*neether, nyther*) and either (*eether, eye-ther*).

Other seat-of-the-pants formulas for spelling include the use of phrase associations. For example, you can remember how to spell *geography* by recalling the phrase *George Elliott's Old Grandmother Rode a Pig Home Yesterday.*

A better method, however, is to learn to recognize words and to have a feel for the sounds of those you don't recognize. It's work, and you had best get to it if you aren't confident of your ability.

EXERCISES

Test your skill on the following exercises. In the following list, write the correct spelling on the blank line. Some words are misspelled, but others are correct. In either case, writing the correct version will be good practice. The answers are on the pages following the exercise, but you are only cheating yourself if you look them up before you go through the entire list.

1. Academic _____

2. Accomodate _____

3. Acheive _____

4. Alotted _____

5. Benefitted _____

6.   Concensus   _____

7.   Conscience   _____

8.   Conveniance   _____

9.   Disperse (money)   _____

10. Dissention   _____

11. Embarass   _____

12. Excede   _____

13. Feasable   _____

14. Guage   _____

15. Grammer   _____

16. Harrass   _____

17. Idealogy   _____

18. Irresistable   _____

19. It's (possessive)   _____

20. Its (it is)   _____

21. Knowlege   _____

22. Liason   _____

23. Maintainence   _____

24. Malleable   _____

25. Mischievious   _____

26. Niece   _____

27. Parallel   _____

28. Perogative   _____

29. Posess   _____

30. Preceeding   _____

31. Principal (money)   _____

32. Principle (rule)   _____

33. Priviledge   _____

34. Pronounciation   _____

35. Publically   _____

36. Reccomend   _____

37. Recieve   _____

38. Restaraunteur   _____

39. Sacreligious   _____

40. Seize   _____

41. Seperate   _____

42. Sherriff   _____

43. Squirrel   _____

44. Tenent (belief)   _____

45. Their (possessive)   _____

46. There (place)   _____

47. Tittillate   _____

48. Turbulance   _____

49. Unnecesary   _____

50. Wierd   _____

Answers

1. Academic   Academic

2. Accomodate   Accommodate

3. Acheive   Achieve

4. Alotted   Allotted

5. Benefitted   Benefited

6.	Concensus	Consensus
7.	Conscience	Conscience
8.	Conveniance	Convenience
9.	Disperse (money)	Disburse
10.	Dissention	Dissension
11.	Embarass	Embarrass
12.	Excede	Exceed
13.	Feasable	Feasible
14.	Guage	Gauge
15.	Grammer	Grammar
16.	Harrass	Harass
17.	Idealogy	Ideology
18.	Irresistable	Irresistible
19.	It's (possessive)	Its
20.	Its (it is)	It's
21.	Knowlege	Knowledge
22.	Liason	Liaison
23.	Maintainence	Maintenance
24.	Malleable	Malleable
25.	Mischievious	Mischievous
26.	Niece	Niece
27.	Parallel	Parallel
28.	Perogative	Prerogative
29.	Posess	Possess
30.	Preceeding	Preceding
31.	Principal (money)	Principal

32. Principle (rule)	Principle
33. Priviledge	Privilege
34. Pronounciation	Pronunciation
35. Publically	Publicly
36. Reccomend	Recommend
37. Recieve	Receive
38. Restauraunteur	Restaurateur
39. Sacreligious	Sacrilegious
40. Seize	Seize
41. Seperate	Separate
42. Sherriff	Sheriff
43. Squirrel	Squirrel
44. Tenent (belief)	Tenet
45. Their (possessive)	Their
46. There (place)	There
47. Tittillate	Titillate
48. Turbulance	Turbulence
49. Unnecesary	Unnecessary
50. Wierd	Weird

12. MAKING IT TIGHT AND CLEAR

Editing and tightening are frequently synonymous. Few written works lack superfluous words. You can find fat everywhere. Pick up a newspaper and see how many words and phrases you can eliminate without damaging the message. Read an advertisement and do the same thing. Do you find a textbook boring? Take a chapter and start redlining all the material that adds length but not strength. Do it with this workbook. The authors, even after years of teaching others the art of editing, do not claim immunity from redundancy, overstatement, or other errors.

Most writers are impatient. They want to finish the job. Thoughts do not wait for precise expression. They flow, often piling atop each other at a pace defying capture by even the fastest typist. The writer records the thought, but the expression may be one of convenience under pressure—not necessarily one of clarity. There is time later for the honing and polishing that form the fiber of editing—or there is no time at all. The author of a manuscript due in a month may have ample opportunity to sharpen the product. A newspaper reporter on deadline literally may have to hurl a rough draft on an editor's desk.

The goal of tightening is to clear away the haze, the fog that obscures the object of expression. You've heard such remarks as "On a clear day you can see forever," and "The mountains look closer on a sunny day." The relative truth of both statements has a parallel in editing. Just as the absence of haze enhances visual perception, the absence of excess wordage enhances understanding.

Readability

For this course, clarity may be considered akin to *readability*, a term that gained great popularity decades ago when researchers began studying relationships between understanding and such factors as word and sentence length. Various formulas were designed to measure readability. The notations at the end of this chapter tell you where to find them. You may find it interesting to test a few formulas on novels, textbooks, newspapers, and advertisements. Different formulas will yield different results, lending strength to the idea that clarity involves more than mechanics.

However, most readability formulas suggest an important common denominator: Relatively short sentences, and words of few syllables, are easier to read and understand than are lengthy sentences laden with polysyllabic expressions. But that is not to say all sentences should be short. A staccato string of one-liners may be fine in a nightclub act, but on paper it can be distracting rather than enlightening. As an editor, you would do well to keep in mind this advice from the pages of Strunk and White's *The Elements of Style:*

> Vigorous writing is concise. A sentence should contain no unnecessary words, a paragraph no unnecessary sentences, for the same reason that a drawing should have no unnecessary lines and a machine no unnecessary parts. This requires not that the writer make all his sentences short, or that he avoid all detail and treat his subjects only in outline, but that every word tell.

Yes, make every word tell. If you want a phrase to serve as your editing motto, you can do no better than that: Make every word tell. Making every word tell enables a novelist to weave a spellbinding story through hundreds of pages. Making every word tell enables a newspaper reporter to produce a story that starts the town talking. Making every word tell enables an editor to help both the novelist and the reporter achieve their goals.

Brevity

Brevity is a good rule of thumb, but not a shrine to be worshipped. Sometimes in their zeal editors take out too much, leaving the copy lifeless. While deft use of a pencil or the *delete word* button can salvage a turgid article or even make it sparkle, heavy-handed editing can destroy style, emphasis, and accuracy. Overediting is as much a mark of amateurism as is overwriting. Good writing demands fullness in the sense that important questions are answered and that proper emphasis is accorded each statement.

Take the following sentence: "The Energy Department has promised a full accounting of the incident but did not indicate a timetable for such a report." A wholesale tightening would dictate: "The Energy Department has promised an accounting but did not say when." Perhaps, however, this is too abrupt. A more charitable editing might be, "The

Energy Department has promised an accounting but did not say when the report would be made." Or take this one: "Don't use a nail that has any rust on it at all" could be tightened to "Don't use a rusty nail," unless the author wanted to point out emphatically that if you use a nail with even a tiny speck of rust you're in for trouble. In tightening your stories have respect and concern for the writer, whose task of communicating is lonely and hard. Help the writer reach the audience, but do not overedit. Above all, have concern for the reader.

Editors also serve the cause of clarity when they eliminate meaningless words or phrases. A good example is *located*. Every time you see the word, try to eliminate it. You'll find it can be done easily, and that your phrase will be every bit as precise without it. "The house is located at 500 South Warren Street." Is that different from "The house is at 500 South Warren Street?" No. You also may purge your vocabulary of *the fact that*. "The fact that Smith has a big nose has no bearing on his intelligence" is no different than "That Smith has a big nose . . ."

Some excellent advice given to writers is "All good writing is rewriting" and "Write the way you talk." These slogans mean that clear expression is hard work and that you should use familiar words. Editors can adopt that advice, but with this word of caution: Not all good editing is heavy editing, and the best word is not always the most convenient. Consider this sentence:

Original: He said he believed the fire was "hotter than hell."
Edited: He believed the fire was hot.

Here the advantage of the edited version is that it saves words. The brevity, however, is offset by two errors. First, we can never know what someone else really thinks, believes, or feels. All we can know is what they *say* they think, believe, or feel. Thus, the saving in words puts the editor in the position of verifying a belief that cannot be verified in the same manner as one can verify that today is Sunday, Monday, or another day of the week. A good editor will never try to save words at the expense of accuracy. Second, paraphrasing and simplifying the quote robs it of its vitality. The statement suggests a degree of heat, a degree that tells us something of the speaker's tone. Even if we cannot know exactly what is meant, we can know that "hot" is an inadequate representation of the speaker's statement. Here are two more sentences:

Original: The boy said, "I was askeered sumpin' would happen to me."
Edited: The boy said he was afraid.

Again, editing has saved words at the expense of vitality. *Askeered* is not in the dictionary. *Afraid* is a simple word known to all. But *askeered*, the exact expression of the person being quoted, gives us a better image of the individual. The fear that "sumpin' would happen" to him is an elaboration on why he was "askeered." Retaining the original language leaves in the life, which is far more important in this example than trying to eliminate fat.

Simplicity

One of the best-known readability experts, Rudolf Flesch, was hired by the Associated Press to analyze the understandability of its writing. He told writers, "Clarity relies almost completely on simplicity." In addition to stressing short words and sentences, he said, "Confusion comes from complex sentence construction, awkward alignment of clauses, unexplained technical terms and other hifalutin words. A complicated lead may be accurate and, with study, intelligible. But the hurried reader probably will not grasp it."

The same habits of writing that result in ponderous instead of talky words also lead to the stilted and almost incomprehensible writing that sometimes characterizes legal, governmental, academic—and unfortunately, even media—communications. "Our language becomes more and more covered, obscure, turgid, ponderous, and overblown," says Edwin Newman, the NBC correspondent who has waged a personal war to, as he puts it, puncture the overblown. "A civil tongue means to me a language that is not bogged down in jargon, not puffed up with false dignity, not studded with trick phrases that have lost their meaning." Newman's two fine books, *Strictly Speaking* and *A Civil Tongue*, are cited at the end of this chapter.

A story that has been going the rounds for years—but whose point seems often to be missed by bureaucrats—tells how a plumber inquired of the U.S. Bureau of Standards whether he should clean clogged drains with hydrochloric acid. The bureau replied: "The efficacy of hydrochloric acid is indisputable, but the corrosive residue is incompatible with metallic permanence." This meant: "Don't use hydrochloric acid—it will eat through the pipes."

An editor also performs a service for both the writer and the reader in deleting words which usually appear only in print—seldom in conversation. For example, a flood of water is almost certain to bring a flood of stories containing the word *inundate*. When was the last time you heard someone use *inundate* about a flood in conversation? *Flood* is a precise, everyday word that means the same thing as *inundate*. So who needs *inundate?* It is a dictionary word but not a conversational word, and editors are wise to eliminate it at every opportunity. "Homes were flooded." "Homes were inundated." Which would you prefer to read, assuming the words mean the same thing? Most likely, your choice would be *flooded*, simply because it is the word you would use in conversation.

In *The Elements of Style*, Strunk and White, in an excellent section entitled "An Approach to Style," urge a concern for the "ear," or the sound of a phrase. The "ear" often overrides rigid rules of grammar. If you like or dislike the sound of a phrase, judge it first against your "ear," and only secondarily against someone else's yardstick. Remember that there are several grammatically correct ways to express most statements.

Are you confused by this discussion? Frustrated because it does not give you a ready reference to proper editing in every situation? If so, perhaps you are looking at editing in a negative way. Don't. Editing is fun and hard work at the same time. Tightening, as part of editing, is both of those things too. No, you cannot tighten everything and call yourself a good editor. While you will do more tightening than stretching, you must always remember that editing involves imagination.

On the following pages, you will find exercises that challenge you to melt the fat from phrases. You also will find phrases where editing seems tempting but is unwarranted. Do not assume the pencil must be used simply because you hold it in your hand. Do not hesitate to use it where the reader will be served. In either case, be ready to defend your changes.

SELECTED READINGS

Bernstein, Theodore M. *Watch Your Language.* New York: Atheneum, 1965. A lively, informal guide to better writing, emanating from the news room of *The New York Times.*

Charnley, Mitchell V., and Blair Charnley. *Reporting,* 4th ed. New York: Holt, Rinehart and Winston, 1979. One of the best of several new reporting texts, readable and comprehensive.

Flesch, Rudolf. *The Art of Plain Talk.* New York: Harper & Row, 1946. A pioneer work by the readability expert whose theories and formula have had a major impact on American news writing.

Fowler, H. W. *A Dictionary of Modern English Usage.* London: Oxford University Press, 1950.

Gunning, Robert. *The Technique of Clear Writing,* rev. ed. New York: McGraw-Hill, 1968. For clear, effective writing—follow these ten principles from the Gunning Formula of Readability.

Hodges, John C., and Mary E. Whitten. *Harbrace College Handbook.* New York: Harcourt Brace Jovanovich, 1977. A grammar book widely recommended by college English departments, with clear and comprehensive rules arranged for easy reference.

Maugham, W. Somerset. *The Summing Up.* New York: Penguin Books, 1946. The great novelist's reflections on the art of writing, still vibrant and relevant for any writer today.

Newman, Edwin. *A Civil Tongue.* Indianapolis: Bobbs-Merrill, 1975. Newman's wry eye focuses on the sorry state of the English language as a reflection of the sorry state of the society.

———————.*Strictly Speaking: Will America Be the Death of English?* New York: Bobbs-Merrill, 1974.

Rivers, William L. *Writing: Craft and Art.* Englewood Cliffs, N.J.: Prentice-Hall, 1975.

Strunk, William Jr., and E. B. White. *The Elements of Style*, 3rd edition. New York: Macmillan, 1979. The "little book" that contains clear, simple guides to effective expression. A classic.

EXERCISES

Tighten the following sentences by

1. Striking out all phrases unneeded because they are self-explanatory:

    Example: Safe car seats are not expensive~~to buy~~.

2. Substituting a single root word for a puffed-up phrase:

    Example: The operation ~~had its origins~~ *began* well before the turn of the century.

3. Eliminating cluttering modish phrases:

    Example: He said controls are not needed ~~at this point in time~~ *now*.

4. Recasting unemphatic constructions:

    Example: ~~There were~~ four ~~of them~~ *were* in the room.

1. Sixty percent of them believed the state should engage in censorship of books.

2. He said there were a few companies in California that were organized for the primary purpose of offering malpractice insurance.

3. The poll was taken during the period from November 4 to November 7.

4. An autopsy to determine the cause of death is scheduled to be performed Monday.

5. Sales rose for the fourth consecutive month in a row.

6. A year will be needed to make a decision as to whether or not to mine the ore.

7. Due to the above facts Rosalie decided to go into the study of music.

8. The senator will rank in the upper one fourth in terms of seniority.

9. The twins were born between 5:30 and 6 p.m. Friday evening.

10. The suspension of service applies only to interstate moves from one state to another.

11. Lumber prices rose sharply last year, with increased building as the major cause of the increase.

12. Police departments operate copters which are capable of flying injured to hospitals at speeds up to 100 mph.

13. The decline in sales is costing the company $25 million a year in revenue.

14. The highway is expected to bring traffic to local businesses for at least another year or more.

15. The toll for September rose to six -- four of them in the past week.

16. He was a public accountant by profession.

17. The copying machine was located in the downstairs portion of the building.

18. She was born in the city of Wichita in the state of Kansas.

19. Within a short period of time he was married.

20. The exercises were so designed that one would use all of the muscles of the body.

Postpone

A public meeting called for the purpose of registering objections to the construction of a proposed shopping center at the corner of 10th Street and 5th Avenue was cancelled indefinitely Tuesday night.

A spokesman for the citizen group against the construction, Hardy W. Stratton, said the group is opposed to the building of the shops, a gas station and a Roy Rodgerd drive-in food shop in the area. He said the meeting was cancelled pending the receipt of more information in connection with possible legal action ordering the Johanson Construction Co. to stop construction.

Stratton went on to say that sufficient publicity had not been given when a zoning hearing was called earlier by the County Commission. He pointed out the construction firm is ignoring a request made on Aug. 26 by the County Ato Attorney, to d cease construction until the matter could be five given further consideration.

#

(Postpone)

A public meeting called ~~for the purpose of registering~~ objec~~tions~~ *to* to ~~the~~ construction of a ~~proposed~~ shopping center at ~~the corner of~~ 10th Street and ~~5th~~ *Fifth* Avenue was ~~cancelled~~ *postponed* indefinitely Tuesday night.

A spokesman ~~for the citizen group against the construction,~~ Hardy W. Stratton, said ~~the~~ group *a citizens* ~~is~~ opposed ~~to the~~ building ~~of~~ the shops, a gas station, and a Roy Rodgers drive-in food shop in the area. He said the ~~meeting was cancelled pending the receipt of more~~ *group needs* information ~~in~~ ~~connection with~~ possible legal action *that would* ~~ordering~~ the Johanson Construction Co. to stop construction.

Stratton ~~went on to say that~~ *said* ~~ins~~ sufficient *notice was* ~~publicity had not been~~ given when a zoning hearing was called ~~earlier~~ by the County Commission. He ~~pointed out~~ *said* the construction firm is ignoring a request made on Aug. 26 by the County ~~Ato~~ Attorney, to ~~d~~ cease construction until the matter could be ~~five given further~~ consider ~~ation~~ *ed*.

(#)

Egg Hunt

RIVERVIEW - A change from the traditional time and age groups for the Riverview Elks Lodge Easter egg hunt were announced by committee members today.

The hunts will begin sikultaneously at 10 a.m. at the City Part and the Riverview Lions Park.

At the Lions Park, youngsters four through seven will participate.

At the City Park, those three and under will be roped off in an area at the northwest section of the park, while those eight through 12 will be in another area.

Todd Ford and Bob Blumer, co-chairmen, said many of the candy eggs will have nickles and dimes attached and several larger eggs wi 11 have dollar bills inside.

All children of the area are invited to participate.

Reward

Riverview -- Riverview High School's two music instructors are recipients of the Riverview Rotary Club's first "Service Above Self" award for their contribution "above and beyond their requirements in their provession.

Brent Anderson adn Sam Richards were presented plawues by Paul Merriweather, director of community services for the club.

Among the accomplishments the pair has to their credit, is the annual community-Christmas musical program presented the Sunday before Christmas. The popular program grew in its second year so much that two performances were required in order for everyone desiring to attend to be able to enter the building.

Over 1,500 persons attended this year's performance which includes the various instrumentation and vocal groups of the high school.

The two men also work with the drama directors of the school in providing music for the annual school musicals, as well as work with and provide entertainment -- individually and with their students -- at various community and club affairs.

In addition, the two talented men have appeared as soloists for community and church programs.

Bond

Spencer City Council has scheduled a $400,000 bond election for Feb. 20 in an effort to raise funds for improvement in the city's water system system

Mayor Wendell Smith said passage of the bond will not increase the city taxes. Although the bonds are being sold as general obligation for lower interest rates, increased revenues from the watrer system is expected to pay cover all costs.

The city serves much of the surrounding area.

Part III

★★★★★★★★★★★★★★★★

Accuracy and Credibility

★★★★★★★★★★★★★★★★

13. ACCURACY

What is accuracy? The answer is as broad as "What is truth?" but this need not discourage us. Throughout this book, we will be looking at this problem in its large dimensions. In this section we will be concerned mostly with the most fundamental precept, factual accuracy, or accuracy as to precise, specific, verifiable details. We will also look at some problems of interpretation and some of omission. In such stories, the facts may not be demonstrably wrong but the story nonetheless may be wrongheaded, as when figures are misinterpreted. Some exercises give you the opportunity to apply knowledge of libel law. Earlier sections dealt with such problems as improper organization and overwriting, which also affect accuracy.

The possibility for error in newspapers, and in all publications, is vast. A typical edition of a metropolitan paper contains perhaps 5,000 verifiable facts. Add to these possibilities for error of commission the countless possibilities for errors in interpretation and omission. Many people have been victimized by the press through an inaccurate statement, be it so casual an error as a misspelled name or wrong address. It's easy to see why on this basis alone the press has a continuous problem of maintaining credibility.

Believability of the Press
How much news that people read, hear, and see do they believe? If disbelief is high, why? If distrust is severe and endemic, what are the implications for democratic government? These questions concern all media. During much of the 1960s, the press excoriated government, asserting that a "credibility gap" existed. By the mid-1960s, the press became vaguely aware that its own credibility was under attack. More recently, the press has faced the job of

convincing readers and viewers that the media are decent, restrained, mature, and accurate. Complaints about the media's presentation may be summarized as

1. A failure to adhere to the ideals and goals of objectivity, by presenting one-sided or slanted news.
2. A propensity to emphasize "bad" news rather than constructive news.
3. Sensation for the sake of gaining readership.
4. Shallow, incomplete, or incorrect reports.

Read the polls. A lot of people say the media present primarily bad news and distorted pictures of life. Government officials often echo this theme, because there is an ambivalent partnership/adversary relationship between the press and public officials. The press works with duly constituted officials to help them reach the public. At the same time, the press is supposed to be the conscience and watchdog of public affairs. Government officials have re-inforced negative appraisals by calling attention to self-criticism by the media and by suggesting that government administrators have sources of information superior to the press's.

Some journalists have written off criticism as the inevitable byproduct of the kind of news the media deal in today: the bearer of unhappy news is often accused of creating it. The press has indulged in much soul-searching on questions of its accuracy and adequacy. This suggests that the number of *deliberate* errors is far fewer than newspapers' detractors suggest, and that lying is rare. Why? First, it is safe to generalize that most publishers, editors and reporters are as honorable as are people in any other profession. They hold membership in trade and professional associations that stress high ethical conduct, and they aim for professionalism in the best sense of the term. There is probably no greater proportion of rascals in journalism than in medicine, law, plumbing, education, or any other field of human endeavor.

Second, the self-righting process in the free and open society's "encounter of ideas" ultimately exposes falsity. The overall impressions of the news over a period of time, rather than the fragments that appear in spot reporting, ultimately prevail in opinion formation. This tends to override the influence of inadvertent inaccuracy and other errors of omission and commission.

Third, publishers are in business for the long haul, and they recognize veracity, honor, and public service as essential to their continued existence. Deliberate slanting is poor business.

Both newspapers and magazines are more inclined than formerly to correct errors, even trivial ones. Some newspapers carry a regular correction column in a prominent, anchored (constant in every issue) position. Some resist the idea of correcting in print all the small errors called to their attention. They argue that a recital of errors conveys an erroneous impression of general incorrectness. Others argue that correcting errors improves credibility.

The most serious criticisms are not easy to redress with a mere correction. They are problems of omission and shallowness. Time or space limitations often are to blame for such errors. There simply is not enough room to print every story in depth. The problem of shallowness is now being corrected to some degree by all media, including the community newspapers, by turning attention from exclusively spot reporting to backgrounding, trying to give what some call the full dimensions of the news. Other problems of inaccuracy result from slipshod reporting, especially haste and misunderstanding. Often a capable editor can correct these quickly.

Factual Accuracy

Checking for factual accuracy means making certain names are spelled correctly, addresses are correct, identifications of persons and places are correct and as complete as needed on first reference, lists of figures tally to sums expressed, and times of events are correctly listed, etc. No fact is too trivial to be correct, if for no other reason than that an error of fact will tend to destroy the credibility of a whole piece.

As Ralph McGill, late publisher of the *Atlanta Constitution*, told young journalists: "You will be dealing in large measure with facts. Even though some of those are the small nuts and bolts of routine reporting of civic clubs and community meetings, they are facts. As such, they merit respect. A good rule is to check all the sources—and then try to find more."

In order to keep a running check on their own standards of accuracy, some newspapers mail to persons named in stories selected at random a clipping of the story accompanied by questions about accuracy, completeness and fairness.

The primary reason for factual inaccuracy is failure to check with a source, such as a dictionary, telephone book, city directory, *Congressional Dictionary*, the *World Almanac*, or an atlas. Standard reference works should be at hand whenever one reads copy for publication. Every metropolitan newspaper desk has them.

Some magazines take extraordinary care, well beyond the assembly-line production from reporter-to-editor-to-copydesk routing of the typical metropolitan daily, in checking out verifiable facts on which conclusions are drawn. The research staffs of some publications check every word to certify accuracy.

In the daily press it is impossible on most desks to doublecheck every name, date, address, or figure. But it is possible to check every *doubtful* fact. Every twinge of doubt one has about a fact should be checked out—by the writer first and by the editor as the court of last resort. Incompetence, laziness, haste, and distraction are the enemies of factual accuracy. These lapses occur in both major stories and relatively trivial ones. In a report of a speech, a reporter wrote that a historian had authored a biography of Sir Richard Burton. The originating editor jumped to a conclusion, wrote the appositive phrase *the actor* after the name, and sailed the story to the copy desk. A perceptive editor recognized that Sir Richard Burton was the nineteenth-century explorer, author, and Islamic scholar, saving the newspaper a serious gaffe, or at least a guffaw. There is no substitute for a good education, but checking rather than jumping to conclusions helps mightily.

Theodore Bernstein cautioned *The New York Times* staff:

> Just as it isn't news when a motorist completes a trip without an accident, so no reporter or writer is ever cited for being accurate. Inaccuracies are as avoidable as accidents; care will usually prevent both. There is no excuse, for example, for saying that a baronet who was killed in a fall from a train had succeeded to a "peerage created in 1611." The nearest dictionary will show that a baronet is not a peer. Nor is there any excuse for saying that James F. Meredith lives at 25 Clermont Avenue when a small amount of checking would disclose that it is Claremont Avenue. The reporter or editor who does check such things wins no medals, but has the reward of knowing that he is doing his job. All of this is by way of bringing to everyone's attention an apt sentence by A. E. Housman: "Accuracy is a duty, not a virtue." Paste that in your hat. Or, if you don't wear a hat, engrave it on your mind.

A precept that is supposed to guide journalists is "get it first, but first get it right." Lapses occur when journalists ignore the kind of evidence that would be required in a court of law, jump to unverified conclusions, and accept hearsay evidence. The Associated Press admonished its staffers, "Don't state as a fact what you do not know to be a fact," after a gaggle of newsmen monitoring the Frank Sinatra yacht off Martha's Vineyard mistakenly identified Mrs. John F. Kennedy as having boarded the yacht. The press corps saw a woman in a black sweater who, by general agreement, appeared to be Mrs. Kennedy. As it turned out the guest was Mrs. Peter Lawford, sister of the late president and then wife of the actor. Newsmen received a tip from a usually reliable source that Mrs. Kennedy would board the yacht that night and they saw a woman go aboard who looked like her. They drew a conclusion that was wrong. Objective newsmen don't draw conclusions. They report what they know.

Occasionally some horrendous mistakes occur that even the barest amount of checking could have avoided. The following news article is self-explanatory:

People don't usually get to hear their death announcement or see it in print. But John P. Johnson, 2245 Marigold Ave., former newscaster, is an exception.

Sitting in front of his television set to watch the Army-Navy football game, he heard the news—John P. Johnson, former news announcer, is dead.

It was at first believed he died in the crash of a DC–3 carrying Brigham Young University fans to Albuquerque. But he didn't.

"When the phones started ringing I had to give up my Army-Navy game," he said.

"I heard from people I hadn't heard from for many years. They would first ask for my wife. When I told them she was out, they expressed condolences to me, because they thought they were talking to my son, who has the same name.

"It's a shocking experience to go through—almost as if I had actually gone through the crash."

The mix-up occurred when a victim of the plane, another Johnson, John R. Johnson, of 2621 Industry Blvd., was identified as being the former well-known newscaster.

John R. Johnson was the plane crash victim.

Errors of Interpretation

Errors of interpretation are more difficult to pin down. They stem also from failure to check—jumping to conclusions, accepting hearsay, getting only one side of a story, ignoring corroborating data, failing to distinguish between an opinion and a fact, and occasionally from jazzing up the facts. Often laziness on the part of editors and reporters is at the root of these problems.

The task of the editor in nailing down problems of interpretation is more difficult than dealing with factual inaccuracies, for the editor does not have access to the sources used by the reporter. But the editor does have the obligation to question the general scope and meaning and propriety of a story. In cases where the editor cannot straighten out the story, he or she can refer it back to the reporter.

In a report commissioned by the News Research Center of the American Newspaper Publishers Association, Dr. David L. Grey of Stanford University analyzed the causes of subjective types of inaccuracies, such as overemphasis and underemphasis and distortions in meanings and omissions. He cited as the causes: reporter's insufficient background information, sensationalism, overdramatization and overemphasis in phrasing, lack of personal contact between the source and reporter and, finally, news desk and editing practices and policies. Grey recommended among safeguards to be taken that reporters and editors work even more closely together to avoid errors in copy editing and revision.

Some monumental blunders have largely been the result of taking at face value "facts" known to be "true" or jumping to unwarranted conclusions. One of the best, or worst, examples was exposed by Edward Jay Epstein in 1971 in the *New Yorker* magazine's

Reporter at Large heading: "The Panthers and the Police: A Pattern of Genocide?" Epstein pointed out that Charles E. Garry, chief counsel for the Black Panther Party, told the press that 28 Panthers had been murdered by the police as part of a national scheme to destroy the party. The charge was widely and uncritically circulated by the press. Epstein said he found in months of travel and research that the number of Panther deaths was actually 19; that the police had nothing to do with nine of the killings; and that six Panthers were killed by seriously wounded policemen who clearly had reason to believe their own lives were in jeopardy; two others had confronted policemen with weapons; and in only one instance (the shooting by police on December 4, 1969, of Fred Hampton and Mark Clark in Chicago) were Panthers attacked by policemen whose lives they were not directly threatening.

Criticism of the newspapers and wire services, as well as television, for the manner in which civil disorders were reported in the 1960s caused some of the media to take a searching look at their own procedures for providing accuracy in both fact and interpretation. The Associated Press updated its guidelines for reporters and editors in the light of the report by the National Advisory Commission on Civil Disorders. The Commission said, "Portrayal of the violence failed to reflect accurately its scale and character. The overall effect was, we believe, an exaggeration of both mood and event." AP then admonished its bureaus:

1. *Be Precise.* Tell exactly what happened without embellishment. The presence of a crowd of 1,000, including Negroes and civil rights demonstrators, and a police force of 1,000 does not mean that 1,000 police battled 1,000 demonstrators . . . choose your words carefully. If it's a minor disturbance, don't call it a riot.
2. *Credibility.* The source of your information is most important. We don't rush out with rumors of impending trouble. . . .
3. *Damage.* We report what qualified and responsible officials say, but we do not state it as fact.
4. *Perspective.* We don't reach for headlines by throwing a story out of focus with an isolated cry of "Get Whitey" or an isolated shooting.
5. *Background* . . . Spell it out. Don't generalize. Get both sides of any grievance.
6. *Staffing.* Get men to the scene at the first hint of trouble.
7. . . . Our reporting and writing should be reasonable, understandable, logical, and orderly.

EXERCISES

In the following exercises, you will find problems of both commission and omission.

The first exercise is designed to test your information and awareness and to help you learn the use of standard reference works, such as the almanac, encyclopedia, and telephone and city directories.

In each of the four paragraphs in the set beginning with "Free" that follows the questions and in the exercise slugged "Bolivia" you will find one error among the facts that must be checked against reference works. The story slugged "Author" contains several misstatements of fact that must be corrected.

In the remaining exercises, the major task is to list the obvious questions a reader may ask but that the reporter has left unanswered. Note the questions at the bottom of the sheet, in the space provided.

Test your information and awareness. Where necessary, look up the information in a standard reference work. Cite the work you used.

1. The population of your state as of the last census, in round numbers:

    _____

2. The names and party affiliations of the two United States senators from your state:

    _____

3. The airline distance from Chicago to New York within 100 miles:

    _____

4. The population of Japan, within 10 million:

    _____

5. One book written by William Faulkner:

    _____

6. The latest recipient of the Nobel Peace Prize:

    _____

7. The first prime minister of independent India (1947):

    _____

8. The capital of Afghanistan:

    _____

9. The world's highest mountain and its elevation within 1,000 feet:

    _____

10. The name of a federal department that regulates the use of public lands:

    _____

11. The size of the 1979 federal budget, within $10 billion:

    _____

12. The branch of service quartered at Camp LeJeune, N.C.:

     _____

13. The opening and closing dates of America's involvement in World
     War I, give or take a year:

     _____

14. The correct name of the president of your college or university,
     as he uses it (and of course spelled correctly):

     _____

15. The correct name of the Smithsonian Institute:

     _____

16. The offices held by Richard Nixon before he became president:

     _____

17. The country in which the most recent Olympic summer games were
     held:

     _____

18. What profession these famous personages followed:

     Edwin Booth: _____

     Henry Luce: _____

     Clare Booth Luce: _____

     Semyon Timoshenko: _____

     Alexander Graham Bell: _____

     James Whistler: _____

19. The name of any endangered species of animal or bird:

     _____

20. The name and formula of Einstein's most celebrated theory:

     _____

Free

Conservationist Joy Anderson, whose book "Born Free" about Elsa
the lioness wakened millions to the plight of vanishing wildlife more
than 20 years ago, was killed by a human attacker.in the Kenya wilder-
ness, police reported today. It was at first believed she was killed
by a lion.

Waldheim

Kurt Waldheim, president of the United Nations, returned to U. N.
headquarters in New York today after a visit to the Middle East.

Rams

Coach John McKay today issued a challenge to the Los Angeles
Rams for Sunday's NFC championship game with his Tampa Bay Dolphins.

Hikers

A wind-driven snowstorm in Washington's remote Pickwick
Mountains tore a tent from its moorings and left two hikers un-
sheltered, battling for survival in the bitter cold last week.

Bolivia

Valley Elementary School students have raised $1,000 from the
sale of popcorn and candles and a paper drive to help build a school
in Rural Bolivia.

Officials said the money will be used to buy roofing material, timbers and windows. The school when built will be the only one in the rural village of Ayata Ajllta, on the shores of Lake Titcaca.

# # #

Author

A Fowler University history professor's study of the Korean Conflict, emphasizing the role of President Harry S Truman, was published this week.

The book, "Harry Truman and the Korean War," was written by Emerson J. Fotheringham, chairman of the history department at Fowler since 1971. Fotheringham served as an army major in the Korean war from 1949 to 1951 and is recognized as an authority on that period.

Fotherham describes the White House decision-making process under the 32nd president. He pays some attention to other major Truman decisions that he says conditioned the president to undertake the Korean "police action." These include the decision to use the first atomic bomb on Hiroshim and Osaka in August, 1945, the breaking of the Russian blockade of East Berlin with the airlift of 1948, and the creation of the North Atlantic Treaty Organization.

The book was published by MacMillan Co. and went on sale Monday.

# # #

Frosts

Record-breaking frosts apparently destroyed most of the state's fruit crop Thursday, with damages, tallied in the millions of dollars in preliminary surveys by county agricultural agents, resulting from the freezing of 50 to 75 percent of the fruit tree blossoms.

Fears for other crops, including peas and alfalfa, mounted as freezing temperatures were forecasted for Friday night. It was the coldest day in May ever recorded here by the Weather Bureau, breaking the previous record of 26.9 degrees of May, 1964.

Fruit Growers in Hennesy County reported 100 per cent loss of chrries, peaches, and apples. Much of the aprocit crop was lost in a heavy frost in March, according to Richard Favorbill, county agent.

A preliminary estimate of loss from Charles Barton, Prince William County agent, was 50 per cent for pears and swett cherries with apricots probably a complete loss.

"In our spot checks we have been unable to find any good apricots," Mr. Barton said. "The condition of sour cherry, apple and peach buds will depend on wether freezing temperatures continue "he continued," and the effectiveness of smudge pots which are in extensive use throughout the county.

The picture for pea crops was a little different, according to George Teeples, Teeples Canning Co., Teeples, Prince William County, who reported that damage was spotty throughout the fields but nothing could be done except to continue watering and to harvest whatever remained to be salvaged.

Unanswered questions: _____

(Frosts)

~~Record-breaking~~ frosts ~~apparently~~ destroyed ~~most of~~ *at least half* the state's
fruit crop Thursday (X) ~~with damages, tallied in the millions of dollars~~
~~in~~ preliminary surveys by county agricultural agents, ~~resulting~~ *indicate damage* from
the freezing of 50 to 75 percent of the ~~fruit tree~~ blossoms *is in the millions.*

Fears for other crops, including peas and alfalfa, mounted as
freezing temperatures were forecast~~ed~~ for Friday night. ~~It~~ *Thursday* was the
coldest day in May ever recorded here by the Weather ~~Bureau,~~ *Service,* breaking
the previous record of 26.9 degrees of May, *?* 1964.

Fruit growers in Hennesy County reported ~~100 per cent~~ *total* loss of
ch~~e~~rries, peaches, and apples. Much of the apr~~o~~*ico*t crop was lost in a
heavy frost in March, according to Richard Favorbill, county agent.

~~A preliminary estimate of loss from~~ Charles Barton, Prince William
County agent, ~~was~~ *estimated* 50 per cent ~~for~~ *of* pears and swe~~a~~*e*t cherries ~~with~~ apricots *were lost and*
probably *were* a complete loss.

"In our spot checks we have been unable to find any good apricots,"
~~Mr.~~ Barton said. "The condition of sour cherry, apple and peach buds
will depend on w*h*ether freezing temperatures continue ~~"he continued,"~~
and the effectiveness of smudge pots*,"* ~~which are in extensive use~~ (X)
~~throughout the county.~~

The picture for pea crops ~~was~~ *is* a little different, according to
George Teeples, Teeples Canning Co., Teeples, Prince William County *x*

(more)

(2/ hosts)

He

~~who~~ reported that damage was spotty throughout the fields but nothing
could be done except to continue watering and to harvest whatever
remained, ~~to be salvaged~~.

Unanswered questions: *How cold? How compare to previous
years' losses? Date in May?*

Boy

A 17-year-old boy was injured seriously Saturday about 6 p.m. when
he slipped and fell 75 feet down the stone face of Old Baldy Cliff in
Buttermilk Canyon.

William Sunday, 17, son of Mr. and Mrs. Dale H. Sunday, of 413 W.
7th Street, was in poor condition at General Hospital suffering from a
fractured right leg. fractured right arm and contusions and abrasions.

The youth and a companion left the picni area at the base of the
mountain about 5 p.m. and climbed up the sawtooth face of the cliff at
the north side of the canoyn. They reached a ridge and when unable to
continue turned around and started down.

After starting down, the Sunday lad lost a handhold as he slipped.
He dropped approximately 60 feet down the near vertical cliff and rolled
another 15 feet to a small ledge, according to Deputy Sheriff B.B.
Vanderpool.

Racing against an oncoming rainstorm, deputy sheriffs, Fish and
Game Department personnel, the County Jeep Patrol and fire department

ambulance crewman bandaged the youth and places splints on his arms and legs, then loweree the victim another 25 feet down the cliff and carried him through heavy brush to the trail and then to a roadway, using an hour to get the injured boy down to the ambulance though only nine minutes to get him from the base of the cliff. Rain began to fall shortly afterward.

Unanswered questions _____

Edit the following story for a Saturday a.m. newspaper.

Stranded

Three young men from Spencer City have been marrooned in two and a half feet of snow on the Shivwits Plateau in eastern Elk county since early Wednesday.

Four others who attempted to rescue them are also stuck in the snow and mud.

Joseph Michaelson, Craig Montague and Norman Root left early Wednesday for a four=wheel drive trip on the highlands near the Shivwits mountains. Their four-wheel drive vehicle stalled in the deep snow about 25 miles south of Mountain Junction near the Elk county-Fremont county border.

Two rescue vehicles with four men got near them on Thursday against the advice of Elk County Sheriff Sam Evans. Both of these vehicles are stalled with broken axles and transmisison trouble.

heriff Evans Friday headed a crew wsith a snow plow and reached
the men about 5 p.m. The men will be brought out during thenight or
early Saturday.

Unanswered questions: _____

_____

Robbery

Daring armed bandits robbed two banks Friday within a two-hour
span, escaping with about $6,742.

A clean-cut, wavy-haired young man who "looked like a college
student" robbed First National Bank at Main and 1st of an estimated
$3,842 about 4:30 p. .

Then about 6 p.m. an older man who appeared to have been drinking
took $2,900 from the Farmer's State Bank at Broadway and 3rd.

The young man involvee in the first robbery appeared "very nervous"
to bank officials, while the older man involved in the second robbery was
described as "very calm." In both robberies a long-barreled pistol was
used.

"He (the robber) was quite unusual looking and I noticed him as
soon as he came in," recalled Miss Cynthia Birch, a teller at the Farmer's
State Bank.

The gunman pulled out a black, long-barreled pistol, believed to be
between 22 and 32 caliber.

When the robber saw the manager, Gerry Campana, he said: "Turn
around or I'll put a bullet between your eyes."

"I looked at that gun and I did like he said," Campana said.

The robber handed Mrs. Betty Nilsson a sack and told her to empty the tils.

Looking away from the bandit, Mrs. Nilsson went to all three cages and scooped the currency into the bag.

The Farmers bank bandit was described as 6 feet tall, with dark, rough complexion, about 40 years old, wearing a dark hunting cap and dark glasses.

The First National Bank Bandit walked up to Mrs. Elsie Quince, handed her a sack, and told her, "Put all your money in there, starting with the hundreds." He whipped out a revolver and pointed it directly at her. "His voice was shakey," Mrs. Quince said. "he was obviously nervous. He tole me not to push any buttons or set of any alarms.

"Me and my buddy will be walking back past the bank and if there's anything unusual going on there'll be trouble," she quoted the man as saying.

Mrs. Quince said she emptied one cash drawer and then showed the bandig there was no money in the other. Then he sauntered out.

##

Unanswered questions _____

_____

Zoo

Just thinking of taking s swim in an outdoor pool in this wintry weather gives goose bumps to humans.

But several of the animals at City Zoo enjoy a winter swim so much they spend plenty of time splashing, racing and playing.

Percy K. Frieren, zoo director, said because the water in the zoo's pools remains fairly constant at 48 degrees, the animals are warmer in the water than out.

Even on days when the mercury dips to a chilly 12 degrees, as it has recently, the water stays warm.

Three roly poly harbor seals spend almost the entire winter in the water. Their heavy layer of "blubber" keeps them warm.

Friskiest of the water animals are the three North American river otters. They can retreat to their den when it gets cold but spend plenty of time in the water, especially at feeding time. Their long fur keeps them warm.

With a constant supply of fresh water entering the sea lion pool, the four sea lions spend plenty of time swimming and frolicking in the water.

# # #

Unanswered questions _____

_____

Meteor

An unusually bright, luminous green and white meteorite was observed Monday at about 5:50 p.m. streaking from south to north across the state.

Observers from as far south as Anderton, Sage County, watched it and all gave similar descriptions.

Besides the main ball, there were one or two smaller greenish balls alongside the main ball and a trail of reddish sparks out behind.

A woman in River Park suburb saw it and at first though it was flying saucer. Employees at the International Airport tower observed the meteorite and described it as bright and beautiful. It seemed to break up in the north, but there were not any reports of its landing anywhere.

Unanswered questions _____

_____

14. FIGURES

You've heard the expression "There are three kinds of lies—lies, damned lies, and statistics." Figures can be twisted to mean anything a user wants them to mean, or they may be used honestly but incorrectly. Hence, an editor always must be on guard when numbers appear in a story. As an editor, you would be wise to keep a calculator handy. It may save you from embarrassment. Beyond that, editors ought to learn something about the use of statistical evidence.

In one recent study reported to the American Newspaper Publishers Research Institute a journalism class examined the news content of 10 daily newspapers on randomly chosen days for two weeks and found that 10 percent of the stories involved statistics. The instructor concluded that "if reporters and editors are to interpret the material adequately, they themselves must be familiar with at least the language of research."

Figures come from government, business, universities, and other institutions. Every major social and economic problem and every trade group has created organizations that make studies and report their findings in statistical terms.

The media are often at the mercy of agencies of government for raw figures and their interpretation, on budgets, wage-price indexes, employment figures, and the like. Many significant figures are buried in voluminous government budgets and reports, and making sense of them requires expertise and zeal on the part of the governmental reporter. The media do wage an unceasing battle for access to such material, often even relatively trivial figures such as numbers of marriage applications and divorce certificates. They are more successful in getting the information than in making it understandable. The copy editor can't do much to dig out this material, but the editor can work to make it appear in meaningful form.

In addition, survey research organizations supply a great deal of statistical information now reaching the press. These stories include the public opinion poll. Most readers are poorly equipped to determine whether a poll has been conducted so as to eliminate or reduce bias. Every poll story should include at least a statement of how many persons were sampled by the surveyors, under what conditions, and how the findings depart from figures that would have been expected had the whole population been questioned. The editor also can do a great deal to assure that the interpretation of the statistical evidence is logical.

More and more newspapers are themselves using what has come to be known as "precision journalism"—the use of figure-oriented social science methods by editors and reporters. Philip Meyer, a reporter with the Washington Bureau of Knight Newspapers, has spearheaded the drive for more of research aimed at reporting on social conditions using the survey instrument, which goes far beyond the one-shot opinion poll. Meyer argues that the press is overly susceptible to anecdotal evidence and the conventional wisdom and needs to go ask people in a systematic, scientific way about trends and conditions. His thesis is that newspaper reporting must become social science in a hurry if the press is to cope with a world of accelerating change. If this is to happen, he says, editors need to develop the capacity for in-house research and hire the talent to carry it out. This statement carries an important warning. Statistical interpretation of social trends should be done by those trained in avoiding bias.

Here are some guidelines that will serve every editor well in appraising most of the statistical stories encountered in the day's news:

1. Figures should be totaled and checked to establish accuracy. All lists of figures should be added to make certain they agree with totals expressed in the story. Percentages should be worked out to verify that they agree with figures indicated in the story. A figure expressed in a headline should always be checked against the story.

2. Remember that figures standing by themselves often mean little or nothing. Comparisons and explanations are vital. Reports on anything from library fines and wage disputes to mill levies and budgets have little meaning in the absence of comparisons with previous situations. The comparisons, however, must be meaningful. You will find at the end of this chapter some stories in which the writer has taken unwarranted liberties in attempting to establish comparative data or has made inappropriate comparisons. The language of statistics, having a ring of authority, often has been used to distort. Writers and editors must be on the alert when sources begin tossing figures around.

3. Round out figures. Cents following large dollar figures generally are confusing. A figure such as "nearly $1 billion" would be appropriate as a roundoff for $995 million. It would be an improper expression for $750 million. A careful editor will know when to approximate and when to be precise. Roundoffs should not be used where no gain in understanding is achieved.

4. Be cautious in dealing with trends or cause-effect relationships derived from statistics alone. Trends usually can't be charted on the basis of comparison of data for only a couple of years. It's useless to talk about trends in divorces vs. marriages, for example, without data from a decade or so—and such data are usually easy to obtain. There will always be some fluctuation in data, a rise or fall, often minute.

Data ought also to be judged carefully as to whether a difference is significant. A drop in the number of calls responded to by firefighters or in the number of building permits granted last month as compared to the same month in the previous year ought to be startling before generalizations are drawn. Stories are most meaningful not when they deal with statistics alone but when causes and effects are assessed by people trained to analyze the variables that led to the difference in numbers between one time and another. In the case of divorce court statistics, those would be people like judges, marriage counselors, and social workers.

5. Challenge all figures that your own knowledge and common sense suggest may be incorrect, misleading, or inappropriate. A columnist once wrote that the Federal Aviation Administration reported the industry's "94 percent safety record." To this a former aviation editor responded:

> No airline official in his right mind would ever brag about a 94 percent safety record. The way this statistic is phrased, it adds up to six percent of the carriers' 13,000 daily flights ending in crashes, or six percent of the nation's 220 million passengers being killed annually. Obviously, there is no six percent crash rate annually, or we'd have 780 airline accidents per day . . . or more than 12 million deaths each year. The U.S. airline industry's safety record for 1976 showed 99.99998 percent of some four million flights taking off and landing safely. *If the rest of the column was as accurate as that opening statistic, I hope readers will take the writer's further discourses on air safety with a large grain of salt.* [Italics added.]

Knowledgeable or suspicious readers will keep you honest in use of figures. One took the time to calculate the fallacies in a report that stated, "The average American who lives to the age of 70 consumes in that lifetime the equivalent of 150 cattle, 24,000 chickens, 225 lambs, 310 hogs, 26 acres of grain, and 50 acres of fruits and vegetables." This seemed strange, so the reader consulted his local butcher. He found the cattle would provide 90,000 pounds of meat, the chickens 24,000, the lambs 12,375, the sheep 1,820 and the hogs 46,500—more than 111 tons. This figures out to 8.7 pounds of meat per person per day. "No wonder our national debt is so much and our hospitals are so full of sick people," the reader concluded.

Note in the following letter how an error might have been avoided had the editor been critical.

> I was quite surprised and disappointed when my wife brought to my attention the story, "The Hazardous Life—Why Addiction and Alcoholism Also Strike Doctors."
>
> This is a quote from the story: "Two U.S. Public Health Service Hospitals provide special care and treatment for addicts. One is in Lexington, Ky., the other in Fort Worth. Officials of these institutions report that 40 percent of the addicts treated in them are physicians, nurses, and pharmacists." I would be most interested in knowing the source of such an erroneous report. The actual figures . . . show that physicians, nurses, and paramedical individuals represent only 1.76 percent of the total addict admissions to both hospitals. This percentage has been quite consistent for many years.
>
> Also in the story was: "On the basis of U.S. Bureau of Narcotics figures it can be estimated reliably that 15 percent of all known addicts are physicians; another 15 percent are found among such paramedical personnel as nurses and pharmacists. . . ." I would also like to know the source of these statistics if we are to believe that 30 percent of known addicts are physicians and paramedical persons. I checked with the Bureau of Narcotics and was informed that the bureau reports a total of 59,000 addicts in the country. Of that number 102 are medical and paramedical persons, with only 66 physicians and 15 nurses. This would be a total of only .171 percent as medical and paramedical individuals.
>
> I have never seen figures such as those in the story and feel they are erroneous. I also feel that this gives a very distorted picture to many of your readers."

6. Graphic presentation often helps clarify complex figures. Newspapers are making increased use of charts, tables, and maps that give important information at a glance.

7. Humanize and simplify figures. Bring them into the home of the reader. If you have a story about a $2 million utility-rate increase, break the total figure down until it bears relationship to an average bill. Tell the reader that a person with a monthly bill averaging $40 will be paying an average of $43.50. Persons with bills averaging $80 or $20 will be able to do some swift calculations of their own. With only the $2 million figure to deal with, they're helpless. While deft use of comparisons is excellent for clarification, an editor must avoid tortured examples. Describing water use as "enough water to cover three football fields 10 feet deep" is clear. Referring to "enough water to float a battleship" is not.

In the following stories you will deal with many kinds of figure problems. Some stories require only that you total figures to the correct sums expressed and make whatever adjustments are clearly needed. Some are correct as written. Others have fallacies of interpretation. The story on the public opinion poll includes some interpretation of results by the story writer not warranted by the statistical evidence expressed. If you reject any story because of fallacies or because the figures can't be adjusted without further information, explain your reasons in a note on the copy.

SELECTED READINGS

Gallup, George. *The Sophisticated Poll Watcher's Guide.* Princeton, N.J.: Princeton Opinion Press, 1972. A guidebook by the most eminent pollster "for those who have occasion to use, interpret, explain or challenge poll findings."

Meyer, Philip. *Precision Journalism: A Reporter's Introduction to Social Science Methods.* Indiana: Indiana University Press, 1973. The book that introduced the concept of using social science survey techniques in gathering and interpreting the news.

Roll, Charles W., Jr., and Albert H. Cantril. *Polls, Their Use and Misuse in Politics.* New York: Basic Books, 1972. Includes good information every editor should have on reliability of poll data.

EXERCISES

Toll

The state's Traffic fatality toll continues to climb at a better than seven per cent clip over last year, statistics showed today.

According to records compiled by the Highway Patrol, 296 persons have become mere statistics on the state's thoroughfares through Friday night. The total this date a year ago was 275. The difference of 21 persons represents a 6.1 percent jump over last year.

So far this year, the state's worst month fatality wise has been September. 45 persons died in driving mishaps during that 30 day period. including a state record 21 persons in a week-long strech between Sept. 10-16.

Other high-rate fatality months have been May, 35; June, 36, and July, 37.

Traffic safety and law enforcement officials are aghast at the calamitious rate at which driving fatalities are increasing.

"There's not much we can do or that money can buy if individual drivers don't stop being so complacent about their driving practices," says Alexander Stretch director of the state Traffic Safety commission. "They cut corners, cross over dividing lines -- they don't seem to care what happens."

Stretch said one of the problems with driving safety is the increasing number of new drivers and cars on the state's highways each year adding that driving skills haven't improved with the rise.

Capt. Kurt Gribley of the State Highway Patrol says there isn't much his officers can do to ensure future highway safety.

"We can clamp down a little more on our written laws, but we can't follow an individual driver around and tell him to drive better," he told the Gazette.

"It's strange," he added. "It's usually the traffic officials and law enforcement personnel who hear the most grief about rising Highway deaths.

But it should be the drivers who get the rude awakening, not us."

(Toll)

State safety officials today expressed alarm over

The ~~state's~~ Traffic fatality toll *which is* ~~continues to~~ climb*ing* at ~~a better~~ *more*
than (seven) per cent ~~clip~~ over last year*s* ~~statistics showed today.~~

~~According to~~ records ~~compiled by the~~ Highway Patrol, 296 persons
had died of injuries in traffic accidents as of
~~have become mere statistics on the state's thoroughfares through~~ Friday
night. The total ~~this date~~ *for the same period last* year ~~ago~~ was 275. ~~The difference of 21~~
~~persons represents a 6.1 percent jump over last year.~~

~~So far this year,~~ the ~~state's~~ worst month *traffic then,* fatality ~~wise has been~~ *was*
September. (45) persons died in ~~driving mishaps during that 30 day period.~~
including a state record 21 persons ~~in a week-long streeth between~~
Sept. 10-16.

Other high-rate fatality months have been May, 35; June, 36; and
July, 37.

~~Traffic safety and law enforcement officials are aghast at the cal-~~
~~amitious rate at which driving fatalities are increasing.~~

"There's not much we can do or that money can buy if individual
drivers don't stop being so complacent about their driving practices,"
says Alexander Stretch, director of the state Traffic Safety commission.
"They cut corners, cross over dividing lines -- they don't seem to care
what happens."

Stretch said one of the problems with driving safety is the increasing number of new drivers and cars on the state's highways each year.
He said
~~adding that~~ driving skills haven't improved with the rise.

Capt. Kurt Gribley of the State Highway Patrol says there isn't
much his officers can do to ensure future highway safety.

"We can clamp down a little more on our written laws, but we can't

follow an individual driver around and tell him to drive better⊗" ~~he~~
~~told the Gazette.~~   (#)

        "~~It's strange," he added.   "It's usually the traffic officials and~~
~~law enforcement personnel who hear the most grief about rising Highway~~
~~deaths.~~

        ~~But it should be the drivers who get the rude awakening, not us~~."

Poll

        State residents generally believe that the present all-volunteer
army is meeting the country's defense needs.

        But the margin was far from decisive, with a bare majority suport-
ing voluntary enlistments over the draft system.

        There was a wide divergence of views between age and sex groups,
depending on who would be affected by the draft. For example, young men
who would be eligible for a draft, support the volunteer army concept
while their fathers of World War II vintage feel the mandatory selection
system would improve the quality of our armed forces.

        The strongest supporters of a volunteer army are young women 18-29
who apparently feel the draft would "endanger" their boy friends or
split up their young families.

        These are some of the highlights from recent state-wide survey on
the draft issue. The survey was sponsored by the Gazette.

        Since there is a controversy in Congress over which method would
best meet U.S. defense needs, the public was asked to join in the debate
with this question:

"As you know, the U.S. now has an all-volunteer army which some say is not producing the quality needed for the U.S. defense needs. How do you feel -- should we continue with the all-volunteer army or go back to the mandatory draft system?"

The findings were fairly close as noted below:

All volunteer volunteer army	52%
Draft system	42%
Undecided	6%
Total	100%

The sex split on the issue with men supporting a mandatory draft and women opting for continuation of a voluneer army.

Young men, however, did not agree with the views of their elders, many of whom felt the effect of the draft in World War II.

While men would be the primary target of a draft, young women displayed the strongest sentiment of anyone on the issue, making it crystal clear that they want their "men" to make the choice and hoping, apparently, they would not leave home.

Here are illustrative break-downs by younger men and women, and older men, many of whom were draftees. (Read across).

	All Volunteer	Draft	Undecided
All men	47%	51%	2%
Men 18-29	56%	44%	--
Men 60-over	44%	53%	3%
All women	56%	34%	10%
Women 18-29	70%	22%	8%

Sex

Less than one per cent of the state's population do not want to receive sexually-oriented advertising, according to figures the United States Postal Service has compiled.

According to Alfred A. Cornwell, officer-in-charge, 4,267 children and 3,597 adults have placed their names on the Sexually-Oriented Advertising Program list of the service. The combined figure is 7,864.

This list allows persons to have their names recorded as not wishing to receive any such advertisements.

Throughout the nation, their are 605,710 names on the list from all 50 states, he added.

What constitutes "sexually-oriented advertising" is pretty much up to the individual. Once the person's name is on the list, any mailer who sends the person unsolicited sexually-oriented advertisements may be subject ot civil and criminal penalities

The big rush to get on the list occured after the law became effective Feb. 1, 1971 he added.

Now, "about one or two persons a day comes in to put their names on the list," Mr. Cornwell said. You can sign up at any Post Office. You fill out a form that you consider the material to be sexually oriented and the process takes about 45 days.

California leads the nation with 56,914 names on the Sexually-Oriented Advertising list, Ohio is second with 50,877, and Pennsylvania is third with 49,429, and New York is fourth with 38,296.

The Post Office keeps a list of the top ten states with the most names on the list, but does not rank them after that.

A householder may also have the Postal Service order his name removed from a specific firm's list under the pandering advertising statute, he added.

Fatal

Four persons were killed and a fifth injured in an early morning collision at the Corner of Street and Evans Avenue.

Two of the dead were from Jonesburgh, the third from Webb City. All were in the same car.

The officer said the accident occurred when a car driven by John Summers, 21, of Webb City, collided with one driven by Cooper B. Frei, 30, of Ferher Corners.

Mr. Summers and his two passengers all were killed. The passengers were P. Frank Nelson, 31, and K. Richard Nelson, 22, both of Jonesburgh.

Mr. Frei was listed in critical condition.

Just prior to the accident, Police Lt. Davis Ernst had given chase to an automobile which had run both a stop sign and a traffic light. He said the vehicle ran five more stop signs in the course of a high - speed chase which reached speeds to 70 mph.

Potatoes

Potato producers have approved a measure to increase the assessment on potatoes for a promotion campaign.

State Agriculture Commissioner Ron Sprague said Friday 399 farmers approved a one cent per hundredweight raise and 413 farmers voted against it.

Although the number of votes cast against the increase was greater, the farmers favoring the extra sssessment produce annually about 19,700,000 hundred-weight of potatoes, compared to 13,270,000 hundredweight of potatoes for the farmers opposed。

A law provides for passage when farmers growing a majority of the potateoes cast approving votes.

The tax goes into effect immediately and will raise the total assessment to three one-fourth cents per hundreweight。

The referendum bill passed the last legislative session after a threatened boycott of potatoes by the United Farmworkers Union.

Backers of the referendum said the additional revenue would be needed to bolster the state's potato sales in the event of a boycott。

Education

A $7,867,085 budget for 1972-73 was adapted Wednesday night by the City Board of Education following a public hearing at which no one showed/

Prior to adopting the new budget the board made an adjustment on the present budget by increasing it $70,750。 The adjustment was made to include additional funds received which the board di dnot anticipate a year ago.

A contract for the construction of two additional rooms to the Davis Elementary School was awarded to the Wong Construction Co., which submitted the low bid of $77,820.

The board set a special meeting for the night of June 28 at 7:15 p.m. to meet legal requirements for selling $620,000 worth of bonds;

opening of bids for aid conditioning the Millicent Junior High School
offices and awarding contract for Tort Liability Insurance.

Expenditures under the new budget -- based upon a 52.15 mill tax
levy which is the same as this year -- are: maintenance and operation,
$4,289,111; capital outlay and debt service, $3,216,198; building reserve
fund, $1,793; school lunch fund, $342,363; tort liability, $6,375; and
recreation fund, $11,245.

Circulation

Circulation by the County Library during October took a big
drop from the same month a year ago, it was announced in the library's
monthly report.

The report showed the circulation totaled 169,735 volumes during
October, 2,564 fewer than in October last year.

Central

Central High School was the "toughest" public school in the city
last year, based on its unenviable record of first-offense student
referrals to the Police Youth Bureau.

In second place for "honors" was Kennedy Junior High Schook, whose
total of 59 first-offense referrals was only for less than that of
Central High.

Wilson High School, which led the parade a year ago with 62
referrals, dropped to the more "respectable" position of sixth place
this year with 19 fewer referrals.

Rounding out the six worst records were West High in third place (57 referrals), Washington Junior High fourth (54) and Northwest High fifth (47).

Also-rans in a race which would be more credit to the community if it never ran were Junior High (32), John Dewer Junior High (28), Barton Elementary (19), Parker Elementary (18), Fuller Elementary (17) and Searview Elementary (16).

Among junior high schools, Washington was highest the year previous with six referrals less than it had last year, while Parker Elementary dropped to second in its category with a big decrease in referrals--31 in the previous year with 18 in last year.

Schools listed by the Youth Bureau as having no first-offense referrals last year include Clark, Dover, Finch, Grand, Harrison, Millicent, Meadow Lane, and Rio Grande, all elementary level.

Captain Wilfred D. Wren of the Youth Bureau said these offenses are listed under 30 categories ranging from petit larceny down to curfew violations, trespassing, pranks, protective custody in the event of desertion by parents and counseling when there is no responsible adult available to carry out this function.

Revenues

State tax revenues are up over $9.3 million so far this fiscal year, members of the legislature's Joint Budget and Audit Committee were told Thursday.

Of the five tax areas for state general and unifrom school fund revenues, only one -- cigarette tax collections -- has fallen below estimates.

Actual collections reported to the committee by the Legislative Analyst's office at the Thursday meeting in the Capital are $210,226,000 from July 1 to May 31. Collections for that same period had been estimated at $200,885,000.

During the same period last fiscal year actual collections stood at $180,313,000, the report noted.

Source of these collections, with estimates listed in parentheses, are as follows:

Individual income tax collected and withheld, $69,621,000 ($65,780,000).

Corporate franchise tax, $10,360,000 ($10,567,000).

Sales tax, $117,223,000 ($112,401,000).

Cigarette Tax, $5,452,000 ($5,520,000).

Liquor profits to April 30, $6,970,000 ($6,617,000).

In other action, the committee adopted a motion by State Senator Vincent Goode, R. Fremont, returning a proposed state employe health and accident program to the drafters as it did not comply with the intent of the legislature.

During the last Budget session of the legislature, a bill was passed aimed at providing this insurance without any employe contribution unless he had more than one dependent.

But the plan submitted Thursday, which was distributed to all employees with their paychecks at the beginning of this month, would actually increase the contribution of a single employe for the same coverage.

Water

The annual report on the distribution of the water supply of the
Oak   River, released this week by Robert B. Dans, commissioner for the
distribution system, revealed that more water was delivered for irrigation, city and industrial use lase year than any other previous year
that records are available.

Mr. Dans reported the distribution of 90,820.9 acre feet of water
during the past season. This compares with $9,607.3 acre feet for the
present year. Of this total amount of water distributed bu Mr. Dans
63,956.50 acre was delivered on direct flow rights held by water users;
26,165.0 on reservoir water rights; and 699.4 acre feet was derived from
the Mountain Power and Light Company No. 1 well at the head of Log Canyon.

The largest user listed among the irrigation companies or individuals
delivered water was the Clark Canal Co., 45,624.0 acre feet, or more than
half the entire total. 25,422.0 acre feet was distributed to the Oak
Valley-Grand Canal Co.

Mountain Power and Light Co. was the largest industrial user listed,
2,072.8 acre feet being delivered to the company for use at its Carbon
Steam Plant generating units in Castle. U.S. Steel Corporation used
1,463.0 acre feet, primarly at the company's coal washing plant at Grand.

Oak Valley City used a total of 2,451.4 acre feet and Grand City
1,098.5 acre feet. Irrigation purposes accounted for 82,148.0 acre feet
of total water used and city and industrial uses, 8,672.9 acre feet.

Mr. Sand said the drainage system's water yield was very close to
that predicted by the snow surveys and that Fielding Reservoir contained
38,550.00 acre feet of water on Dec. 31, slightly less than the previous

year. Capacity of the reservoir before spilling occurs over the top

spillway is almost 66,000 acre feet thus assuring a 100% delivery of

reservoir water for next year.

15. TASTE

The modern living section of a metropolitan newspaper ran a cover story on the rewards of breastfeeding, together with a picture of a young woman with an infant nuzzling at her breast. An irate reader fumed, "Topless waitresses I'll tolerate, bare-bosomed show girls I'll sanction, but a nursing mother on the front page of my beloved society section turns my veins to ice. What happened to the days when this page displayed beautiful brides, happy families on excursions or civic-minded women readying charity functions?"

Taste never was static, but judging it has become complex. Public protests against portrayals of sex, violence, and social aberration in the media—especially in movies, television, and magazines—are frequent. Audiences have become more worldly and have overwhelmingly accepted greater candor than that in the breastfeeding article. One by one, the taboos have toppled.

Yet the newspaper is in a special position. It is a trusted friend, often a very old friend, with known habits and character, invited into the home and accessible to everyone. What this means is that the editor must know readers—their education, tastes, and dispositions and their changing tolerance, receptivity, and need for broader exploration of issues. To determine community standards is not easy—the United States Supreme Court has given up after a generation of cases involving obscenity controls and left standards up to each locality. Newspaper editors must judge not only what the proverbial little old ladies in tennis shoes, or even children, need to be protected against, but also what can and should be explored by intelligent, discerning readers.

X-Rated Language. Not only are once unmentionable subjects treated today frankly and in considerable detail, but language has assumed a new directness that would have amazed, and repulsed, people of other generations. It has been only in recent years that relatively tepid words such as *syphilis* and *rape*—rather than their euphemisms *social disease* and *criminal assault*—have appeared in print. Today, print available at any magazine stand carries words that once might have made a longshoreman blush.

Frankness has social value. When suffocating social problems—like venereal disease, teen-age pregnancy, drug addiction, suicide—find refuge in vague words under a blanket of prudery, we avoid dealing with problems that mature people should discuss.

Most newspapers have abandoned circumlocutions, but most print profanity reluctantly—if at all. The AP/UPI Stylebook says: "Do not use obscenities, profanity, vulgarities, etc. in stories unless they are part of direct quotations and there is a compelling reason for them. When they are used, flag the story at the top." (The usual warning reads: "Editors, the following story contains words or phrases that some readers might find offensive.")

Many reporters, particularly young ones who are less inhibited than veterans because they have grown up in permissive times, often insist that it is hypocritical to avoid honest language as it is expressed by the person quoted. They commonly use *damn* and *hell* and other such expressions. Some words, however, still have not been permitted in general news writing and may never be. Seven are specifically prohibited in broadcasting by Federal Communications Commission regulations. Many editors say they believe firmly in the axiom that the press should not say in print what one could not say as a gentleman or lady. They contend that current issues can be discussed honestly without resort to the vulgarisms that might be employed in the dialogue swirling around those issues. These editors are on guard against even such expressions as *screwed up* and *shack up*, phrases creeping into common parlance. They say restraint in language is a mark of maturity. (One daily editor, aghast at seeing a torrent of four-letter words in the college newspaper he had edited as an undergraduate, suggested that students put all the words in a box on the back page. He argued that readers who wanted them could see them all in one place, and the staff would have gotten the words out of its collective system.)

Is refusal to succumb to faddish vulgarities mature? Editors should recognize that dignity in language is a foundation stone of respectful human relations and serves the cause of intelligent dialogue better than do expletives. But what happens when public personages, even public officials, make statements in language that cannot be ignored? A secretary of agriculture is fired for telling a racist joke in gutter language; the president of the United States uses vulgar words in private conversations that are taped and ultimately help drive him out of office; a vice president is photographed making an obscene gesture; an astronaut laces his broadcasts from space, to which millions listen, with gamy expressions; activists use racy rhetoric as weaponry at public meetings.

UPI carried Billy Carter's comment about American Jews ("they can kiss my ass") because, it explained, members of the president's family are public figures and their excesses should be chronicled. On the other hand, UPI said, "We do not feel bound to carry every utterance of minor political party leaders who decide to take vulgar swipes at Billy Carter or anyone else." Several years earlier, George McGovern, the Democratic presidential candidate, whispered a similar remark to a heckler and a news service reported it as "kiss my＿＿." This prompted one newspaper to tell its readers drily that McGovern said "kiss my dash." In 1979 President Carter's remark that if Senator Kennedy ran for president "I'll whip his ass" was of course reported just that way.

Newsworthiness must be the deciding element. But even then, the bald quotation can sometimes be softened so as to be inoffensive. Often the context can perfectly well convey the meaning without the explicit words. Generally, a word can be eliminated without doing any violence to the essential thought.

Good newspapers recognize that reports can be honest and fair and give the reader a clear picture without torturing the images, even when obscenities are not used. Often a few quick slashes of the pencil are all that is needed. In reporting on a rock concert, one newspaper had to make a judgment as to whether one bizarre sidelight was important enough to report. Having decided that the event could not be ignored, it edited the paragraph, left, to appear as it does on the right:

One sidelight of the performance: A boy and girl stripped naked, jumped into a vast square of foam and made love amid a watchful sea of faces. The unscheduled love making by the naked teens shocked some of the audience, but no move was made to stop the display of the full sex act.	One sidelight of the performance: A boy and girl jumped into a vast square of foam and made love amid a watchful sea of faces. The act shocked some of the audience, but no move was made to stop it.

Some newspapers have developed policy statements on how touchy language is to be handled. The policy of the *Philadelphia Inquirer* is worth quoting at some length here:

The Inquirer's policy on the use of profanity, obscenity and blasphemy in its columns is based on the premise that the newspaper should be acceptable in all kinds of households.

Unlike the movies, whose rating system warns potential viewers of the kind of language they will be exposed to, newspapers serve a broad general audience that expects a G-rated product every day.

It is true, of course, that society's attitudes are ever changing and that we now freely use some language that a few decades ago was thought to be too frank. Still, there is danger of getting out in front of our audience; we should carefully monitor the use of profanity, obscenity and blasphemy and restrict it to extraordinary circumstances.

This is an area in which only the broadest sort of guidelines can apply. A word or a phrase that may be used in one context may be entirely objectionable in another.

Central to any decision is this question: Is an important journalistic purpose served by the use of the questionable language?

The more harsh the language, the more important and serious purpose must be. This means that we have to decline to publish some quotes that we ourselves find very funny; in the interest of simply entertaining our readers, we should not resort to language that will offend many of them.

Beyond those involving mild expletives, decisions about profanity, obscenity and blasphemy should be referred to the executive editor or managing editor. If neither is present, the decision must be made by the ranking editor on duty in the news department.

The following guidelines are intended to help editors make decisions in this area, including the crucial one of when to refer a case to higher authority:

1. The use of any questionable language is almost exclusively limited to quoted material. It should be rare indeed that our own writers should use it. This means, among other things, that columnists should not make casual references to the Deity merely to lend emphasis to their own statements.

2. Generally, when a news subject utters profanity, obscenity or blasphemy in an interview with one or two reporters, we will not use it. The question becomes more difficult when the number of listeners grows larger and the personage of the speaker more important.

3. The part of the paper in which the language would appear also has a bearing on whether it should be permitted. An expletive that would be excised from a Page One story, where the casual reader might see it, possibly could be used within a long, thoughtful piece in Review and Opinion or Today Magazine.

4. Line editors may decide when the circumstances warrant the use of mild expletives such as "hell" or "damn." When the speaker is a reasonably important person or the audience a fairly substantial one, line editors may also authorize the use of such terms as "goddamn," "son of a bitch," "bastard" and "Christ." When the circumstances are not clear-cut, or if stronger language or a question of taste is involved, a ranking editor must be consulted.

5. Sometimes language that is not in itself profane, obscene or blasphemous might be objectionable on grounds of taste, and a ranking editor must be consulted. On the other hand, we should not hesitate to write in clinical terms on matters pertaining to the human anatomy, sex and excretory functions when relevant to the news.

6. In most cases, when language is deleted from a quote, an ellipsis will be inserted to indicate that something is missing. Occasionally—and on approval of a ranking editor—it is permissible to suggest the word or phrase used without

actually publishing it. This is done by using the first letter of the word, followed by an em dash: "The mayor told the reporter, 'If you print the story, I am going to kick your a—!'" The use of *bleep* and *bleeping* as substitutes for profanity is restricted to the sports pages.

When in doubt about whether any language is appropriate, ask for guidance. The practice of referring these decisions helps us maintain uniform standards throughout the paper.

Taste in Pictures. What has been said about tasteful use of words applies equally to pictures. Scarcely a day goes by when editors are not presented with questions of propriety in pictures either taken by the staff or transmitted on the news service wires. (The news service editors move material they might find personally objectionable but that they say editors should have the opportunity to consider for their own audiences.) A picture of an auto victim's decapitated torso, of the mutilated body of a war victim, or of starving children in Asia is repulsive, but such pictures have been run by responsible newspapers and magazines to make a point or because of the overwhelming news interest involved. The question comes down to whether a legitimate point is made or whether the picture is run gratuitously to pander to baser tastes. A spectacular set of pictures made by a *Boston Herald American* photographer at a 1975 fire showed a mother and child plunging to their deaths from a balcony. The pictures got front-page play across the United States and predictably, the papers got many calls protesting the pictures as outrageous and in incredibly poor taste. "Our choice," said one editor, "and the complaints that resulted, reflect the delicate balance—often highly individualized—between reader interest and editor responsibility." Another said,

> If it were a mistake to run them, it would likewise have been a mistake not to run them. Those are the horns of the editor's dilemma. Most of them regard human life as precious, human dignity as more precious. But in addition to their strengths and weaknesses, editors do carry about with them somewhat self-consciously a professional dedication to the proposition that their job is to pass on news as it truly is, within the bounds of integrity and responsibility.

The "streaker" craze of 1974 presented editors with a different situation but essentially the same problem. *Newsweek* carried several full-color pages of streakers. Most newspapers carried pictures illustrating the epidemic of nude persons running in public singly and in groups. However, almost none used full-length frontal views. The craze ended as abruptly as it began. Most newspapers were able to ponder quietly the large problem of whether publicity had helped popularize the fad.

Some Other Problems of Taste and Ethics

Racial Identifications. The responsible editor does not give offense to groups any more than to individuals. This includes religious, racial, and national groups. A good general policy is not stating race, color, or creed of a person unless there is reason for it. This applies even to stories of success or achievement as well, though often the identification of a minority race, for example, in such stories is essential—it is doubtless pertinent that a black homecoming queen at a university is the first of her race so chosen. (The term *black* now is preferred to *Negro*, although a generation ago the opposite was true. When most racial designations are used, they are capitalized: Caucasian, Oriental, Indian; but *black* and *white*, when used to denote race, are usually lower-cased today.)

Blood and Gore. Many stories of crime and tragedy have some seamy details that need not be expressed in print and usually are not. A few years ago a dozen or so tabloids of the sort sold in supermarkets exploited these details in the most lurid way: "I Cut Out

Her Heart and Stomped On It." Most of these papers found that violence didn't sell as well as celebrities, health, and the occult, and their readership formulas have been considerably changed, although a freaky fringe of magazines still panders to a morbid curiosity about crime for the sake of mere sensation. Because they are read by millions, these journals deserve the serious attention of journalism students.

Unless they are inescapably a part of the story to which the reader is entitled, the descriptions of victims and scenes of violence should be muted. Even then, restraint dictates what is reported, even in so compelling a tragedy as the 900 deaths in Jonestown, Guyana, in 1978. A question for editors to ask themselves: Can it be read at the breakfast table?

Many news organizations have codes and many newspapers have expressed or implied policy statements that spell out broadly how to deal with such details. The Code of the American Society of Newspaper Editors says, for example,

> A newspaper cannot escape conviction of insincerity if while professing high moral purpose it supplies incentives to base conduct, such as are to be found in the details of crime and vice, publication of which is not demonstrably in the general good. Lacking authority to enforce its canons, the journalists here represented can but express the hope that deliberate pandering to vicious instincts will encounter effective public disapproval or yield to the influence of a preponderant professional condemnation.

A Final Word

Your own good sense, integrity, and conscience will be constantly involved in making judgments on taste problems and other ethical concerns. The key word in this discussion is *responsibility*. You will have a responsibility to your reader: On the one hand, is the story misleading or cryptic because it may offend? On the other, is it offensive to fair-minded people? You will have a responsibility to the subject of the story: Does it unnecessarily strip away privacy or needlessly inflict pain? You will have a responsibility to society: Does the public have a right to know whether a dirty joke told by a Cabinet member is so gross as to warrant his removal from public life? Responsibility involves decisions as to where the greater good lies and whether compromises can or should be made in the selection and presentation of a story to protect the rights of all.

SELECTED READINGS

Hulteng, John T. *The Messenger's Motives: Ethical Problems of the News Media.* Englewood Cliffs, N.J.: Prentice-Hall, Inc., 1976. Includes chapters on taste and pictures.

Merrill, John C., and Ralph C. Barney. *Ethics and the Press: Readings in Mass Media Morality.* New York: Hastings House, 1975. Excellent readings on credibility, objectivity, and bias.

Rubin, Bernard, ed. *Questioning Media Ethics.* New York: Praeger, 1978. A research report of the ideas of 22 media professionals and critics dealing with concrete problems of ethical values under the stress of professional necessity.

EXERCISES

In judging the following stories, use the standards you believe that the editor of a community daily in your own locality would follow in making responsible decisions as to whether a story should be used and how it might be edited.

Pilot

ESTES PARK -- Searchers recovered the body of a 45-year-old aldwell, Idaho, man Monday from the wreckage of his helicopter in a rugged mountain area north of here.

The Larimer County Sheriff's office identified the victim of the Sunday crash as James Smithers, a pilot for Helicopter Service, Inc., Boise.

A Civil Air Patrol (CAP) spokesman said the helicopter crashed Sunday after trying to pick up a surveyor on a charter assignment.

The wreckage was spotted Monday morning by the CAP plane and was reached shortly afterward by a sheriff's ground party.

The huma remains were taken to the coroner's office here.

Pilot

ESTES PARK -- Searchers recovered the body of a 45-year-old Caldwell, Idaho, man Monday from the wreckage of his helicopter in a rugged mountain area north of here.

The Larimer County Sheriff's office identified the victim of the Sunday crash as James Smithers, a pilot for Helicopter Service, Inc., Boise.

A Civil Air Patrol (CAP) spokesman said the helicopter crashed Sunday after trying to pick up a surveyor on a charter assignment.

The wreckage was spotted Monday morning by the CAP plane and

was reached shortly afterward by a sheriff's ground party.

~~The huma remains were taken to the coroner's office here.~~

Scotus

Editors: the following includes material that may be offensive to

some readers.

WASHINGTON - Over the objections of Chief Justice Warren E. Burger,

the Supreme Court has given a former New Jersey high school teacher and

two other people a chance to upset their convictions for saying "m_____

f_____" in public.

Burger said the court had taken steps "to return to the law of the

jungle."

The ex-teacher, David A. Rosenfeld, used the phrase while imploring

whites attending a school discussion at Hightstown, N.J., to pay heed to

the grievances of blacks.

He was convicted of disorderly conduct under a New Jersey law that

prohibits loud and offensive or profane or indecent language in public

and was fined $80.

By a 5-4 vote, the court ruled Monday that Rosenfeld was entitled

to reconsideration under other high court decisions limiting prosecution

for using curse words in public.

Burger, in a strenuous dissent, said; "If continued, this permissive-ness will tend futher to erode public conficence in the law-that subtle but indispensible ingredient of ordered liberty."

The other dissenters were Justice Harry A. Blackmun, William H. Rehnquist and Lewis F. Powell.

In a second case, the court ordered reconsideration of conviction of Mallie Lewis, a black New Orleans woman, who used a similar phrase when police were arresting her son. She was convicted of violating a city ordinance and sentenced to $10 fine or 10 days in jail.

The vote in this case was 6 to 3, with Powell swinging over to the majority.

In a third case, the court ordered reconsideration of the conviction of Wilbert Montell Brown for saying "m_____f_____" facist pig cops" in a talk to a group at the University of Tulsa in Oklahoma.

Burger, said: "It is barely a century since men in parts of this country carried guns constantly because the law did not afford protection.

"In that setting, the words used in these cases, if directed toward such an armed civilian, could well have led to death or serious bodily injury.

"When we undermine the general belief that the law will give protection against fighting words and profane and abusive language such as the utterances involved in these cases, we take steps to return to the law of the jungle . . .

"I cannot see these holdings as an advance in human liberty but rather a retrogression to that men have struggled to escape for a long time."

#

Nip

Little Carrie Dudley, year-old daughter of Mr. and Mrs. Ron Dudley, 221 W. 4th St., must wonder if the debut into the "playmate world" is worth it!

Ten days ago she got curious about the queer things her brother and sisters, Shawn, Kelli, and Rae, were playing with, so she put one of them into her mouth. It was a jack. It caught in her throat and choked her.

Her mother beat her on the back and shook her by the heels, but Carrie continued to choke, and she turned blue.

He mother poked with her fingers into Carrie's throat. All she got out was blood--and little pieces of flesh. She poked again. This time she brought out the jack--and more flesh.

Later the doctor jokingly asked her mother why she didn't jerk out all of Carrie's tonsils while she was at it.

If Carrie could understand, she'd undoubtedly feel lucky, though. That same day her little playmate, Jennie Jones (daughter of Mr. and Mrs. Larry Jones) choked on some of her brothers' peanuts. One of them didn't come out. It got into her lung, and she had to be rushed to the hospital to have it removed surgically.

Both Carrie and her playmate recovered quickly, and things went smoothly enough for a few days--until Sunday afternoon.

He daddy was on the couch nursing intestinal flu; her mother was in the kitchen peeling potatoes; Carrie and her brother and sisters were having noisy fun in the bedroom.

Suddenly someone banged the bedroom door shut--hard. Everybody started to scream--especially Carrie. The door had slammed tight on her tinly left finger and cut the end of it right off.

Her mother got there first, then she started to scream too.

Her daddy came running. He turned white and headed for the bed. (Later her mother said it might have been the flu or the blood that made daddy faint, but most likely it was the memory from his boyhood when a lawnmower cut off four of his own fingers.)

Somehow Carrie's mother, with the help of neighbors Chris and Dick Stevens got her to the doctor's office. He sutured the finger, but warned that because it was so badly smashed it might not "take."

Carrie's parents think it will, though. After all, when the lawnmower cut off four of her daddy's fingers, he gathered them and ran home with them. The doctor sewed them back on, and all but the baby finger grew back together.

If Carrie's finger doesn't "take," though, she will really have something to talk about when she is old enough to talk. After all, what other little girl will have a stubbed baby finger--just like daddy's?

Stomp

A Fraternity Council stomp Friday night in the Union Ballroom ended with a broken window, backed-up toilets and other minor damage. No one was injured, but many people were sick and vomited on the floors.

The window was baroden when a person was pushed against the glass. There was no fight involved and the breakage appeared to be an accident. The damage will amount to approximately $250.

Vandalism appeared to be the cause of the other damage to the Union. Toilets in the north wing of the Union were backed up when they were stuffed full of rags. The total damage will not be covered by the rent payed by the Council for the Union Ballroom, approximately $125.

Another minor incident occurred when a person with vomit on his shirt ran into the restroom, screaming, "I need a fix." Campus Security was unable to find any of his friends to take him home, but the yourth ran away when the police were driving him home.

Many campus groups use stomps as their major source of income. The Fraternity Council has had several successful stomps within the last year. Other groups use the same method. The problem stems from the fact that, to get the most money, the groups have to cater to the high schools students in the valley. Usually the advertisements say "No ID required."

The typical security at a stomp is two Union managers, and three or four policemen from the University Police. At Friday's stomp, eight policemen were on duty. The sponsors pay for the security and usually provide additional help.

One solution proposed by some people is to require Univerisity ID to get in. Presumable, University students would have more respect for Union property, since they would pay for the repairs. But high school students don't really have any other place in town to hold stomps and cheap concerts.

-2/Stomp

Larger rent for the Union Ballroom? More security? No more
high schoolers? No one yet knows what the reaction by the Union
Administration will be to Friday's stomp.

Version A

Flier

A package arrived Saturday for Mrs. John Peterson Jr. along with a
letter from her husband. He hadn't forgotten their second wedding
anniversary--May 1.

Sunday, Mrs. Peterson received another message: "The Navy regrets...
Lt. (j.g.) John Peterson Jr. has been killed in a training accident..."

Lt. Peterson, navy pilot flying from an aircraft carrier, the USS
Hancock, was killed when his plane plunged and burned at sea near San
Diego during training exercises. His body was not recovered.

Mrs. Peterson, the former April Johnson, and a son, Gary, one-year-
old, live with her parents Mr. and Mrs. Sidney Johnson, 2924 Lincoln Ave.
Mrs. Peterson is expecting another child in early summer.

Parents of Lt. Peterson, Mr. and Mrs. John Peterson Sr., live at
254 4th St.

Lt. Peterson was killed Friday on his RF8-A. He was a member of
VFP-63 photo squadron.

He had celebrated his 25th birthday the previous day.

His father recalled Monday that "Jack" had always been interested

Flier 2:   and

in flying. He joined the Naval Reserve Officers Training Corps gradu-
ating in 1963. He was educated in the city and graduated from Central
High School.

He earned his Navy wings at Corpus Christi, Tex. He had been
stationed at Miramar, Calif., until being assigned to the aircraft
carrier five months ago.

Lt. Peterson was born in Elm City April 2, 1954, a son of John and
Ruth Wallace Peterson. He had lived here all his life until he joined
the Navy.

He was an active member of the Methodist church.

He married April Johnson May 1, 1978.

He is survived by his wife, a son, Gary, his parents; two brothers
Roger and Michael; two sisters Martha Peterson and Mrs. John (Loretta)
Ganet, both of San Bernadino, Calif; grandparents, Mr. and Mrs. Clyde
Peterson, both of this city.

Memorial services will be held Wednesday at 1 p.m. in the Methodist
Church, 553 Industry Blvd.

Version B

Flier

An Elm City navy pilot died in a jet crash off the coast of
California, his wife and parents have been advised.

Lt. (jg) John Peterson Jr., 25, was killed when his RF8A plane

crashed on a training mission Friday as a member of the VFP63 photo
squadron operating off the carrier USS Hancock.

His widow, April Johnson Peterson, resides at 2924 Lincoln Ave. and
his parents, Mr. and Mrs. John Peterson Sr., reside at 254 4th St.

Educated in Elm City schools and a graduate from Central High
School, Lt. Peterson joined the Naval Reserve Officers Training Corps.

He earned his Navy wings at Corpus Christi, Tex. He had been
stationed at Mirarmar, Calif., prior to his assignment to the
Hancock.

He was an active member of the Methodist Church.

He was born April 2, 1954, in Elm City, a son of Mr. and Mrs. John
Peterson, Sr., and married April Johnson May 1, 1978.

His survivors also include a son, Gary, his parents; two brothers
Roger and Michael; two sisters Martha Peterson and Mrs. John (Loretta)
Ganet, both of San Bernadino, Calif; grandparents, Mr. and Mrs. Clyde
Peterson, both of this city.

Memorial services will be conducted Wednesday at 1 p.m. in the
Methodist Church.

Zenith

A prposal that could stop the construction of more than 200
condominium units in Buttermilk Canyon was given prelim inary approval
Monday afternoon by the Zenith Town Planning Commission.

The proposal is a draft policy declaration stating Zenith desires to annex 25 acres of land where the development is planned in order to insure proper planning.

According to Mayor Ferrol G. Waters, Zenith is not necessarily trying to stop the development. "If we don't have a policy declaration, then Magic Mountain can do whatever they want," he said.

The developers, Magic Mountain Properties, want to construct 226 condominium units over a 10-year period. The site is about a half-mile above Zenith's current city limits in the canyon.

There is sharp disagreement as to the purpose of the policy declaration. The Town Planning Commission members agree that the purpose is to give Zenith some control over development to insure proper planning.

Others thi-nk the purpose is to stop Magic Mountain development. "That's the whold damn purpose of it, no ifs, and's or but's about it," said Magic Mountain president John Gertz. According to Charles Hullinger, owner of the Restaway Lodge in Zenith, "the sole purpose is to screw the Magic Mountain guys, and I want everyone to understand that."

# # #

Fatal

Two persons were kelled when the pickup truck in which they were riding swerved out of control on state Highway 4, crashed through a cement retaining wall and landed upside down in Canyon Creek, the State Police reported Friday.

The victims were identified as Rhonda Bates, 21, and Paul Tregeagle, Jr., both of Elm City. The accident occurred Thursday night.

Authorities could not immediately identify Tregeagle because he was
eject ed from the truck and was last seen floating downstream in the
creek. His body has bot yet been recovered.

#

Rustlers

Cattle rustling conjures up pictures of the old west, but a
$500 reward has been offered for information leading to the arrest
of a modern cattle rustler who killed and butchered a young steer in
the National Forest August 19 or 20.

The steer, which belonged to Kenneth Wells, was found Tuesday
near Herd Hollow, a range area located between Fork Canyons east of
Fielding. The animals had been stripped of its hide and meat and
had only the head and fron legs remaining.

Suicide

The death of a 34-year-old man Wednesday at 12:20 p.m. on the
Union Pacific Railroad mainline tracks, 10 miles south of here, was
termed an apparent suicide by the County Sheriff's Dept.

Edward Pollard was killed instantly as he walked into the boxcars
of a southbound freight train. Three fellow employes witnessed the
accident while having lunch.

Homo

Children should be taught the dangers of homosexuality from the time they are old enough to leave their own front yard, believes Capt. Clive Spritzer, City police officer.

"I'm not an expert in these things but I used to work on the vice squad," he said. "It's an unfortunate fact of life that a few homosexuals don't restrict their activities to consenting adults.

"Often the way it is found out that someone else is a homosexual is because he entices children," he said. "This is what I really object to. I don't want to argue their right to be what they are when only consenting adults are involved, either morally or legally."

Persons involved in this type of activity also do not restrict their work to private places, said Capt. Spritzer. There are many serious problem areas in bus stations, public parks and other area with public restrooms.

"I feel parents have a responsibility to make their children aware these things happen," he said. "Thus, if some stranger calls the child over and says something like 'Hey! Want to feel something nice and soft, that child will know how to respond."

Precisely what the parent should say depends upon the age, maturity and intelligence of the child, the head of the training division said.

"Most parents are sold on the idea of sex education in the home, but too few are doing it," he said. "This is a phase of training that shouldn't be neglected.

#

16. LIBEL

The very mention of libel in a newsroom will cause heads to turn. Libel is the legal term for a statement made visually, as in print, that is damaging and untrue. It is to journalism what malpractice is to the medical profession or fraud to business. It smirches the standards that ethical practitioners hold dear. More than that, it can tear down in moments a reputation that has taken years to build, and that is sometimes more precious than life itself. Thus, good editors are always alert to the implications of their work and to the damage that can be done (through simple carelessness as well as willful neglect) both to the media and also to the good name of an individual or corporation.

The number of court actions involving media has skyrocketed in recent years. And where libel law has not changed much in the past decade, how the principles are applied in the courts is changing rapidly. You should keep abreast of legal developments; libel law is only one battleground. The press must be ever vigilant against harassment through libel actions and threats of libel and be willing to endure them to report the news. It also wages an unrelenting fight to gain open access to court deliberations, to strike down gag laws, to get cameras and artists into the courtrooms, and to protect confidential sources of information. But libel is the legal area that most concerns the media as a daily practical concern. Furthermore, it is the one area in which the copy editor is expected to be directly concerned and about which the copy editor can do the most.

When you select and edit materials according to the news story standards of accuracy and taste set out in the previous chapters, your chances of being sued for libel and slim and your chances of defeating a libel action are good. The cardinal rules in avoiding a libel proceeding are to be *fair* and *impartial*, *complete* and *accurate*. These precepts will especially help you avoid the trap of *malice*, which is a crucial factor in whether a defamatory story can stand on one of the legal defenses. Malice can be established when there is personal ill will in printing a story. It can also be presumed by courts when grossly insulting words are used or when negligence can be found that is so great as to betray a lack of concern for reputation. These criteria are especially needed when sensitive matters such as arrests and investigations are involved. Be dogged in your attempts to insure utmost factual accuracy; have concern for reputations by making sure the reporter has obtained all sides of a story.

Here is some advice in the event you are confronted with a challenge to a story you have edited. You should assume the positive role of information collector rather than the defensive stance of respondent to questions. Ascertain the nature of the complaint, plus the name, address, and telephone number of the complainant. Do not answer questions about the story beyond the material in print. Simply tell the complainant you will see that the matter is checked and that a response will be made. Do not make apologies. Do not promise corrections. Many callers have legitimate complaints, but no complaint requires an immediate, off-the-cuff response. Every complaint must be checked. And there is always time to check. You may promise a response—any caller is entitled to that—but no more. The caller may be in error or may be fishing for additional information to strengthen a contemplated legal action. You must not be persuaded, in the heat of the moment, to act in a manner that may be detrimental to you or your employer. This applies whether you are dealing with private citizens or officials. A lawyer cannot require you, over the telephone, to appear in an office. Neither can a court clerk, a mayor, or a judge. Any such demands should be referred immediately to superiors or to counsel. The legal process is a paper process. You are under no obligation to work outside that process, and you should resist any suggestions that you are being uncooperative by choosing to work within it.

The exercises at the end of this chapter will challenge your ability to recognize potentially libelous information and to make editing changes accordingly. Before you attempt to edit these stories, read carefully the Libel Manual in your stylebook. If you wish to pursue libel in more detail—and the more you learn about it, the better—numerous texts are available. Some are cited at the end of this unit. Also read carefully the chapter in this book on "Police and the Courts," p. 203. The following well-established points will help you work with these stories.

What Is Libel?

Three matters have to be established in a court of law before libel can be proved: publication, defamation, and identification.

1. Publication. Remember that an item printed need not necessarily have been prominently displayed. It is only necessary to have printed (or aired) it so that it could have been seen or heard. The smallest item on the bottom of page 42 is as potentially libelous as a Page One article. For you as a practicing journalist, publication means having been printed or aired, for broadcasts also are treated as libel. (Oral defamation usually is treated as *slander*.) Technically, any "fixed, visible representation to the eye" could constitute libel, including skywriting, hanging in effigy, graffiti, or letters.

2. Defamation. A good short definition of defamation is "that which tends to make others think less of a person." A little broader is the typical definition that defamation is that which tends to prejudice a person's right to social contact, business, profession or calling, or merely general reputation in the community. Reputation is not necessarily the same as character. It is the opinion others hold of a person. A false statement is not necessarily defamatory in itself. It must be damaging as well.

Courts have ruled that some words are always libelous on their face (*libel per se*). To accuse anyone of a breach of ethics or committing an unlawful act is always libelous, whether the offense is a misdemeanor or higher crime. Some words not clearly defamatory on their face can be construed to be libelous because of special circumstances (*libel per quod* or *libel "by extrinsic fact"*). To say falsely that a Mormon bishop is a smoker would, for example, be defamatory of him, because that faith forbids use of tobacco. Generally it is not libelous to say a person is something he or she has a legal right to be, but there are exceptions. To accuse a person of having a loathsome disease would prejudice his or her right to social contact and could be deemed defamatory. American courts have ruled that to call someone a Communist or Nazi is defamatory.

One statute reads that defamation is an "expression tending to impeach the honesty, integrity, virtue or reputation of one who is alive and thereby to expose him to public hatred, contempt or ridicule." (Defamation tending to blacken the memory of one who is dead can be prosecuted as criminal libel, but the AP Libel Manual wisely refrains from an extensive treatment of criminal libel. Generally speaking, the same considerations govern criminal libel proceedings as the more common civil libel, and criminal libel actions are very rare.)

3. Identification. A defamatory expression that is exposed to public view is libelous if it identifies the person defamed. Identification can be made indirectly. Often to prove libel it is not necessary to identify a person accused in a story by name if that person can be identified by indirection—by description, by relationship, or even by a nickname.

Special care must be taken to make certain all identifications are correct. Many libel awards have been won by persons incorrectly identified. Hence, in stories about crime and other antisocial behavior, the name and address of the accused are always used as a point of identification, and of course these should be carefully verified.

In one of the following exercises a person clearly defamed is not directly identified, but there can be no question about whom the piece refers. Your job is to determine whether there is any defense to publishing the allegations.

Defenses

It would be impossible for any newspaper worthy of the name to avoid publishing all defamatory matter, as, for example, news stories from the courts or police stations or branches of government. The law recognizes that it is sound public policy for such matters to be examined, and consequently allows several defenses.

The three most basic defenses—*truth*, *fair comment and criticism*, and *statutory* or *qualified privilege*—are briefly described in the Libel Manual. Where any of these can be established in defense to a libel action, they are *complete defenses* in the sense that they will completely defeat recovery of damages by the plaintiff.

1. Truth. Once upon a time truth was no defense at all. The old common law axiom three centuries ago was "the greater the truth, the greater the libel." Today it is the most complete defense—it will totally defeat recovery of damages in a libel proceeding if it can be established. In some jurisdictions the truth is not a complete defense in civil libel cases when malice can be shown, and malice always destroys the defense of truth in criminal cases. So the truth must be published "for good ends and justifiable motives."

If you are really sure of your facts, you can tell complainants threatening a libel action, "We aren't sued when we tell the truth." That will usually stop them dead in their tracks. However, the matter really isn't that simple. As the AP Libel Manual emphasizes, the truth must be provable—you have to have evidences admissible in a court of law—and that might be quite a different matter from your just knowing something to be true. Three main points are emphasized in all discussions of truth as a defense:

a. The truth must be published without malice.
b. The truth must be as broad as the charge. It is not enough merely to show that the person named has a bad reputation, nor is it any help to show that a charge was common knowlege. Even the word *alleged* is of marginal effect here, mostly useful in showing absence of malice and qualifying a charge as a report rather than as a matter of fact.
c. The literal charge must be true. It is not enough to show that a quotation was accurate—that charge itself must be provable. What a police officer or other court functionary tells a reporter outside a privileged court proceeding is not defensible except on grounds of truth—the truth of what was said, not merely of the fact that it was uttered.

In one of the following exercises the neighbors are quoted as telling about threats made by a husband against his wife. In all likelihood a court would not allow these neighbors to say the same thing on a witness stand, where the charges might be treated as hearsay, gossip, or innuendo. It's safer, in fact it's good ethics and good sense, to reject these off-the-cuff statements until they come out in a privileged court proceeding.

2. Privilege. The key to privilege is the word *qualified*. Privilege is always qualified by the absence of malice. It is not the same as the absolute privilege enjoyed by a public official in an official proceeding. The official can say anything in a courtroom, subject to the judge's tolerance, or on the floor of an official proceeding in the legislature. The reporter's privilege is limited to making a fair and true, nonmalicious, report of the public and official proceeding and not going beyond the proceeding.

a. *The guideline on what is public:* Was the public actually invited to attend, and were there in fact people from the casual or open public in attendance? Was the document actually open to inspection by the public?
b. *The guideline on what is official:* Is there a provision in law saying that the board or group should meet—a city ordinance, for example, prescribing

when and how the city council should convene? Is there a legal provision
that a document be kept?

If the meeting or document meets these tests, there's no doubt that you can safely
use anything from it. Semiofficial meetings, such as those of Parent-Teacher Associations,
probably don't qualify for this defense, or at least the defense is weak here.

In the following exercises, you'll encounter much privileged material from criminal
complaints filed in court, open proceedings of legislative and judicial bodies, and the like.
This material can safely be used as long as the reporter has not gone beyond the proceedings by, for example, injecting a personal evaluation. All that takes place in open court can
be reported.

In some of the following stories the privilege is tenuous. The bar association of a
state, for example, is not a public organization in the sense recognized by libel law. You
may decide the story is worth carrying because it is too newsworthy to be ignored, but be
prepared to defend your judgment.

In some of the privileged proceedings dealt with here, you may decide that on grounds
of ethics a story ought not to be carried or should be muted, even if the material is privileged.
Again, be prepared to defend your judgment.

Remember that *investigations* themselves are not privileged. In most cases the police
dispatcher's record, detective's report, jail inmate lists, and the like are not open to public
inspection. On the other hand, a complaint formally signed by a magistrate and sworn to by
a police officer is privileged, and you may freely quote from it. Again, on ethical grounds
you may not wish to do so; many newspapers refuse to carry most civil complaints simply
because a plaintiff can swear to almost any allegation and have it made a matter of public
record. You may decide that the story on the county roads director's public intoxication
should be carried. But you should question whether the action against him is privileged at
this juncture of the proceedings and whether the offense is grave enough to warrant stig-
matizing him.

3. Fair Comment and Criticism. The defense of fair comment and criticism is available when the press comments on any matter that presents itself for public approval, such as
a governmental action, an artistic performance, or a sports event. Three cautions:

a. The opinion need not be charitable but it must be the writer's true opinion—
    it cannot be actuated by malice or contain words so scurrilous that malice
    can be presumed;
b. It cannot go beyond the action or performance itself; you could safely say a
    boxer was inept in his bout, but to accuse him of showing cowardice prob-
    ably would be a charge so broad as to destroy the defense of fair comment;
c. The factual foundation for the opinion must be accurate. All opinion stems
    from factual grounds. You could not safely accuse even a public official
    of dereliction of duty if the duties did not include, say, supervising the
    sewer system about which you are complaining.

You may find the play review included in the following exercises something short of
a professional evaluation. Your job is to help the writer. You will, of course, judge the
review from every standpoint, but you should not do violence to the judgment of the author.
What you need to do is help the writer avoid any libelous imputation in judging the artistic
merits of the play.

4. Other Defenses. In addition to the three primary complete defenses, the law recognizes the defenses of *consent* and *reply*. A plaintiff cannot sue successfully when consent
has been given for publication of a libel—as, for example, when a celebrity consents to having

his unvarnished memoirs published. If, as in one of our exercises, a person has freely and openly admitted being a Nazi, there can scarcely be a complaint about that characterization when applied to him in the story. One may reply to a libel, just as in defending against a physical attack. But the reply cannot go beyond the charge, any more than a defense to an attack can go beyond what is necessary to repel it.

5. Partial Defenses. Finally, there are some "partial defenses" that will reduce damages awarded by a court. In general, anything the writer or editor can do to show that the story was published without malice—"for good ends and justifiable means"—or that care was taken in the preparation of the report will mitigate damages. You could plead in a court that a report came from a reputable newsgathering agency and that therefore you had reason to believe that it was accurate.

One important partial defense is *retraction*. In many states the law provides that if a retraction is made in the way the law specifies (usually meaning that it must appear within a specified time after a demand is made and in the same position as the offending article), the award of damages is limited to actual damages—those the plaintiff actually sustained—rather than providing for general damages that make the person "whole" again or for punitive damages that punish the press. Unfortunately, some papers knuckle under and print retractions even where they have a strong case, simply because fighting a libel charge can be an expensive business, sometimes more costly than the award of damages itself.

But editors sometimes feel warranted in taking a calculated risk in publishing libelous material, even when they have no firm defense, on grounds that the material is of such overriding public interest that withholding publication would be a disservice to the reader and to society. These decisions have to be made on an individual basis. Libel defense has been widened to make it difficult for officials to sue unless "knowing falsity" or "reckless disregard for the truth," in the language of the Supreme Court, can be proved. This is a recognition in law that the widest possible public discussion of the acts of public persons, especially public officials, is consistent with the democratic ideal.

SELECTED READINGS

General Texts

Devol, Kenneth S., ed. *Mass Media and the Supreme Court,* 2nd ed. New York: Hastings House, 1976.

Francois, William E. *Mass Media Law and Regulation,* 2nd ed. Columbus, Ohio: Grid, Inc., 1978.

Franklin, Marc A. *The First Amendment and the Fourth Estate.* Mineola, N.Y.: Foundation Press, Inc., 1978.

Gordon, David. *Problems in Law of Mass Communications.* Mineola, N.Y.: Foundation Press, Inc., 1978.

Nelson, Harold L., and Dwight L. Teeter, Jr. *Law of Mass Communications,* 3rd ed. Mineola, N.Y.: Foundation Press, Inc., 1978.

Pember, Don R. *Mass Media and the Law.* Dubuque, Ia.: William C. Brown Co., 1977.

Specific Books on Issues of Concern to Editors (e.g., Libel, Privacy, etc.)

Ashley, Paul. *Say It Safely,* 5th ed. Seattle: University of Washington Press, 1977.

Pember, Don R. *Privacy and the Press.* Seattle: University of Washington Press, 1972.

Sanford, Bruce W. *Synopsis of the Law of Libel and the Right of Privacy.* New York: Newspaper Enterprise Association, Inc., 1977.

Stevens, George, and John B. Webster. *Law and the Student Press.* Ames, Ia.: Iowa State University Press, 1973.

EXERCISES

Probe

A 20-year-old mother was killed Sunday at 8 p.m. on Industry Boulevard at 21st Street when she was flung from her husband's car as it made a violent U-turn.

Ironically, two County Sheriff's deputies were half a block away and witnessed the accident.

Sharon Miller, 1540 21st Street, was dead on arrival at General Hospital. Her husband and driver of the car, Jaines, 25, was treated for contusions and abrasions. The couple's son Donald, two, was hurled into the back seat in the accident, but escaped injury.

Deputies Sam Berger and Ed Ashton, who witnessed the incident, said the car made a wild U-turn and Mrs. Miller was jurled onto the roadway. The careening auto continued in a circle and ran over the victim as she lay helpless in the street.

Neighbors of the Millers had minutes before called police following a violent argument at the Miller home. They told police Mr. Miller had dragged his wife and child into the car and sped off. Because Mr. Miller had a long felony record for similar assault, they feared for the wife and baby's safety and called police.

Officers said an autopsy will be ordered on the victim because of a strange wound was found in her head. A recently fired 22-caliber pistol also was found in the car. Officers said facts in the case will be turned over to the County Attorney's office.

# # #

(Probe)

A 20-year-old ~~mother~~ *woman* was killed Sunday at 8 p.m. on Industry Boulevard at 21st Street when she ~~was flung from~~ *fell from a car driven by* her husband~~'s car as~~ *and was run over.* ~~it made a violent U-turn.~~

~~Ironically, two County Sheriff's deputies were half a block away~~ ~~and witnessed the accident.~~

The victim, Sharon Miller, 1540 21st ~~Street~~, was dead on arrival at General Hospital. Her husband, ~~and driver of the car~~, Jaines, 25, was treated for ~~contusions~~ *bruises* and ~~abrasions~~ *cuts*. The couple's son Donald, (two), was hurled into the back seat ~~in the accident~~, but ~~escaped injury~~ *was uninjured.*

Deputies Sam Berger and Ed Ashton, who witnessed the incident, *from half a block away,* said the car made a ~~wild~~ U-turn and Mrs. Miller ~~was jurled on~~ *fell* onto the roadway. The ~~careening~~ auto ~~continued~~ *careened* in a circle and ran over the victim ~~as she lay helpless in the street~~.

Neighbors of the Millers had minutes before called police following a ~~violent~~ *an* argument at the Miller home. ~~They told police Mr. Miller had dragged his wife and child into the car and sped off. Because Mr. Miller had a long felony record for similar assault, they feared for the wife and baby's safety and called police.~~

Officers said an autopsy will be ordered, ~~on the victim because of a strange wound was found in her head. A recently fired 22-caliber pistol also was found in the car. Officers said facts in the case will be turned over to~~ the County Attorney's office *will handle the case.*

(# # #)

Principal

   Johnson City --The JohnsonCity Board of Education voted Friday not
to offer a contract of employment to Norma Darcy, Monroe School principal,
for the next school year.

   Mr. Darcy's attorney, Janet Brown, said the "board's decision will be
appealed to Federal District Court "as soon as we get written notification
of the decision."

   The principal charged with insubordination and inability to continue
in the position.

   Ms. Brown said her client denies the allegations and feels it is a
"difference in philosophies in education" which led to the board action.
She said she and Mr. Darcy had been told the board would not make a
decision until June 14. "He wasn't in town today and I was tied up in
federal court," the attorney said.

   She also said many hours had been spent in two hearings (closed to
the public) and that the evidence against her client "just slipped away
to nothing."

Dear Editor:

   About six months ago, my brother, along with three other young men,
between the ages of 13 to 15 were convicted of burglary. Two of the boys
weren't even put on probation, and the other two might as well not have
been.

   Right now these two are up to be released from probation for good
behavior. But how these officers figured these boys were being good is

beyond me. Between both boys, they have seen an officer four times (one visit for one boy and three visits for the other). So there is no way these officers could know how the boys are behaving. All they know is that they haven't been arrested again.

The other day, this probation officer phoned my dad and asked him what he thought about his son being released from probation. My father told him it didn't matter if the boy was left on probation or not, since the officers don't work with him anyway.

This officer told my father that they don't have time to work with boys who aren't in a lot of trouble. I guess the courts and the probation officers feel it better to wait until these boys are totally uncontrollable before they step in and do anything. By then, it's too late.

If these officers were doing their job they would see each of these boys at least once a week. And if the courts pronounced some stiffer penalties on these boys when the break the law--they could, for instance, take 10 of them at a time and make them clean a section of road for about two hours--at least it would serve as some kind of punishment and perhaps help the boys.

But as the juvenile court and probation system is now, the boys think it's just a big joke, and it is.

Dennis Keith
1254 First Street

Lodge

LAKE WAHEPETO -- A letter to the operator of Marina Lodge was sent from National Forest headquarters in Elk City warning the operators that

unless several violations of their special use permit are corrected within two weeks of the warning, action to close the lodge operation will be
taken.

Rodney Webster, branch chief of recreation lands for the forest,
said the lodge permittee, Otto Bruce, has received previous letters
warning that seven specific items of his operation are in violation of
the use permit. "We have received no response from Bruce concerning
these violations and are now taking action to require him to either
correct them or risk having his permit revoked" Webster stated

One of the major violations is the operation of a youth camp at
the lodge. Webster said that when the permit was by the forest headquarters here on May 27 it was specifically stated the the would be
no youth camp allowed. A request from the permittee earlier had been
made and a decision not to allow the camp followed from the Forest
Service.

Webster said, however, that on June 10, the first contingent of
youngsters arrived and he alleged there have been groups there since
that time.

"We feel there are groups booked for the entire summer, mostly
from the Las Vegas area," Webster said.

In addition to the youth camp, other complaints have been outlined
by the Forest Service, including corporation structure information,
business address information and health and safety measures.

Webster said the permit requires that all health and safety regulations of the state be met as well as specific areas outlined under Forest

-more-

Lodge 1st add/

Service regulations

The letter sent to Bruce stated that if compliance was not met, the permittee must show cause why the permit should not be revoked.

"There are three basic alternatives which can be taken," Webster said. They are compliance with permit by the permittee, obtaining of an injunction from court more by the Forest Service to close the lodge if the permit is revoked and in the event of revocation, an injunction for the permittee to continue to operate.

"We expect litigation to be involved before the incident is settled," Webster said. "We would, of course, hope that the permittee will comply to the terms of the permit to avoid any further action on the part of the Forest Service."

                                     #

Bar

The state bar is investigating allegations that a deputy prosecuting attorney uses public facilities and employes in his private law practice.

B. Gale Voorhees says he had given an explanation to the bar and denied any wrongdoing. Raymond P. Hullinger, executive director of the state bar, confirmed the investigation but refused to elaborate saying it was a confidential matter.

The charges were made in a letter written by four women to selected state offices questionning whether the tax-payers are paying for Vorhees' offices, secretary and stationary for his private practice.

Three of the four women who wrote the latter, Elnora Gooden, Sally
Schmeckpfeffer and Heidi Hough, have recentlybeen involved in eviction
proceedings in which Voorhees acted as a private lawyer for the plain-
tiffs.

Copies of that letter were sent to Attorney General Humbert Dowell,
the State Bar and the State Human Rights Commission.

Voorhees has denied making a practice of using county-employed
secretaries to assist him in his private practice. He noted occassion-
ally he has asked the county secretary to do office work for him.

He acknowledged using official prosecuting attorney stationary in
private law correspondence and also said he used his public office
space to conduct his private practice.

#

Prison

A complaint charging assault by a convict with malice aforethought
was signed Thursday against a 57-year-old convict serving time for a
second degree murder conviction.

John Ross Grant, who was committed to the prison Jan 11, 1978 for
the murder of his wife, is named in the complaint signed by Sheriff's
Detective Thomas Sandoval before City Judge Taylor Trapp.

The complaint accuses Grant of stabbing Joe T. Sherwood, 33, twice
with a knife June 15 at the prison. Sherwood is serving time for assault
with intent to commit murder of his wive. He was committed to the prison
February 18.

Booked

A 48-year-old man has been booked into the county jail for investigation of second-degree murder in the shooting of his son-in-law.

Gerald Lusty, 48, of 211 10th Street, was arrested following an incident in a pool hall monday afternoon which left dead Vaughn Warr, 31, 1525 Airport Drive.

Police responded to a fight-in-progress call from Bud's Tavern, 521 10th Street, and when they arrived Warr was lying in a pool of blood in the rear.

The victim was still alive when officers checked his condition but was gasping and retching blood and having difficulty breathing. He was dead on arrival at General Hospital at 5:30 p.m.

Police said witnesses reported that Lusty and his 21-year-old daughter were in the pool hall when Warr entered and started arguing with his wife。

Warr picked up a pool cue during the quarrel and Lusty intervened between the couple but Warr then turned on his father-in-law.

Police said Warr backed Lusty into a corner of the pool hall whereupon the younger man was shot with a small caliber automatic pistol.

Vagabond

by Matthew Arnold
Staff Writer

Somewhere close to the end of Act II this production comes alive, but it is a long time getting there。

It is not intolerably long, because there are enough rousing moments

-2-

and decent performances to tide one over if he does not just dismiss a silly script out of hand.

"The Vagabond King" is, however, a silly script and as such could only have succeeded if the production had risen above it by way of an infused, energetic style.

The sort of style I am talking about was consistently embodied only by Tricia Playford as one of the minor characters, Lady Mary. She struck just the right balance between contrived elegance and sincerity.

I say contrived not because it appeared so but because it was an artificial framework which became real through the conviction and stage presence of the actress.

The rest of the cast was not so tuned in, the most obvious failure being Lunel McAlister as Francois Villon, the vagabond king. I am the first to admit that he caught fire in Act II, causing the whole cast to abruptly rise to a challenge which was completely unexpected by this viewer.

Before that, however, it was obvious be was struggling in the same trap he has been in for some time: things are too easy for him. McAlister has years of experience behind him, so it is too great ex-penditure of effort for him to perform passably.

He does everything passably. His golden voice lets little real emotion through, but it is nice to listen to and is supplemented by 10 or 11 gestures which few City Repertory Theatre patrons have not seen umpteen 100 times before.

He has a favorite stance too, one leg back, lock-kneed, the other

-3-

forward, a bent knee allowing him to bounce up and down on the ball of his foot. This pose, he seems to feel, is particularly attractive in the one-quarter position which he assumes regardless of how badly it interferes with his relating to the other characters.

I suggest he can do better than this and challenge him to take some risks in order to break out of a very dangerous rut. An initial strategy might be to allow the awesome energy present in the final scenes of the show to serve as a guide for finding a similar release throughout, restrained and focused according to the immediate demands of the script.

It would also do him no harm to dispense with the unending shifting about of weight which is, I assume, meant to remind us that there is life in his character. It is also true that we know in our hearts that he is attentive to what is happening on stage and his frequent head-cocking isn't necessary.

As I have said, something happened late in the playk an incident which inspires confidence in his ability to deal with these difficulties, all of which have afflicted his acting for several years now.

His leading lady, Gladiola Perry, delivers a steady performance as Katherine De Vauxelles. Her problem comes when she is required to sing. It is next to impossible to catch a single word of her lyrics. Listening to her sing was rather like hearing a sustained "ah" with the necessary fluctuations up and down the scale.

Most of the cast, in fact muddles the lyrics. I congratulate Richard Duncan as the Captain for leading the cast in the "Archer's Song" and making it the only fully comprehensible song of the evening.

-4-

As for the others, Ronald Huntington distinguished himself by pulling of f some nice character work as Louis XI. His Louis was sly and calculating, and he sent a few chills through the audience by dropping his voice to a spooky whisper from time to time. He also has a curious habit of speaking out of one side of his mouth.

As Tristan L'Hermite aquat little Ray Frantz follows Huntington about like a pet aardvark. I did not think the stage lights were particularly bright, but I could find no other reason for his constant squint, unless he was trying to read concealed cue cards somewhere, a circumstance which would also explain his infantile line readings.

The program reminds us that hs has 40 years of acting experience, but in this instance he seemed incapable of anything beyond loudness and Drama I intonation. It might be worth noting that Frantz is a local butcher when he's not trodding the Repertory boards, and he seems incapable of everything away from his ham.

Dennis Noble was looser and more relaxed than I have ever seen him, and his Guy Taberie was a high point of the evening when his distinctive strut did not interfere.

Lueretia Meriwether needs more maturity in projecting the words of her songs, but her Hugette Du Hamel stood out with sheer youthful energy and feminine charm。

A gruff, lusty sincerity made Casin Chloet thoroughly convincing, and Mergatroid Dav is as the villainous Thibaut D'Aussigny was appropriately sinister even if he did seem a bit spaced。

Director Emilio Baccarot sets up from nice pictures and some adept

-5-

rhythmic builds but has recurring problems with focus. The show opens
with a sprawling choral number after which two characters converse.

The blocking is so badly mismanaged that one's eyes stray about the
stage for several seconds before spotting who is talking. When staging
songs he and choreographer Nick Broadhead like to line everyone up in a
more or less straight line across the front of the stage, a technique
which noticeably diffuses everyone's attention.

Whether Baccarot let it happen or caused it to be, there are two or
three instances when the otherwise excellent lighting by Natalie Lux
promote focus all wrong for the show. One is during a ballet in the song
"Nocturne." It is danced in comparative darkness while an inconsequential
cluster of characters is highlighted.

The non-lighting designers were relatively immune from the director's
murky vision. John Turner's settings are flawless and, except for a
certain red cape donned at one point by McAlister, Krisca Watson has
really outdone herself in constuming.

The one item of significance I have not mentioned is the script,
beyond saying it is silly. I stick to that assessment and must really
question the value of a university affiliated theater producing such
tripe, especially if unable to overcome it with the kind of style that
was lacking here.

The usual response is that such things are demanded by the public.
I can go along with that up to a point and gladly accept the inclusion
of Rodgers and Hammerstein, Lerner and Lowe, Cole Porter, Gilbert and
Sullivan or Irving Berlin in a season, but Rudolf Friml?

-6-

I won't push the point。 Repoertory's selections are noticeably improving. I only hope no one really believes that a not very good operetta like this qualifies as serious theater.

#

Smathers

By Andrew Walters

Staff Writer

District Attorney Robert Smathers is "a lame duck," Judge W. Robert Borland of District Court, said Friday, adding "we will be well rid of him."

The judge also objected to a number of criminal cases the attorney's office had filed involving minor offenses

The judge made the comments while handling a calendar of criminal cases that involved arraignments, sentencings and motions。 Eighty-three cases were on the calendar。

"There are a lot of petty offenses here today because the district attorney is trying to push this on me," Judge Borland said. "His time here is short. Fortunately for our fair city he is not running again. "We will be well rid of him and his indeptitude," he said.

Several persons charged with petty offenses appeared without lawyers。 The judge asked if one man had a lawyer and was told no。

"Well, don't go to too much expense。 This is a small deal," the Judge said。

One case that the judge objected to hearing Friday involved three men charged with "hunting over unshucked corn" or allegedly using corn as a bait to lure waterfoul so they could be shot.

"This is a great big serious offense. Listen to this: these men are charged with hunting over unshucked corn. Dammed if they didn't," Judge Borland said.

Judge Borland also noted later in the hearings that one attorney was nodding agreement with some arguments lawyers were making to him.

"I'm getting some signals from counsel at counsel table," the judge said. The judge warned that if the man "did that in front of a jury, you will be eating some of those great 15 cent meals at the jail."

#

Merritt

The University is reported to be preparing a law-suit against Charles Merritt, former president of the Associated Students for embezzlement and fraud. The final decision to press charges or not has not been made yet.

The question stems from the rock concert last April. The concert was an experiment in using a huge closed-circuit television screen to show the concert live from Chicago. The Williams Bak ing Co., sponsors of the event, hired Mr. Merritt to handle much of the public relations work and to solve minor problems on campus.

At the time of the event, the advertising announced that some of the proceeds would go to the University's scholarship fund. Williams donated this money because they needed to guarantee the University something for the use of its facilities and to appease the Henry Concession Co., Inc., which has the franchise for University events.

But only about $200 actually made it into the fund. Allegedly the rest of the $2,000 was absconded with by Mr. Merritt.

During spring quarter, Mr. Merritt had been having some financial troubles, mostly caused by his campaign for president. After he paid his election debts, Mr. Merritt went to New York to work for the summer.

Mr. Merritt is back in town now, working full-time. He has been advised to obtain a lawyer by Legal Services of the University. This is the normal procedure when the University has received a complaint.

Raymond Spratt, the lawyer working on the case, is out of the country for the next few weeks. When he returns, a decision to prosecute will be made. Whether the University Scholarship Office will have to sue Merritt to get the money will also be decided at some other time.

#

Hire

A 24-year-old woman arrested early Friday about 2:10 a.m. at 459 W. Center Street for soliciting sex acts for hire.

She is Taffy Barr, who gave her address as Joe's Motel, 242 W. Center Street.

Police Officer Nelson Knight, who arrested the Barr woman, said in his report that she approached him on the sidewalk and propositioned him.

In the report, Officer Knight said the Barr woman asked him if he was a police officer and, according to Officer Knight, he replied "no."

After the proposition had been arranged, however, Officer Knight did identify himself as a police officer and placed the woman under arrest.

She will be arraigned in city court Monday at 10 a.m. before city Judge Rodney T. Thorgmorton.

#

Wiley

The director of the County Roads Department was arrested by sherrif's officers at 10:15 P.M. Friday forpublic intoxication but he will not have to face formal charges due to a policy by a City Court judge.

E. Robert Wiley, 53, 1022 East 42nd Street, was discovered by the officers asleep behind the wheel of his car about two blocks from his home on 42nd. The officers booked him into the County Jail for public intoxication but as this was his first offense he was released without a fine or court appearance being imposed on him.

City Court Judge Sterling Stanton said a "standard order" from the court that has been in effect for up to 10 years allows first time public intoxication offenders to be released without being fined or being required to appear in court. He explained that after the first offense they are required to go through the full judicial process.

Mr. Wiley was not in his office Saturday and could not be reached for comment.

#

Nazi

State Univeristy fired its first tenured professor in all its 103 years Saturday ordering history instructor Nunley T. Griffin dismissed immediately for calling for the extermination of Israel.

As Griffin and 100 supporters chanted in a drizzeling rain outside, the Board of Regents voted 10-3 to adopt the recommendations of a faculty panel and President James Rutherford Maxwell to fire the 32-year-old self-proclaimed Nazi.

Maxwell called it "A landmark in a difficult but essential effort for higher education" to protect itself against those who would destroy American universities. The Board's resolution said:

"Resolved: that the Board of Regents hereby concurrs ... that Professor Nunley T. Griffin be dismissed from the faculty immediately ...

Griffin had already been suspended from his teaching duties and barred from the campus by Maxwell but had been on full pay.

The Board heard no witnesses in its 2-hour session, but spent the time considereing a 168-page report from the faculty committee and the concurring recommendation by Maxwell.

#

Senate

State Sen. Harvey Brooks, D-Spencer City, pointed his finger at Jeffrey Roebuck, president of Consolidated Industries of Elm City, Wednesday and said he had a "gut feeling" that Roebuck committed perjury in his testimony about campaign contributions to Gov. Fred W. Harper.

The sharpest exchange yet in the Senate Standing Committee on government Ethics' 2-week-old hearing occurred after Roebuck changed the story he gave a week ago.

He testified then under oath a personal loan of $25,000 made to

Roebuck had been consummated long before the governor, then a consolidated vice president, announced his candidacy in February last year.

Roebuck Wednesday, said he got the dates mixed up and the unsecured loan had actually been made after Harper won the party nomination last August.

He testified Wednesday that, after a telephone call from an un-identified source asking them to check his records, he found they were in error and that the loan had been finalized in August.

Brooks charged this was a direct contradiction and he cited other "discrepancies" between Roebuck's testimony and that of other witnesses.

"Somebody's not telling the truth," he said, "just listening to this conversation over the last couple of hours, your credibility has dropped from 100 to zero.

Brooks then looked up over his glasses and grew more agitated.

"You smile, sir, but if what you said here and before the press, and if my impression is correct, you committed perjury. I have that feeling in my gut."

"If my smile is offensive to you, I'm sorry," Roebuck said.

"If my credibility has gone to zero in your eyes, then it must be 100 percent in the eyes og others."

Roebuck sais he never discussed campaign financing with Harper and that the loan was a personal matter negotiable solely to help Harper out of "some temporary financial contretempts."

"You expect this committee to believe that?" Senator asked.

"All I can state is the truth as I understand it," Roebuck said.

Brooks seemed incensed over Roebuck's contention that he did not know where the telephone call came from that prompted him to recheck his records and change his recollection.

He said his secretary did not ask who had called and he added, "I don't honestly know, Senator, where the call came from

#

Dismiss

ELM CITY -- In a terse statement to the press, City Manager Nate Feldmann said Thursday that police officers Larry Jones and Nate Bonham have been dismissed for disloyalty and subterfuge.

"It is my opinion that irreparable damage would be caused to the police department by reinstating these officers," Feldman stated.

Jones and Bonham had been suspended without pay since last Wednesday after contacting other police officers in an effort to change police administration.

Other charges that the two officers participated in partisan politics and failed to attend manditory meetings were not serious enough to warrant dismissal and were not considered, said Feldman.

A closed-door meeting to consider dismissing the officers was held Tuesday with some policemen participating. Norman Eisely was attorney for the two officers.

Feldman said that charge of disloyalty made dismissal the only course of action open for the police department to operate efficiently.

#

Housing

Investigators from the County Sheriff's Office hope to hire an auditor to examine the books of the County Housing Authority.

Lt. Hobart Esplin said his office will ask the county commissioners to provide funds for that auditor in order to verify complaints of mismanagement and criminal conduct made against Housing Authority executive director R. Perry Swarthout.

The investigation, which had originally been handled by the County Attorney's office, is now being conducted by the sheriff's detective division.

It involves allegations made by a group of Housing Authority employees that Swarthout overpaid landloards, violated the agency's policy on use of the Housing Authority car and used employes on agency time to move his personal belongings.

Complaints of a lack of training and general mismanagement were also made.

Swarthout has denied all of the charges.

Esplin said he anticipated the investigation will last from two to three weeks.

Thieves

Mary Ellen Lundberg complained to sheriff's deputies that former tenants of a trailer house she rents on 2510 Mockingbird Street left with $1,800 worth of her home furnishings.

Missing was a refrigerator, a gas stove, a chandlier, a dining room set, bedroom set, tables, chairs and light bulbs.

#

Indecent

Prof. Joseph W. Wignell, 57, of 233 Third Street, a State University professor of journalism, pleaded guilty in City Court Wednesday afternoon and was fined $150 for indecent and obscene conduct.

#

Death

A couple was booked into the County Jail Tuesday on suspicion of first degree murder in connection with the death of a 10-month-old boy.

The victim was identified as Davey Bybee, son of Mrs. Leta Allen, 25, of 248 Marianne Circle. He was dead on arrival at County Hospital at 6:10 a. m.

The boy's mother and step-father, Scott P. Allen, 22, were arrested by police for questioning following his death.

Asst. County Atty. Thomas Ryan ordered an autoposy performed.

Frank Rutledge, Youth Division detective, said the boy had a number of bruises on its head and body, several toes appeared to be broken.

The youth had been rushed to the hospital, according to patrolman Dennis Kopp, when the mother called an ambulance service at 5:59 a.m.

Police had placed the victim and his four-year-old brother, Greg Bybee, in a shelter home on two previous occasions. The last time was July 14.

An investigation then of a child beating case involving the victim, followed by a hearing in Juvenille Court, resulted in he and his brother being placed in a shelter home for the second time.

Mr. Allen was donvicted of battery against the child in city court last Sept. He was fined $50 by Judge Dave Bertram and released.

The children were subsequently returned to their mother who married Allen last week under the supervision of the family services division.

Police Tuesday placed Greg Bybee and a four-month-old sister, Judy Allen, in a shelter home pending the outcome of legal action against the couple.

#

Part IV

★★★★★★★★★★★★★★★★

News Stories

17. BUSINESS

Until recent years, business news was a blind spot in most of the American press. Coverage was meager, sometimes slipshod, and inexcusably dull. Often business news was handled by reporters with little understanding of the business community and little appreciation of its impact on people. In the late 1970s, newspapers took a harder look at business news coverage. It was expanded and improved. Today people are looking to newspapers and magazines to cover business news informatively.

One reason is the consumer movement. Buyers are demanding more and more information about goods available, their prices, their quality, their use, and who makes them. Another is a collision between the news media and the business community over social responsibility. Businessmen have become vocal about what they regard as a bad press and a lack of understanding of economics and of their work. (The National Association of Manufacturers has suggested that reporters be sent back to school to bone up.)

Then there are the stunningly successful examples of the business journals that reach an intelligent and influential lay audience, from *Fortune*, a spinoff from *Time* magazine in the early 1930s, to the *Wall Street Journal*, which has grown in less than half a century from a small chronicler of the stock market's movements to one of America's great newspapers. These publications recognize that business news is important and interesting to decision makers.

Most important, economic and business news stories have become essential to everyone. They touch people in all walks of life. That means business news is developing on a new level, reaching persons who have little or no direct interest in such traditional news as the securities markets or the columns of specialized statistical information on the business page. Taxation, interest rates, the fate of the dollar, the recall of autos and other defective merchandise, the safety of products, the construction of buildings in the urban environment, industrial pollution, government regulations affecting prices and employment, the tax laws, the availability of oil and other essential goods—all these are vital everyday concerns. The news services have considerably expanded financial news wires, including interpretive columns. News staffs are sprouting specialists in real estate, autos, aviation, agriculture, and other areas.

Some critics have suggested eliminating the business page as such, or retaining it only for specialized business news or for reporting on securities markets, one of its traditional concerns. They argue that business news is hard news and ought to compete with all other news for position in the paper. The likelihood is that top business stories will be measured by their impact and interest and take correspondingly important positions in the paper. But it's also likely that the business page itself will continue to expand to reach a general readership.

What kind of readership is the business page getting? Surveys indicate that about one-fourth of all readers turn to it regularly, though readership is highest among males, people over 50, college graduates, and those earning more than $20,000 a year. As you work with business stories, here are some guidelines to reaching and widening this affluent, educated audience.

Readability

Business news is becoming a great deal more readable because readers want it to be interesting, understandable, and even entertaining despite its complexities. As in all good editing, you should fight against obscure in-jargon and cliches. It serves no purpose to report that a new oil well "spudded in on a four-inch choke," a reference remote from the experience of almost all your readers.

Too many stories about interest rates appear to be written for business community insiders, playing up the names of banks and subordinating plain-talk explanations. The general public is far more interested in what the figures mean than in the bond market or which banks are raising or lowering prime rates, since most citizens are not prime-rate borrowers. Also many people assume that mortgage rates must be at least equal to or higher than the prime rate. Because mortgage seekers outnumber prime-rate borrowers, mortgage figures always should be mentioned in stories of this type. Precision also is important. The original of the following example does not reveal the previous prime rate, nor does it specify the mortgage rate in noting the predicted reductions. Linking figures is tedious work, but a good editor should take the time to do it.

Original

NEW YORK (NS) — Several major banks reduced their prime lending rates to 18 percent Tuesday, reflecting sharp declines on the bond market and prompting White House officials to say the long-expected recession has become a reality.

"Business activity is slowing down, no doubt about it," said a White House spokesman who asked not to be identified. "The rates are still too high."

U.S. Bank and Trust, the nation's fourth largest bank, was the first to announce the reduction. It was quickly followed by California Surety, the nation's largest, and dozens of others soon made similar announcements.

There were predictions that home mortgage rates would fall by 2 to 3 percentage points by the end of the year.

Revision

NEW YORK (NS) — Several major banks reduced their prime lending rates by 1 percent Tuesday, lowering to 18 percent the rates charged their most credit-worthy customers. White House officials said the cut reflects a reduced demand for money by the business community and indicates a recession is in progress.

There were predictions that home mortgage rates, now averaging 16 percent, would fall to 13 or 14 percent by the end of the year if lenders become convinced the rate of inflation is slowing and that the public will not seek loans at higher rates.

(Follow with White House comment and further explanation of the recession, subordinating the names of banks and the bond-market situation.)

The key to writing in understandable fashion is first of all understanding on the part of the writer and editor. Technical words should be reduced—accurately—to plain talk. Dialogue, anecdotes, and other talky, concrete devices are appropriate, as the *Wall Street Journal's* readable and informative feature pieces indicate.

Objectivity

Traditional newspaper objectivity dictates that news be separated from advertising as well as from opinion. Therefore, mere puffery and propaganda have no place in business news. The day has gone when the business page was no more than a sop to the advertiser with a new product or model to trumpet.

The press has a legitimate adversary role in holding the business community to account. Most business is public or quasi-public, increasingly regulated by public agencies, owned by vast numbers of people who buy publicly offered stocks, and presumably responsive to public needs. If what a corporation does affects your readers, its doings should be reported with candor.

Newspapers have often been accused of bowing to advertiser pressure because they depend on advertising revenue. It is true that the press and business share the same monetary pressures and motivations, but business advertising benefits by being seen in a journal readers regard as fair, impartial, and accurate. As a rule, it can be said that advertisers have small influence over the news columns of dailies, particularly where the newspaper is itself economically strong enough to resist pressures.

Trade Names

It is scarcely possible to write effectively about business without using corporate names and trade names. The new emphasis on business news has dictated a more enlightened and open approach to their use than was typical only a few years ago. There's a new openness about brand names even among advertisers, who more and more are using names of competitors in comparative advertising.

Use trade names whenever they are pertinent. Would leaving a trade name out of a story deprive the reader of needed information? Would its obvious deletion seem petty? Would including it enhance imagery? (Formerly, editors often went out of their way to take out brand names simply because publishers and business managers insisted that they were in the business of selling advertising, not giving it away.)

The same applies to use of corporate names. Is the name of the architectural firm that designed the building pertinent? Is the name of a law firm that filed a suit pertinent? Is the name of an engineering firm information the reader needs?

Localize Stories
   Almost every national story has a local dimension. How has the change in the interest
rate affected home building in your area? How is the consumer price index reflected in a
basket of groceries at your own markets? How has the energy crisis affected service at your
gas stations? Be alert to opportunities to help make your business page relevant to your
readers.

SELECTED READINGS

Kirsch, Donald. *Financial and Economic Journalism: Analyses, Interpretation and Reporting.* New York:
        New York University Press, 1976. Includes a list of important reference sources on companies,
        individuals, and industries. Deals with training reportorial minds to be financial detectives.
Rubin, Bernard, and associates. *Big Business and the Mass Media.* Lexington, Mass.: D. C. Heath and Com-
        pany, 1977. Analyzes the problems corporate executives and the press corps encounter as they
        interact in presenting news to the public.

EXERCISES

X-Wing

   BURBANK, Calif. -- An X-shaped wing that rotates for v vertical

takeoff like a helicopter and then locks in place for high speed

horizontal flight is being developed by Lockheed=California Company.

   Ben R. Rich, vice president of the firm's Advanced Development

Projects organization, the famed Skunk Wordks, said the company has

received initial funding for the $2.5 million development program

sponsored by the Defense Advanced Research Projects AGency (DARPA).

   Under the program contract, Lockheed will building and ground-test

a full-scale, 25 ft. (7.6 m) diameter X-wing and control system.

   Rich said that if the concept proves valid, it may be possible

to build an aircraft with unique characteristics.

   With the wing rotating, the aircraft will take off and land

vertically like a helicopter, and attain flight speeds to 233 m.p.h.

(407 km/h). With the wing locked into a fixed X position, transonic

speeds equivalent to those at which commercial jet airliners fly, may
be attained. Conventional takeoffs and landings can be made in the
fixed-wing configuration if a runway is available.

Air Force Colonel Norris Krone, Jr., of DARPA, the overall program
manager, said a one-quarter scale model of an X-wing aircraft is currently being tested in the David Taylor Naval Ship Research and Development Center's high speed wind tuhnel at Carderock, Maryland.

# # #

X-Wing

BURBANK, Calif. -- An X-shaped wing that rotates for ~v~ vertical
takeoff like a helicopter and then locks in place for high=speed
horizontal flight is being developed by Lockheed~California Company.

Ben R. Rich, vice president of ~the firm's~ Advanced Development
Projects organization, the ~famed~ Skunk Wor/ks, said the company has
received initial funding for the $2.5 million development program
sponsored by the Defense Advanced Research Projects Agency ~(DARPA)~.

~Under the program contract,~ Lockheed will build and ground-test
a full-scale, 25=ft=~(7.6 m)~ diameter X-wing and control system.

Rich said that if the concept proves valid, it may be possible
to build an aircraft with unique characteristics.

With the wing rotating, the aircraft will take off and land
vertically like a helicopter, and attain flight speeds to 233 m.p.h.
~(407 km/h)~. With the wing locked into a fixed X position, *the aircraft may attain* transonic
speeds equivalent to those at which commercial jet airliners fly, ~may~

more

(2/ X-Wing)

~~be attained~~. Conventional takeoffs and landings can be made in the
fixed-wing configuration if a runway is av~~i~~lable.

Air Force (Colonel) Norris Krone, Jr., ~~of DARPA, the~~ overall program
manager, said a ~~one-~~quarter scale model of an X-wing aircraft is ~~cur-~~
~~rently~~ being tested in the David Taylor Naval Ship Research and Development Center's high=speed wind tunnel at Carderock, (Maryland).

# # #

Walpool

Walpool Brothers registered a substantial profit for the first 9
months of the fiscal year compared to a loss in the same months last
year, Mr. Rupert Wal pool, Chairman and Chief Executive Officer of the
specialty department store, announced today.

For the nine months ended October 31, earnings after taxes totaled
$236,981 or 32¢ a share based on the 747,111 common shared outstanding.
This compared iwth a loss of $24,040 or three cents a share one year ago,
figures adjusted for the five-for-four stock split paid February 23.
Sales advanced to 25 million dollars, a gain of five percent.

For the 3 months ended October 31, earnings were $102,924 or 14¢
per share as against a deficit of $38,460 or 5¢ per share in the 3rd
quarter last year. Sales volume increased to $8,810,035 from the
$8,016,014 recorded in the comparable period one year earlier, an in-
crease of 10%.

Mr. Walpool said: "The retailing climate in our area has improved

significantly. Further, we are continuing to benefit from our new expense control system. The gain in earnings reflects good incremental
profits on sales increases."

#

Recall

WASHINGTON (NS) -- The U. S. Department of Transportation has
again asked Ford Motor Co. to explain why problems have ariseh in connection with a court-ordered recall campaign involving 1968 and 1969
Mustangs and Cougars with defective bucket style driver seats.

After an initial inquiry into the problem by Jean Claybrook,
administrator of the department's National Highway Traffic Safety Administration (NHTSA), Ford provided assurances that the campaign would
be run properly, however consumer complaints have continued to arrive at
NHYSA. These have ben predominan associated with a shortage of
replacement parts at Ford and Lincoln-Mercury dealers, where the
automobiles are supposed to be repaired.

Ford had assured Ms. Claybrook that parts would be send to dealers
during the week of May 16. But according to reports received from
around the country, the dealers have all but run out, and the owners
are forced to continue driving dangerously defective vehicles.

After a two-year legal battle, a U. S. District Court found that
the defect in the driver's seats of the Mustangs and Cougars could result in the seat back suddenly falling backwards at speeds of up to 60
miles-per-hour. When this happens, the driver could fall into the back

seat and lose control of the car. The court found that the seat failures
present "a severe threat to moto vehicle safety" so some 500,000 owners
of the vehicles.

For their safety until the repair is made, a large, firm object
such as a suitcase should be proped behind the seat, NHTSA says.

# # #

Ads

MINNEAPOLIS -- A spokesman for the newspaper business today called
upon educators to help raise the level of professional skills in advertising, and thus serve both sonsumers and advertisers more effectively.

Otto A. Silha, president of the Minneapolis Star and Tribune
Company and Chairman of the Newspaper Advertising Bureau, Inc., told a
dinner meeting of the American Academy of Advertising that this is
necessary because the consuj-er's reliance on information from from ad-
veritsing is increasing.

Mr. Silha spoke in the University of Minnesota Campus Club on the
topic, "The Reading of Advertising -- Some New Thoughts." With respect
to newspapers, he said, the utility of their advertising to readers
"is my nomination as one major secret to future newspapedr success.

He made the following points:

Last year all U. S. media amassed advertising revenues totaling
more than $33 billion and upwards of 170,000 people worked in jobs that
require a considerable knowledge of advertising.

In today's world, everybody needs advertising and consumerism puts a premium on information. The more educated, the more affluent and the more sophistical individuals consume more advertising as well as more of other goods and services, and eeucational levels and income levels are in a steadily rising trend.

Redent United States Supreme Court decisions have underlined the importance of advertising to the individual as well as the advertisedr, and the restrictions on advertising in the ethical codes of various provessional groups are under attack.

-30-

Crops

Crop growing conditions were generally favorable during mo most of June, states the state Crop and Livestock Reporting service.

Hot, dry winds the last week of June rapidly depleted the soil moisture and caused some stress to dryland crops. As of the first of July, cros were showing good growth and were a week to ten days ahead of last year.

In most of the state June precipitation kept the winter wheat in good condition, however, in the North moisture was on the short side. At present the crop is maturing ahead of normal. The crop was forecast at 34,000,000 bushels. This is 2% more than last month but 13% below last year.

Spring wheat crop is expected to total 19,030,000 bushels, a decrease of 34% from last year. This sharp drop is attributed both to decreased acres which at 370,000 acres declined 31% and lower yield prospects which at 52 bushels is 2 bushels from last year. The crop was seeded earlier than usual but spotted stands were common due to dry planting conditions.

Even though harvested acres are expected to be greater than last year by 14%, production prospects at 42,100,000 million bushesl are for a 3% reduction in barley. This is a result of a drop of 8 bushels in yield prospects -- 46 this year versus 54 last year. The crop was planted earlier than usual but in dry soil.

The cherry crop is expected to be slightly less than last year at 2,700 tons. Apples at 110,000,000 pounds and pears at 1,800 tons are expected to be down from last year. Peach production should be greater than last year with prospects for a crop of 12,500,000 pounds.

# # #

Mortgages

A total of $12.0 billion of home mortgage loans were closed in April, 40 percent more than in April of last year, the Department of Housing and Urban Development reported today.

Savings and loan asociations accounted for 59 percent of the home loan originations, compared to a market share of 58 percent a year ago.

Commercial banks accounted for 18 percent and mortgage comparnies for 15 percent.

Originations of long-term apartment house loans aggregated $1.1

billion, up 30 percent over last year. Savings and loan asociations

made 54 percent of these multi-family loans and commercial banks 24

percent.

Construction loans for homes at $2.8 billion were 31 percent

higher than in April, last year, while multifamily construction loans

increased by 33 percent.

# # #

18. PUBLIC RELATIONS

Much information from business, government, and other institutions is generated by public relations practitioners. Every large company has one or more of these who deal with the press regularly. Usually they are known as public relations specialists, although they go by a variety of titles.

Public relations is more than press relations. It's really the whole art of maintaining good relations between the organization and its consumers or other publics. However, working with the press is central, and PR people—especially those in government—often justify their existence by maintaining that the information coming out of their offices otherwise would never reach the public. While traditionally looking askance at public-relations people who seek what is called a free ride in the form of a news story as opposed to paid advertising, editors and reporters also know they would sometimes have great difficulty obtaining important information or reaching vital company sources without the aid of these people.

Relations between PR people and editors are at their best in a climate of mutual respect. Most PR people are trained communicators, who more often than not have been newsgatherers and editors themselves. In the best situations they function as a two-way connection between management and media, interpreting one to the other. They help management speak out, and they recognize that misunderstandings are fostered by a close-mouthed mistrust of the press by businessmen or officials. They have been seeking professionalism and developing ethical standards for the past 50 years, since public relations took the place of mere press agentry.

Much of what comes through these PR persons is legitimate news and most is non-controversial: the story of an appointment, plans for a building, the opening of a branch office, the development of a new product. In these cases, you can use their information without fretting. Where the news is controversial, PR information should serve as no more than a statement of the official position of the company or agency, as an account of one position. What you get, of course, is one version of the truth. In all such cases, the company's PR handouts should be no more than a departure point for a story that treats all sides with fairness, balance, and depth. In every case, good newspapers insist on rewriting handout material so they do not become mere conduits between a special interest and its public. The rewriting should produce a better written story, should adhere to newspaper writing standards, and should contain more or better information. With some experience in judging news releases, you should be able to weed out stories that are mere public relations promotions and those that are interesting and relevant to your audience. No story should sound like an advertisement or publicity puff.

Publicity people also are largely responsible for what has become the "media event," or what is referred to in the chapter "What Is News" as the pseudo-event. A press conference is called, a demonstration is staged, or a public contest is held. It is a truism that people who understand media often are able to use the media for their own purposes. A butcher, baker, or candlestick maker may have a good story idea, one of significance to the community, but a ready-made, easy-to-cover event such as a test-firing of a rocket will bring a swarm of reporters much more quickly.

Media are vulnerable to the appeal of a now event, as opposed to an idea or suggestion that may or may not turn into a story. This is not to say that stories generated by publicity people are devious. In the end, editors make the decisions on what gets printed, and it would be unprofessional for them to guarantee space to any self-serving organization any time it desired publicity.

The sheer glut of free, unsolicited news furnished through PR channels also poses dangers. Handout news also can preempt space that might be used for more generally valuable news. It can even discourage staff initiative. Most large papers therefore use handout information sparingly. On a typical news day the business editor of a large paper receives at least 50 news releases through the mail. Most go unopened. If the name on the envelope is a label or if the return address itself doesn't suggest that a *news* story is inside, it can safely be discarded. Good PR people recognize the value of direct, personal relations with editors; they write to them personally and their mail is individually addressed.

Conflicts of interests must be avoided. Gift-giving is common in public relations work. Most newspapers forbid the acceptance of gifts, and newspaper staffs follow self-policing policies to avoid actions that would compromise their objectivity.

SELECTED READINGS

Cutlip, Scott M., and Allen H. Center. *Effective Public Relations*, 5th ed. Englewood Cliffs, N.J.: Prentice-Hall, Inc. 1978. The standard textbook for public relations students.

Nolte, Lawrence H. *Fundamentals of Public Relations*, 2nd ed. New York: Pergamon Press, 1979. A widely used textbook.

Newsom, Doug, and Alan Scott. *This Is PR: The Realities of Public Relations*. Belmont, Calif.: Wadsworth Publishing Co., 1976. A practical guide for PR people, especially PR consulting firms.

Simon, Raymond. *Public Relations Concepts and Practices*. Columbus, Ohio: Grid Publishing Co., 1980. Like Cutlip and Center, a text approved by the Public Relations Society of America.

EXERCISES

In the following exercises, you will have the opportunity to judge how handout materials should be handled. Rewrite the Mercury story. Otherwise merely describe on the story what kind of newsworthiness each story has and how it might be used, if at all. Remember the rule that handouts should be rewritten, not merely edited, so do not attempt to edit any of these.

Rewrite the following sample press release, retaining only the essential information:

Mercury

Mercury Corp. reported Tuesday its sales for the fourth quarter were $3.2 million, an increase of $200,000 from the same quarter of last year.

"This shows the continued strength of Mercury Corp. in a competitive market," said company president Robert M. Willard. "We are confident the demand for our products will grow as we develop new lines."

Mercury Corp. earnings for the fourth quarter were 27 cents per share compared to 29 cents per share in the previous fourth quarter.

For the year, Mercury had total sales of $15.2 million and net earnings of $1.15 per share. This compared to sales of $18.4 million and net earnings of $1.39 per share the previous year.

"Once again," Willard said, "we had a tremendous team effort. Our experienced staff benefited from the contributions of several outstanding new people. At Mercury, we will continue to recruit the best people available in an effort to reward the confidence our stockholders have placed in us."

#

Family Entertainment
Centers

FARMINGTON RESIDENTS SURVIVE CALIF. TIDAL WAVE

Santa Clara -- Judy and Clyde Jackson, and Dalene Hansen and Jarrad
Van Hutten of Farmington, Utah survived "The Tidal Wave", the world's
tallest roller coaster at Marriott's Great America in California. The
friends experienced the gigantic thrill ride while on holiday at the
Santa Clara theme park.

It was different from what they expected. They were catapulted
out of the station from zero to 55 miles per hour in just 5 seconds.
Then they whirled around a 360 degree vertical loop and soared skyward
up a 142.5 foot-high coaster incline, the world's tallest. Once at the
summit, there was only one way to return, to repeat the ride through
the loop--BACKWARDS!

Mrs. Jackson said that she kept her eyes closed through the entire
trip. Mrs. Hansen said that "the whole sensation was so neat."

The Jacksons, Mrs. Hansen and Van Hutten were in California with
nineteen young members of the Mormon Church. The youngsters were in
the Clint Pagaent In Oakland.

-30-

Contact: Bruce W. Burtch
         Public Affairs Manager

P. O. Box 1776
Santa Clara, California 95052
408/988-1776

STANLEY CONSULTANTS, INC.

NEWS RELEASE

Contact: D.N. Haerer, Marketing
Communications Coordinator

Phone: 319/264-6207

For Release   IMMEDIATELY

IRIS BAUERBACH ELECTED CORPORATE SECRETARY

MUSCATINE, IOWA -- Richard H. Stanley, president, Stanley Consultants,

Inc., announces that the Board of Directors has elected Iris M. Bauerbach

as Corporate Secretary and Assistant Treasurer of Stanley Consultants, Inc.,

effective January 3, 1977.

Mrs. Bauerbach joined Stanley Consultants in January, 1962. During

her fifteen years with the firm, she has held positions as Personnel

Assistant, Head of Communications Department, and Administrative Assistant

to the President.

* * * * * * *

Stanley Consultants, Inc., a Muscatine, Iowa-based professional con-

sulting firm, offers multidisciplinary services internationally in the

fields of engineering, architecture, planning, and management. The firm

is completely employee-owned and currently employs approximately 600 full-

time professional, technical, and administrative support staff members at

six domestic and six overseas locations.

- 30 -

STANLEY BUILDING, MUSCATINE, IOWA 52761 USA
Atlanta • Chicago • Cleveland • Indianapolis • Washington, D.C.
Bolivia • Dominican Republic • Liberia • Malaysia • Nigeria • Philippines

INTERNATIONAL CONSULTANTS IN ENGINEERING, ARCHITECTURE, PLANNING AND MANAGEMENT

SCOTT NEWS

FOR RELEASE: **IMMEDIATE**

CONTACT: Ms. Jane Balzereit - 215/521-5000
                  (after 6 p.m.)   - 215/887-4066

DECORATED PAPER TOWELS

FEATURE WESTERN DESIGNS

PHILADELPHIA, PA. -- Decorated paper towels featuring Western themes are now available in stores throughout the area.

Scott Paper Company has introduced three new designs of decorated ScotTowels, called "Western Selections."

The three new border designs are named Western Flowers, Early Western Kitchens and Wicker Baskets to reflect the collection theme. All three are available in green, curry, poppy and blue designs imprinted on white.

The designs actually were chosen by towel users following consumer-preference testing of a variety of designs keyed to western culture. They are being marketed in the West, Northwest, Dakotas, Minneapolis and Omaha.

The "Western Selection" series brings to six the total number of border designs available in ScotTowels. The towels also come in three solid colors -- green, yellow and white.

#   #   #   #   #

#7726
PUBLIC AFFAIRS DIVISION • SCOTT PAPER COMPANY • SCOTT PLAZA, PHILADELPHIA, PA 19113 • 215/521-5000
NOTE TO EDITOR: See reverse side for location of facilities and statement of business

News from **Journal** (LADIES' HOME)

Downe Publishing, Inc., 641 Lexington Avenue, New York, New York 10022

CONTACT: Howard Greene/Greene Inc./71 Park Ave./New York, N.Y. 10016
          (212) 725-2660   Home: (516) FR 4-4230

FOR RELEASE: 6:00 PM, EDT, WEDNESDAY, JULY 20

PSYCHOLOGIST SAYS CHILDREN HURT BY PARENTS'

'INCOMPETENCE IN COMMUNICATING'

Children 'Need Information Without Derogation'

NEW YORK, July 20 -- A noted psychologist today professed amazement at "how many parents will label their child stupid, lazy and a cheat, yet expect him to be bright, industrious and honest."

Dr. Alice Ginott stated in the current (August) issue of LADIES' HOME JOURNAL that through "incompetence in communicating" parents frequently distort their children's self-image.

"The easiest way to make a child feel that there is something wrong with him is to criticize," the psychologist said. "Even constructive criticism diminishes a child's image of himself. Instead of criticism, a child needs information without derogation."

As an example, Dr. Ginott told of the mother who saw her 13-year-old son ladling "almost the whole pot of chocolate pudding into an oversized bowl. She was about to rebuke him: 'You're so selfish. You only think of yourself. You are not the only one in this house!' But she had learned that 'labeling is disabling' - that to talk about a child's negative personality attribute does not help him develop into a more caring person. So she said: 'Son, this pudding has to be divided among four people.'

"'Oh, I'm sorry,' he replied. "I didn't know that. I'll put some back'."

more ...

PSYCHOLOGIST   - Page 2 -

   According to Dr. Ginott, "Most of us love our children. What we lack is a
language that conveys love, that mirrors our delight - and that makes a child
feel loved, respected and appreciated."

   The psychologist stated in the JOURNAL article that parents sometimes teach
children to do the exact opposite of what they want. She told of a four-year-old
girl who couldn't help the way she felt and told her mother she hated her grandmother and wished she were dead. The horrified mother answered, "No, you don't.
You love Grandma. In this home we don't hate. Besides, she gives you presents and
takes you places. How can you even say such a horrible thing?"

   When the child persisted in her original statement, the mother spanked her.
Not wanting to be punished more, the four-year-old decided to change her tune:
"I really love Grandma, Mommy," she said. And Mommy kissed and hugged her and
praised her for being such a good girl.

   According to Dr. Ginott the mother taught the child, "It is dangerous to tell
the truth. When you lie, you get love. When you are truthful, you get spanked.
Mommy loves little liars. Only tell her what she wants to hear."

   The psychologist stated in the article that to encourage the child not to lie,
the mother could have answered, "I understand how you feel. You don't have to love
Grandma, but I expect you to treat her with respect."

                              #   #   #

NEWS RELEASE

From: The National FFA Center -- P. O. Box 15160
Alexandria, Virginia 22309   Phone: 703 360-3600
Dan Reuwee, Director of Information

FOR IMMEDIATE RELEASE

_____*Davis*_____ FFA MEMBER ATTENDS NATIONAL CONFERENCE
(TOWN OR CHAPTER)

_____*Flint Richards*_____ of the
(Name)

_____*Davis*_____ FFA Chapter at _____*Davis*_____
(Chapter)   (Name of High School)

High School is attending a National FFA Leadership Conference in Washington,

D.C., this week. The week-long Washington Conference is being held at the

National FFA Center near the Nation's Capital.

The FFA Conference program is designed to improve leadership skills, develop

an understanding of the national heritage, and prepare FFA members for more

effective leadership roles in their chapter and community. The Conference is

also a forum for the exchange of FFA Chapter activity ideas among members from

across the nation.

Besides the training sessions, the   program includes visits to

Mt. Vernon Plantation, the National Archives, Smithsonian Institution,

Arlington National Cemetery, and several other historic monuments and

memorials in and around the Capital.

A highlight of the Conference was a Thursday morning visit to the office

of Congressman _*Evan McKay*_____ of _*Huntsville*_____.
(Congressman's Name)   (Town or District)

Later participants attended a Capitol Hill luncheon featuring a question and an-

swer period with Congressmen, and Washington leaders in business and industry.

_____*Flint Richards*, __*17*__, is the son/~~daughter~~ of Mr. and Mrs.
(Name)   (Age)

_*Aaron Richards*_____ of _*Farmington*_____.
(Parent's Name)   (Town)

His/H~~er~~ vocational agriculture instructor is _*Larry Golking*_____.
(Instructor's Name)

= 30 =

University of Puget Sound

news release news release news release

office of public relations, 1500 north warner, tacoma, washington 98416 (206) 756-3148

FOR IMMEDIATE RELEASE

      Robert C. Averett   , son/~~daughter~~ of
Henry M. Averett of _3799 S 9ᵗʰ E #1_ ,
was among the more than 400 students who received undergraduate degrees
at the University of Puget Sound's spring commencement exercises held
recently.

      Former governor of Oregon, Tom McCall, delivered the commencement
address and was recipient of the honorary degree of Doctor of Public Affairs.

      Dr. Thomas Davis, dean of the university, presented the undergraduate
candidates to Dr. Philip M. Phibbs, UPS president, who conferred the degrees.

      The University of Puget Sound is a privately endowed, liberal arts
institution with an enrollment of approximately 2,800 students on the main
campus representing every state in the nation and 21 foreign countries. It
offers a wide variety of academic programs in the liberal arts and sciences
and Schools of Business and Public Administration, Education, Law, Music and
Occupational and Physical Therapy.

      Founded in 1888, UPS is located in Tacoma, Wash.

            #####################

KM

VETERANS ADMINISTRATION
INFORMATION SERVICE (202) 389-2741
WASHINGTON, D.C. 20420

IMMEDIATE RELEASE

A grant of up to $25,000 is available for seriously disabled veterans interested in "wheelchair homes."

This word came from Administrator of Veterans Affairs Max Cleland who, himself, lost both legs and an arm during the Vietnam conflict.

He reminded eligible veterans the grant can be applied to a new home, used to remodel an existing dwelling or to pay off the balance owing on a home the veteran has modified at his own expense.

Under the law, eligible veterans may obtain a VA grant of up to half the cost of a specially adapted home to a maximum of $25,000.

Basically, eligible veterans are those who have suffered permanent and total military service-connected disability due to the loss (or loss of use) of both legs; blindness, plus loss of use of one leg; or other injury which prevents them from moving from place to place without the aid of a wheelchair, braces, crutches or canes.

Cleland urged disabled veterans to consult their nearest Veterans Administration office for detailed eligibility requirements.

-more-

-2-

He pointed out other eligibility requirements include
a provision that the veteran must be able to afford purchase of the
"wheelchair home" with the assistance of the grant and that
it must be medically feasible for the veteran to live there.

To qualify for a VA grant a new housing unit must have
at least two entry ramps located to avoid fire hazards, doorways
at least 36 inches wide, hallways at least 48 inches wide,
specially equipped bathrooms, specially located electric switches
and outlets, an automatic smoke detector, and other features.

Cleland said VA field specialists will help eligible
veterans in choosing a suitable lot for the housing unit, in
obtaining the services of an architect, securing construction bids
and arranging financing.

The VA Administrator also reminded veterans that some
states provide special tax relief for owners of "wheelchair homes"
and up to $40,000 mortgage life insurance is available to most
veterans who receive the housing grant.

# # # # #

Evans

for further information contact:
        Jessica Zive
        Jessica Dee Communications, Inc.
        160 Central Park South
        New York, N.Y. 10019
        (212) 581-5757

RELEASE AT WILL

                    "Fur Glossary"

     Furs are being worn by everyone these days. Women of all
sizes and shapes, men, even kids are warming their hearts (not to mention
their bodies) with fur garments ranging in style from full length coats
to mittens and in type from rabbit to lynx. Never have furs been as
accessible as now.

     And the more people who join the fur parade, the more they
need to know about the garments they are buying. What's a reasonable price
range for a particular kind of fur? What does "let-out" mean?   What's
underfur? Guard hair? According to David Meltzer, president of Evans, Inc..
the world's largest furrier with 90 leased and wholly owned retail outlets
in addition to manufacturing facilities and a wholesale division, it's
important to know what you're getting into -- literally.

     Less than fifty species of animals (out of a total of 4,000
mammals) are cultivated for their fur value. Some are found only in their
wild state, but most are ranched or farmed. The American fur industry no
longer manufactures furs from <u>endangered species</u> such as leopard, tiger and
cheetah, but other furs have rapidly taken their place.

                    -more-

glossary/add 1

Protected animals such as sable remain expensive because
the quantity of pelts is limited. As a fur gains in popularity, its
price rises quickly, and raccoon coats costing only $800 ten years ago
now sell for $3,000 and up. Some furs go out of style, as did silver fox
in the fifties and sixties, with ranchers turning to other species such as
mink.

The quality of pelts has a lot to do with price. All fur consists
of leather (tanned or dressed) and hair or fur. Hair may be full and thick
like mink or flat like antelope. Guard hair is the long, lustrous outer fur
that shields the animal. Underfur is the fur seen by parting the guard hair.
Sometimes the guard hair is plucked, leaving a soft underfur. This can be
sheared or plucked to improve overall texture. Other types of processing
include dyeing and bleaching.

Furs can be worked many ways into coats depending upon the style
and pattern of the coat and type of fur. Some of the terms you should know
about furs are:

Skin-on-skin: pelts sewn together.

Let-out: a single pelt is deftly worked into narrow strips and
reset and then sewn into a much longer strip for less bulk, more variety
in styling, and the look of one unbroken line. Let-out furs have more
suppleness, they are lighter, and have greater beauty than any other fur.

Pieced: those furs made from pieces cut away from the pelt are
collected and sold to furriers who recut them and sew them into clothlike
plates which are then manufactured into fur garments. Some of the world's
finest furs, such as mink and Russian Sable, are made this way.

When selecting a fur, the three key considerations are texture,
color, and suppleness of leather. Flat fur should never be sparse and curly and
should have a consistent pattern. The color should be uniform and clear
with the best furs showing a bluish cast. A reddish cast is the first
indication that the fur is of poor quality.

\#   \#   \#   \#

1740 Broadway, New York, N.Y. 10019   (212)245-8000

AMERICAN ✝ LUNG ASSOCIATION
The "Christmas Seal" People

for release: IMMEDIATELY
        Contact: Mary Matson Kelly
                   Ext. 512

Have you ever been bothered by smoke in a restaurant, theater or other place? Do you want to know what to do about it?

Calm -- rather than timid or belligerent behavior -- is the answer, an American Lung Association pamphlet says.

Over- or under-assertiveness will only result in a negative response from the smoker, writes Frances E. Cheek, Ph.D., in a new Christmas Seal publication, "Facts and Features for Nonsmokers & Smokers." Dr. Cheek is director of the New Jersey Neuropsychiatric Institute's Behavior Modification Program.

"For many of us nonsmokers who are becoming increasingly alarmed by new information regarding the effects of smoke on the nonsmoker -- and are attempting to stand up for our rights in public places and personal spaces -- protecting ourselves is not so easy," says Dr. Cheek.

more...

Two kinds of errors are usually found, Dr. Cheek writes.
"Some of us -- the under-assertive -- come on too tentatively.
We don't really feel we have a right to interfere with the pleasures
and activities of others, our manner is diffident, we are easily turned
aside. Others -- the over-assertive -- come on too strongly. We
attempt to get our way too vigorously, our manner is often seen as
rude or abrupt. People resent our requests and refuse to cooperate. "

Dr. Cheek gives an example of an effective approach:

"The scene is a fashionable restaurant at the dinner hour.
One couple has been seated. At the table beside them are an elderly
well-dressed man and his wife who have just finished dinner. The
man is puffing contentedly on a cigar.

"After several moments, the woman in the newly arrived
couple says with great charm to the smoker:

"Sir, we have a problem.

"What do you mean? ' is the response.

"In order for you to enjoy your dinner, you must smoke your
cigar, but in order for us to enjoy our dinner we must be free of cigar
smoke.

"The elderly man laughs and puts out the cigar.

Although this type of assertiveness does not always work, says
Dr. Cheek, it will "raise your batting average. " She concludes the
article with guidelines for correctly assertive behavior.

more...

3- facts & features

Other features in the Christmas Seal people's new publication

for nonsmokers and smokers alike are:

"How Not to Love Your Kids" (smoking during pregnancy and

parental smoking)

"What You Can Do" (tips for smokers)

"Q & A" (questions and answers about nonsmokers' rights)

"The Incredible Donna Shimp Story" (an interview with a New

Jersey woman who won her right to a smoke-free workplace

in court)

"Smokers and Nonsmokers vs. Smoking" (the results of a

nationwide survey on smoking)

Copies of "Facts and Features for Nonsmokers & Smokers" are

available from Lung Associations throughout the country or by writing

the American Lung Association, GPO Box 596, New York, N.Y. 10001.

Requests sent to ALA headquarters will be referred to local associations.

\#   \#   \#

Western Airlines *news release*

6060 Avion Drive, Los Angeles, California 90009– (213) 776-2345 or 646-4321

WESTERN AIRLINES INTRODUCES NEW ALASKAN FOOD SERVICE

LOS ANGELES, June 28--A tasty new Alaskan food service offering the robust flavor of Alaska mixed with the rich heritage of the Pacific Northwest is now on all Western Airlines' flights between the Pacific Northwest and Alaska.

Known as the Pacific Northerner, a name which according to Dick Ensign, senior vice president of marketing for Western, "will recall fond memories for many old-time Alaskan travelers who used to travel on Pacific Northern Airlines, now a part of Western."

The new service features gourmet bits, such as Petersburg cocktail, Fairbanks salad, veal Kodiak, Cold Bay crab, filet Sitka, club steak Juneau, Kodiak king crab, Bristol Bay Salmon, Reindeer sausage, all topped off with Klondike'koffee'.

In first class there is custom chinaware designed in bold red, white and blue, complimented with Western's exclusive "miner's skillet" for choice of individual entree, bright colored linens, menu, and seat reservation cards bearing the Pacific Northerner logo.

In coach there will also be a choice of entree, plus silverware wrapped in colorful linen blending with the specially designed napkins and placemats. And, as in first class--a last minute refresher before deplaning--hot towels.

More . . . . . .

19. THE NEWS SERVICES AND "WIRE COPY"

The most influential and least understood of all news organizations are the two major world-wide news agencies, The Associated Press (AP) and United Press International (UPI). Commonly called the wire services, because their copy originally moved over telegraph circuits, AP and UPI would prefer to be known as news services. Their business is news. They are the wholesalers of the news industry, providing copy to virtually every news outlet in the United States and thousands more overseas. They receive their revenue from newspapers and from radio and television stations that subscribe to their services. They sell no advertising and they own no newspapers or broadcasting stations. The news media outlets they serve make the final decisions on which AP and UPI stories will be printed or broadcast, and in what form. There is always a decision-maker between the news services and the public.

The history and development of the news services is well documented in journalism literature. What is important for you, as an editor, is a fundamental understanding of how the news services operate and how they fit into the newsroom. There are structural differences—AP is a cooperative and UPI is privately owned—but the two operate similarly in serving their clientele. Both have headquarters in New York with offices scattered all over the world. They compete for the newsmarket in much the same way that Ford and General Motors compete for automobile buyers. They produce a great deal of original copy from Washington, D.C., New York, and major foreign cities. Still, much of their production results from a clearinghouse function—rewriting stories from clients (the AP calls them "members") and distributing them to other clients. Some of these client newspapers can feed copy directly into the news service computers. Others provide stories to the news services by telephone or by making copies of their stories available. The decision of a municipal governing body may be front-page news in that city but worth only a paragraph or two in another newspaper 200 miles away in the same state. The news service office may rewrite the local newspaper story, boiling it down to bare essentials for distribution elsewhere. The story is transmitted into a computer and appears simultaneously on teletype machines or is received into electronic storage at newspapers all over the state. Another version is prepared for distribution to broadcasting clients. Editors throughout the state make independent decisions on how much, if any, of the news service copy will be used and in what form it will be presented.

The decision by a newspaper or broadcasting station on whether to subscribe to AP, UPI, or both frequently turns on one or more of several factors: perceived quality of the product in a given geographical region, ability of the sales staff, and price. Price quite often is the only factor seriously considered by many small broadcasters and newspapers that have limited time or space for wire news. The larger the news organization, the more likely it is that it will pay for the services of both agencies.

The wires have separate reports for an array of special areas such as national and international news, regional and state news, sports, and financial news. A media outlet may receive as many of these services as it is willing to pay for. A small broadcasting station or newspaper typically will receive a single report combining the key items from the various specialized files. At the other extreme, a large newspaper or broadcaster may receive virtually everything the news services have to offer. Hundreds of thousands of words may be transferred from computer to computer in mere moments. Editors may rely upon indexes they call up on the video display terminal—rather than teletype printers—to determine what is waiting for review.

There are other news services in addition to AP and UPI, but none provides the same type of comprehensive coverage. A number of so-called supplemental services, generally offering column, background, and feature material, are available from major newspapers, such as *The New York Times* and the joint *Washington Post–Los Angeles Times* service, and from syndicates. This material also may be received electronically.

Wherever you work or study, make arrangements to visit the state headquarters office of AP or UPI. The bureau chief or correspondent in charge can explain the operation. To attempt to outline a typical office here might serve the cause of confusion rather than clarity. Offices range in size from one person to dozens. The pattern of how news moves to and from bureaus also differs widely among states (see the figure on p. 187 for a typical model). A firsthand visit is the best way to gain an understanding of the wire-service operations with which you'll deal. Editors at newspapers generally are not good sources on how wire services operate. They see only the end result.

Very important to you, as an editor in the electronic age, is the flexibility with which copy may be edited. Now, and in the future, you will have an opportunity to edit and reshape wire copy in a fashion that simply wasn't practical until the mid-1970s. You should be aggressive in taking advantage of this opportunity, because enlightened news service personnel will be the first to admit that their copy—because of the sheer volume and the speed with which it must be prepared to meet deadlines—sometimes contains errors and always deserves careful reading. Large bureaus have fulltime editors. Smaller ones may not. The person who writes a story in a small bureau may also edit it and move it on the wire, without review by another set of eyes. As far as the reader and the law are concerned, what appears in your newspaper is your responsibility. So if you permit a wire service error to get into print, it is likely that your reputation—not the wire service's—will be blackened in the reader's eyes.

Traditionally news service copy has received relatively little editorial scrutiny in comparison to locally produced copy. That is because the development of TTS (teletypesetter) tape made correcting news service copy costly and time-consuming. In the 1950s, TTS became a laborsaving device for newspapers, enabling them to feed news service copy into linecasting machines in paper tape form. Simultaneously with the reception of stories on teletype printers, newspapers received paper tape versions. This meant the copy could be typeset without human hands. Any corrections or changes had to be typeset locally, thereby impinging upon the labor and time savings gained through the implementation of TTS. By and large, then, newspapers tended to give news service copy a quick once-over, looking primarily for typographical errors that would be obvious to readers instead of reading closely for shortcomings in content and phrasing.

In the electronic age, you can do anything with wire copy that you choose to do. The copy is on your videoscreen and at your mercy for correcting, rearranging, rephrasing, tightening, or combining with whatever related copy is available. Newspaper editors frequently combine the best elements of AP and UPI wire stories or use the wire copy as the basis for local stories.

In theory, the electronic age has brought about a complete change in the practical flexibility of wire editing—from limited to unlimited. In reality, it is not working as well as it might. Editors at many newspapers have become proofreaders as well, on the theory that computers will typeset exactly what appears on the screen. There is no need to worry about mistakes by human hands operating typesetting machines in the backshop. This additional burden has slowed the editing process, and now editors in many cases have the capability—but not the time—to edit wire copy. The result is the same as before the introduction of videoscreens—wire copy is only lightly scanned. But as newspapers gain experience in the new electronics, as equipment becomes more sophisticated, and as duties are redefined, it seems likely that wire copy eventually will undergo the same careful scrutiny that local copy receives.

Some of the best writers and editors in the news industry work for the news services.

However, all copy benefits from a second look. Additionally, a significant portion of the material transmitted by the news services is based upon information from stringers (free-lance newsgatherers), whose reliability all too frequently proves inadequate. One cannot assume that all copy that carries the AP or UPI credit goes through a common editing journey. One piece may have been written by a veteran reporter, perhaps a specialist in a given field, and edited by a person with an equal reputation. The next story on the wire may have been written by a brand-new staffer, working from the notes of a brand-new stringer, and edited by a brand-new and nervous editor.

These are realities of the news service business. They do not tarnish the well-deserved reputation the news services have built through long years of hard work in pursuit of accuracy and reliability. However, the realities should convince you that news service copy is vulnerable and should be treated as cautiously as is any other material that comes to your attention.

Because wire copy is being received electronically by more and more newspapers, it is possible, as we have seen, that you will do all of your editing on a videoscreen—without reference to paper. However, many papers continue to receive hard copy in upper-and-lower-case TTS style. Some examples are included here. Also included are examples of all-cap wire copy, still common, especially from the supplemental services.

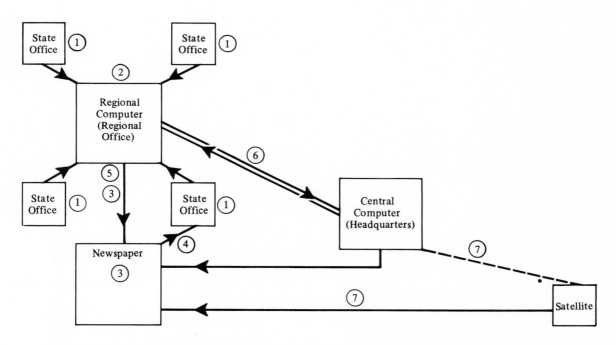

An Example of News Service Operation. State offices (1) are connected by telephone lines to regional offices (2), which have computers through which news copy is electronically relayed to newspapers (3). Newspapers also may file copy electronically to state offices for consideration as wire copy (4). A regional office also may relay copy to a newspaper from the news service's central headquarters (5). The central office files national and international news to newspapers by sending it through the regional computer (6). The central office also may send copy via satellite (7). Technology is advancing rapidly and this illustration does not represent a standard. It reflects general principles, but there are a number of different configurations within the operations of the news services. Photographs are transmitted on a separate but similar system.

The increasing sophistication of transmission and reception techniques makes it possible for wire copy to appear in a newspaper office in a form that requires little cutting and pasting. For instance, it was once common for news services to send a number of leads, inserts, and adds that had to be fitted into place in the original copy. Now, with high-speed delivery, the news services frequently retransmit an entire story, even if only minor changes are being made, because it is easier for the newspaper desk to handle a single piece of copy than two or more. Still, an editor should know how to handle running stories that include new leads and pickups.

Slug designations have changed over the years. For many years, the initials of the filing bureau were included at the top of the story ("CX" indicates Chicago in AP copy). Now, however, technological change has replaced that with single-letter designations for wires and four-digit, consecutive numbers for stories as they move on the wire. A story that years ago might have been slugged "CX69" now could be "a6900."

SELECTED READINGS

Baillie, Hugh. *High Tension.* New York: Harper & Row, 1959. Reminiscences of a United Press executive.
Cooper, Kent. *Barriers Down.* New York: Farrar and Rinehart, Inc. 1942. AP's long-time general manager tells how he helped bring down the worldwide news cartel.
Gramling, Oliver. *AP, the Story of News.* New York: Farrar and Rinehart, Inc., 1940. The standard historical work covering the American news cooperative from its earliest years to the eve of World War II.

EXERCISES

In the following exercises, you have the opportunity to edit several kinds of news service copy. The first story, "Board of Trade," is typical all-cap copy. You will need to underscore all the letters to be capitalized in type. Make any other corrections you feel are needed. Delete the news service coding marks such as B3021 (the number and priority code of the transmission) and 120 (the approximate number of words transmitted). If no end mark is included, be sure to add it. (Often in wire service stories the time when transmission of the story on the teletypewriter ends is used as the end mark.)

"Telephone" is an example of a regional teletypesetter (TTS) story. Each line of this story corresponds to a line of type that will be set by the perforated tape delivered simultaneously with the teletypewriter copy. Again, edit this story thoroughly from every standpoint. You will find some incomprehensible figures that the teletypewriter has misprinted. You cannot supply the missing figures, of course. You can challenge them, however, so the story can then be referred back to the originating service.

"Accused" is not an easy story, but you can help to make it more understandable for your readers. Edit it thoroughly to improve understanding. And in particular, make the mandatory correction.

The last story, "Hostage," is a running story or sectional story in which new leads, adds, inserts, and corrections follow the initial report right up to and even beyond your deadline. To put together one final complete story from all the material that has moved on the wire before you must commit yourself at deadline, simply follow the directions on the copy itself. Consider here that you have a 4 P.M. deadline. (Remember, the time the story transmission was completed appears at the bottom of the copy, together with the date, as the end mark.) Working from the latest part of the story back to the first, pick up from one story to the next, eliminating and discarding superseded material as dictated by the directions on the story segments. Paste the usable portions of the story together to make the single complete story.

Many more new leads will move on the wire before this story reaches a point of resolution. After the first-day story segments, you will find a story, "AM—Hostage, lst Ld," which moved the following day. It picks up into a previous segment that has moved on the wire but is not included here. You need not edit this final story unless asked to do so by your instructor. In that event, delete the continuation line at the bottom and treat the story as a self-contained whole.

In addition to the running story itself, you will find available for your use just before your 4 P.M. deadline a typical sidebar, or related story, "Media Embargo—With Hostage." You may treat it as a separate related story or incorporate the material into your main story at some logical place, as your instructor may ask. Notice in the running story and sidebar how a confused situation gradually becomes more meaningful and factually correct as well as complete through successive leads.

Remember, in this age of electronic transmission, you may not have to piece stories together in the manner required in these exercises. Because of the speed with which copy can be delivered, and because it is mechanically easier to replace an entire story than to slice in leads, adds, or corrections, news services often retransmit an entire story with the appropriate changes rather than send a short top or correction. Still, the exercises will be valuable to you because sometimes you will want to combine stories from various sources or rearrange news service material in a manner not suggested by the transmissions themselves.

B3021

Board of Trade, 120

CHICAGO (NS) -- A LAST_MINUTE BUYING RALLY BY LOCAL TRADERS IN

WHEAT AND CORN FUTURES REVERSED DAY-LONG TRENDS MONDAY AND CAUSED

GRAIN PRICES TO CLOSE HIGHER IN CONCERT WITH SOYBEANS ON THE CHICAGO

BOARD OF TRADE.

SOME TRADERS SAID SOYBEAN PRICES WERE RISING ON NEWS OF

EUROPEAN INTEREST AND BECAUSE SELLERS DUMPING WHEAT AND CORN CON-

TRACTS WERE TRYING TO COVER THEIR COMMODITITIES SHORTAGES.

TALK THAT THE INTERNATIONAL LONGSHOREMAN'S UNION IS CONSIDERING

SOME TYPE OF BOYCOTT OF GRAIN SHIPMENTS TO THE SOVIET UNION APPAR-

ENTLY CONTINUED TO WORRY TRADERS.

CORN P:RICES WERE BOUYED BY SIGNIFICANT BU YING BY A LARGE

COMMERCIAL HOUSE.

223P CS

~~B3021~~

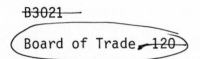
Board of Trade ~~120~~

    CHICAGO (NS) -- A LAST=MINUTE BUYING RALLY BY LOCAL TRADERS IN
WHEAT AND CORN FUTURES REVERSED DAY-LONG TRENDS MONDAY AND CAUSED
GRAIN PRICES TO CLOSE HIGHER IN CONCERT WITH SOYBEANS ON THE CHICAGO
BOARD OF TRADE.

    SOME TRADERS SAID SOYBEAN PRICES WERE RISING ON NEWS OF
EUROPEAN INTEREST AND BECAUSE SELLERS DUMPING WHEAT AND CORN CON-
TRACTS WERE TRYING TO COVER THEIR COMMODIFITIES SHORTAGES.

    TALK THAT THE INTERNATIONAL LONGSHOREMAN'S UNION IS CONSIDERING
SOME TYPE OF BOYCOTT OF GRAIN SHIPMENTS TO THE SOVIET UNION APPAR-
ENTLY CONTINUED TO WORRY TRADERS.

    CORN P.RICES WERE BQUYED BY SIGNIFICANT BUYING BY A LARGE
COMMERCIAL HOUSE.

R 5050

ACCUSED, 520

    WASHINGTON (NS) - JOSEPH C. "JOE BANANAS" BONANNO, A REPUTED NEW
JERSEY MAFIA CHIEFTAIN ONCE UNDER FEDERAL GRAND JURY INVESTIGATION FOR
UNAUTHORIZED POSSESSION OF RAILROAD BOXCARS, WAS ACCUSED THURSDAY OF
TURNING A SMALL FLORIDA RAILROAD INTO A BOXCAR REPAIR SERVICE.

    REP. HARLEY O. STAGGERS, D-W. VA., CHAIRMAN OF THE HOUSE COJMMERCE

COMMITTEE, BERATED THE INTERSTATE COMMERCE COMMISSION FOR GRANTING

BONANNO'S PETITION TO TAKE CONTROL OF THE RAIL LINE IN JUST THREE DAYS,

AT A TIME WHEN THE GRAND JURY INQUIRY WAS STILL UNDER WAY.

"THIS IS A FIASCO," FUMED STAGGERS AT A COMMITTEE HEARING. HE SAID

THERE HAD BEEN NO RAIL SERVICE ON THE 27-MILE MARIANNA AND BLOUNSTOWN

RAILROAD, A FREIGHT FEEDER LINE IN THE FLORIDA PANHANDLE, SINCE EARLY

DECEMBER, PARTLY BECAUSE THE TRACKS WERE CHOKED WITH 118 BOXCARS BEING

REFURBISHED.

STAGGERS SAID WORKERS ON THE FLORIDA LINE WERE REPAINTING OLD

BOXCARS WITH THE NAME OF THE MARYLAND & PENNSYLVANIA RAILROAD SO THEY

COULD BE LEASED AT A HIGHER PER DIEM RATE THAN BEFORE ON THE INTERSTATE

RAIL SYSTEM.

"WHY AREN'T THEY WORKING ON THE TRACKS?" A RED_FACED STAGGERS

SHOUTED AT ICC CHAIRMAN GEORGE STAFFORD, WHO TESTIFIED BEFORE STAGGERS'

SPECIAL COMMERCE SUBCOMMITTEE ON INVESTIGATION ALONG WITH A DOZEN OTHER

AGENCY OFFICIALS.

THE ICC WITNESSES SAID BONANNO'S REQUEST TO PURCHASE CONTROL OF

THE MARIANNA AND BLOUNSTOWN WAS APPROVED SEPT. 10 WITHOUT KNOWLEDGE

HE WAS STILL BEING INVESTIGATED BY THE GRAND JURY.

NO CRIMINAL CHARGES WERE BROUGHT AGAINST BONANNO, BUT HE WAS

ORDERED BY A FEDERAL JUDGE TO PAY $150,000 TO PENN CENTRAL FOR RENT

OF RAIL CARS IN HIS POSSESSION WHEN FBI AGENTS RAIDED THE TINY LASALLE

& BUREAU COUNTY RAILROAD IN ILLINOIS LAST MARCH.

A NUMBER OF PENN CENTRAL BOXCARS WERE FOUND TO HAVE BEEN MARKED

OVER WITH LS&BC INSIGNIA, AND IT WAS LATER LEARNED THAT ABOUT 350

BOXCARS HAD BEEN SHIPPED TO LS&BC, WHERE BONANNO OPERATED A RAILROAD

REPAIR SHOP UNDER THE NAMES DIVERSIFIED PROPERTIES, INC., AND MAGNA

EARTH ENTERPRISES. BONANNO DENIED ANY WRONGDOING, SAYING HE HAD

BOUGHT SOME BOXCARS WHOSE LEASES TO PENN CENTRAL HAD EXPIRED.

STAGGERS ASKED THE ICC TO INVESTIGATE THE FLORIDA RAILROAD

SITUATION AND REPORT BACK TO THE SUBCOMMITTEE WITHIN 30 DAYS. HE

CHARGED THE ICC HAD NOT GIVEN THE BONANNO APPLICATION PROPER CONSIDERA-

TION.

"THERE HAS BEEN A WHOLESALE BRINGING IN OF EMPTY BOX_

CARS -- FOR REPAINTING AND REFURBISHING," SAID STAGGERS. "MEANWHILE,

THE PEOPLE WHO DEPEND ON THAT RAILROAD ARE IGNORED."

STAGGERS SAID THE ICC STAF APPARENTLY HAD DISREGARDED

REGULATIONS AND PROCEDURES FOR CONSIDERATION OF BONANNO'S

APPLICATION FOR CONTROL, WHICH WAS REQUIRED BECAUSE OF HIS

CONTROLLING INTEREST IN ANOTHER RAILROAD, CADILLAC AND LAKE CITY

OF MICHIGAN.

R 5060

URGENT

ADVISORY 30

EDITORS: PLEASE HOLD THE BOXCARS DISPATCH WASHINGTON R5050. WE

HAVE MISIDENTIFIED THE PRINCIPAL INVOLVED IN THE STORY. A MANDATOR

1ST LEAD AND CORRECT WILL MOVE SHORTLY.

NEWS SERVICE/WASHINGTON

835 PES

R5057

ACCUSED

URGENT

MANDATORY 1ST LD AND CORRECT R5050, 120

WASHINGTON (NS) - A MAN ONCE UNDER FEDERAL GRAND JURY INVESTIGATION
FOR UNAUTHORIZED POSSESSION OF RAILROAD BOXCARS WAS ACCUSED THURSDAY
OF TURNING A SMALL FLORIDA RAILROAD INTO A BOXCAR REPAIR SERVICE.

HE WAS IDENTIFIED AS JOSEPH C. BONANNO, WHO WAS NOT CHARGED
FOLLOWING THE GRAND JURY INQUIRY BUT WAS ORDERED TO PAY RENT ON THE
BOXCARS IN HIS POSSESSION WHEN FEDERAL AGENTS RAIDED HIS FACILITY LAST
SPRING.

BONANNO IS A BUSINESSMAN WHOSE ADDRESS WAS LISTED AS ESSEX FELLS,
N. J. HE IS NO KNOWN RELATION OF JOSEPH "JOE BANANAS" BOANNANO, THE
REPUTED MAFIA CHIEFTAN ONCE BASED IN NEW JERSEY.

X X X REP HARLEY: 2ND GRAF R5050

930 PES

m 1524

Telephone, 200

BOISE, Idaho (NS) - The
Idaho Public Utilities Commis-
ion Monday approved a plan to
provide telephone service to
a remote area of Southern Idaho

ranches in the Three Creek
and Murphy Hot Springs areas
of Twin Falls and Owyhee
Counties.

Under the prposal to serve
the remote ranches in the area,
individuals from the two areas
have agreed to provide the
lines and other necessary construction for the telephone service which will be operated by
Rural T$_e$lephone Co. of California.

Residents who wish service
will ray an initial $ 00 advance
and the project will not begin
until $,000 is collected.

In addition, several ranchers
will act as guarantors for a
second loan of $ 0,000.
For farmers and ranchers in the
Three Creek and Murphy Hot
Springs area the decision means
the end of a long wait.

1015 a

e 6119

PM - Hostage, 110

Urgent

RIVERVIEW (NS) - A man with a bomb tied around him barricaded himself inside ahouse this morning with three children, police said.

Sheriff's Capt. Harry Stevenson said a bomb was also found in a milk box at the man's house in another part of the city.

Stevenson declined to identify the man, whom he described as 30 years old. The officer said the man's wife had been in the house, but escaped and was with police on the front lawn.

Officers blocked off the neighborhood around the house at 1252 Arbor St.

The sherriff's department received the first call as a bomb threat shortly after 8 a. m.

- - - - - -

07-07   9.24a

e6129

PM - Hostage, 1st Ld, 250

Urgent

RIVERVIEW (NS) - A man with a bomb tied around him barricaded himself inside a house today with his three children and threatened to set off the bomb if he heard a broadcast report of the incident, police said.

Several radio stations immediately stopped live coverage. Some
which had been reporting it dropped it from the next hourly newcast.

Sheriff's Capt. Harry Stevenson said a bomb was also found in a
milk box at the man's house in another part of the valley. That device
was detonated by bomb experts, he said.

Capt. Jack Green said it was believed the man, separated from his
wife, had at least one additkonal bomb in the house. Officers said
shots were also fired.

Green said his demands were unclear. "The guy hasn't been too
communicative," he said.

The man was, however, negotiating on the phone with his brother,
a police officer and a psychiatrist, Green said.

The man was described as 28 years old. One witness said he was
wearing military fatigues.

The officer said the man's wife had been in the house but escaped
and was with police on the front lawn.

Officers blocked off the neighborhood. Fireme, paramedics and
members of the police bomb squad stood by.

- -------

07-07 10.32a

e6156

AM-Hostage, 480

RIVERVIEW (NS) - A man with a bomb strapped around his waist
barricaded himself and his three children inside his father-in-law's

house today and threatened to set off the bomb if he heard broadcast reports of the incident, police said.

Across town, police detonated a crude bomb at the man's house, where he had left a sign saying it was a small nuclear device and that the house was "wired so no one can enter, or it will go."

At the request of the sheriff's department, several radio stations blacked out news of the incident after broadcasting initial reports. Neither KRPT nor KUU television mentioned the incident on noon newscasts while the drama was taking place.

Sheriff's Capt. Jack Green identified the man as James Witt, 29, a vacuum cleaner salesman. He said the children were 2, 4 and 6 years old

Police said the children had not been harmed. The nam, negotiating with police and a psychiatrist by phone, claimed one was asleep, said Green.

Green said the man had made no specific demands except that he would kill the children if he heard news reports. He said it was believed the man had at least one bomb in addition to the one tied around his waist.

Neighbors were evacuated, Police, firemen, paramedics and bomb experts stood by.

The man's estranged wife and her parents had been in the house earlier when three shots were fired at the father-in-law, police said. It was not clear how they got out.

Green said it was believed the hostages were being held in the basement of the large house in a well-to-do neighborhood.

He said the incident began as a bomb threat report at 8:11 a. m.

Police found two signs at the man's house across town - one in the mailbox and one next to the milk box.

One written in felt-tipped pen on yellow cardboard said: "This home is wired with electric, battery operated plastic explosives. So are other locations in this area. Plase evacuate the area."

A second sign said, "Look at the milk box. Have the bomb squad come and gently disarm it." On the other side it said, "A small nuclear device inside. Don't use your radios. Advise public not to use FM channels."

But Capt. Robert Mullen said the milk box bomb appeared to be made of black powder taken from shotgun shells found in the home. He said it had wires running into the house and attached to a clock.

Mullen said it appeared Witt had "some experience with explosives." He said Witt was at one time in the National Guard.

When the bomb squad detonated the device, he said, there was "a very large flash of fire and lots of smoke. It was not sophisticated. It was more of a scare device."

- - - - - -

07-07 12:46 p

e6316

AM - Hostage, Sub, 140

RIVERVIEW, to expand, with identities of wife and parents, sub 6th, 7th and 8th grafs: Green said...got out.

Green said the man had made no specific demands, except that he would kill the children if he heard news reports, and to ask for food and cigarettes. He said it was believed the man had at least one bomb in addition to the one tied around his waist.

Neighbors were at the father-in -law's home were evacuated. Police firemen, paramedics and bomb experts stood by.

The man's estranged wife, Betty, 27, and her parents, Sydney and Carol Walters, had been in the house earlier when three shots were fired at Walters, police said.

Officers said Walters and his wife were able to flee the home when the shots were fired and notified authorities. They said that shortly thereafter, the telephone rang in the Walters home and Mrs. Witt apparently was told to answer it. Instead, she left the house, officers said.

Green said, 9th graf.

07-07 02.19 p

e6318

AM-Hostage, 1st Add, 180

Riverview: scare device."

The Witt home is across the street from Valley Elementary school. School officials said the school was not evacuated.

Linda Jeffs, Witt's next-door neighbor, said Witt had come over to her house Sunday afternoon and talked with her husband, Jerry, for about four hours. She said Witt "told him that his wife had filed divorce proceedings and he seemed pretty upset.

"I was going to ask him to stay for dinner. He seemed really lonely," she said.

Mrs. Jeffs said the Witts moved into the neighborhood last April 1 and "kept pretty much to themselves," although her children played with the Witt children.

Bradley Jones, sales manager for the ABC Vaccuum Co., said Witt quit his job at the firm's Riverview office about a week or 10 days ago. Jones declined to say why Witt quit.

Jones said he had not talked to Witt in several weeks but "at that time he was very friendly and outgoing."

Mrs. Jeffs said Witt had told her husband that he wanted to buy a target range.

07-07 02.24 p

e6333

AM - Hostage, Sub, 30

Riverview: to add names of children, CORRECT children's ages and CORRECT Green's rank from captain to major, sub 4th graf: Sheriff's Capt...years old.

Sheriff's Maj. Jack Green identified the man as James Witt, 29, a

former vacuum cleaner salesman. He said the children were David, 7,
and his brothers Mark, 4, and Sean, 2.

    Police said, 5th graf.

07-07   03.47 p

e6334

AM - Media Embargo

With Hostage

    RIVERVIEW (NS) - Television and radio stations voluntarily
complied with a police request for a news embargo Monday after a man
holding his three children hostage threatened to set off a bomb if he
heard broadcast reports of the incident.

    Nearly all neews directors interviewed said they were frustrated
by not being able to report the story, but they said they didn't want
to be responsible for the children's deaths.

    "I understand the potential problem," said Art Fitzgerald, news
director of KTQR Radio. "I try to relate by thinking if it were my
kids I sure as hell wouldn't like anybody to report anything."

    Between 40 and 50 reporters and cameramen monitored the situation
from a vantage point about 100 yeards from the house. Television
stations fed tapes back to their station but the noon news came and
went with none being aired.

Radio stations broadcast early reports Monday morning based on
sketchy information, as did one of the two television stations.

But at the request of the sheriff's department shortly after
10 a. m., those reports stopped after the man barricaded inside his
father-in-law's house told police he would detonate the device strapped
around his waist if he heard broadcast reports of the situation.
Meanwhile, the two daily newspapers reported the story.

The man was identified as James Witt, a 29-year-old former
vacuum cleaner salesman.

07-07   0.3^{55} p

e6141

AM - Hostage, 1st Ld, 250

RIVERVIEW (NS) - A man who held his three children hostage for
more than a day changed from Army fatigues to a blue blazer, shaved
and walked out of a suburban house with his 7-year-old son at his side
Tuesday.

Sheriff's deputies led the man, James Witt, 29, to a police car,
and the boy, David, was reunited with two younger brothers, Mark, 4,
and Sean, 2, who were released five hours earlier. The youngest
reportedly had begged his father to let him back in.

Sean said it had not been determined whether Witt actually had the
bomb he told police was strapped around his waist. He did not have it

when he emerged from his father-in-law's weapon-laden house 32 hours after he first took the children hostage.

Monday, sheriff's deputies detonated a bomb found at Witt's home across town.

Witt, estranged from his wife, told negotiators he took his three children hostage because he feared he wouldn't see them again when he and his wife are divorced, said a psychiatrist who h-lped police negotiators.

Stevenson described Witt as "apologetic" after the incident. "He wanted to come out. It was just getting over that step and fear," he said.

He said Witt cut himself while shaving, which further delayed the end of the drama.

Chief sheriff's: 5th graf

- - - - - -

07-08   0.350 p

20. POLICE AND THE COURTS

In an era when lawyers are alert to file motions claiming that publicity has prejudiced their clients' cases, editors must exercise special care in handling stories about the law. There is no blanket rule to apply in deciding whether to use information that may be in the public interest but at the same time may be prejudicial and perhaps inadmissible as evidence in court. Caution is always a good guideline.

Some police departments, in their eagerness to have the public believe they are doing good work, release information that is tempting to use but that may be more self-serving than informative. Statements such as "We've got our man" are prime examples. An editor should never fall for stories that convict individuals of crimes. Let the reader draw conclusions, but do not draw the conclusions yourself. If the copy says, "A robber was captured today only moments after holding up The First National Bank," change it to "A man was arrested today only moments after a holdup at The First National Bank." Based upon other details provided, the reader may or may not conclude the charged person likely is the guilty party. At least, you will not be forcing a conclusion to be drawn on the basis of information that may later be found erroneous.

Legal language, loaded with Latin phrases, is difficult for the layman to follow. For instance, do you know what is meant by a *writ of mandamus* or *habeas corpus?* If you don't—and even if you do—you can hardly expect a casual reader to be capable of translation. It is your job, when a story includes such terms, to make certain they are defined. This may seem to be a tedious process, especially after the hundredth time, but you must not forget the general reader neither sees every story you edit nor makes a point of remembering esoteric language of little personal application.

As an editor, you also should reduce the chances for confusion. For instance, the term *not guilty* frequently is used in the courtroom, but *innocent* means the same and is much preferred in media. Why? Because the word *not* is too easily dropped in typesetting, or missed in broadcasting. In either case, presence of the word *guilty* leaves the danger of confusion. In handling legal stories, use *innocent* and relegate *not guilty* to the spike.

Be sure, also, that verdicts are carefully explained. Litigation is often complicated, and it is worth whatever extra wordage is necessary to make sure the story is clear. Reporters on court beats frequently are inexperienced, and that increases the responsibility of the editor to guard against imprecision.

EXERCISES

Porno

A guilty verdict was returned against the Peek-a-Boo Book Shop, in a civil action in District Court Friday.

The five man, three woman jury declared in an 8 - 0 decision that all 47 items submitted as evidence by district Atty. Robert Smothers were obscene.

A 6 - 2 majority was all that was needed to convict in the case, according to Smothers. He said the unanimous verdict reflected public opinion on the subject.

The jury's ruling will prohibit the future sale of the items previously banned under a temporary restraining order but won't affect other merchandise at the store.

Hubert R. Knight, Attorney for defendants David Brumbaugh and the Newman Corp., said that an appeal will be filed within 30 days with the State supreme court.

It took the jury about two hours of deliberation to come up with the verdict against the films, magazines, books, a recording and deck or cards.

The materials were either confiscated by police during raids or voluntarily surrendered by the store on four separate occasions, according to Smothers.

Two criminal trials are scheduled against Brumbaugh and the Newman Cor. in city court Nov. 15.   #

(Porno)

A ~~guilty~~ verdict was returned against the Peek-a-Boo Book Shop, in a civil action in District Court Friday.

The five=man, three=woman jury ~~declared in an 8 - 0 decision~~ *brought in a unanimous verdict* that all 47 items submitted as evidence by district (Atty.) Robert Smothers were obscene.

A 6 - 2 majority was ~~all that was~~ needed ~~to convict in the case, according to Smothers~~. *Smothers* ~~He~~ said the unanimous verdict reflected public opinion ~~on the subject.~~

The ~~jury's ruling~~ *verdict* will prohibit ~~the future~~ sale of the items previously banned under a temporary restraining order but won't affect other merchandise at the store.

Hubert R. Knight, Attorney for defendants David Brumbaugh and the Newman Corp., said that an appeal will be filed within 30 days with the State supreme court.

~~It took~~ the jury *deliberated* about two hours ~~of deliberation to come up with~~

(more)

(2/ Verdict)

~~the verdict against the~~/films, magazines, books, a recording and deck
                                                                    f
o~~r~~ cards.

    ~~The materials~~ were ~~either~~ confiscated by police during raids or

voluntarily surrendered by the store on four ~~separate~~ occasions,

according to Smothers.

    Two criminal trials are scheduled against Brumbaugh and the Newman
      p
Cor. in city court Nov. 15.   (#)
      1

Drugs

    A 26-year-old woman was arranged here in Circuit City Court today

on a charge of uttering a forged instrument resulting from a Monday

incident at a drug store.

    Peggy Boston, 560 Larkspur Lane, was arrested Tuesday. She hae

been sought for trying to obtain some 30 pain-killing tablets from

the Prescription Pharmacy, 2100 Industry Blvd., with a bogus

prescription.

                              # # #

Typewriters

    Robbers broke into Wheel and Bearing, Inc. offices at 3213 Industry

Boulevard Wednesday night and stole three electric typewriters and a

typewriter table worth a total of $6,440, according to police reports.

                              #

Condition

    FREMONT—A 23-YEAR-OLD CONSTRUCTION WORKER WAS LISTED IN POOR
CONDITION AND IN INTENSIVE CARE BY CURTES COUNTY HOSPITAL OFFICIALS
THURSDAY, FOLLOWING AN ELECTRICUTION WHILE WORKING AT A CONSTRUCTION
SITE WEDNESDAY IN FREMONT.

    JOHN TIMOTHY, 23, AN EMPLOYEE OF THE CHRISTENSEN CONSTRUCTION CO.,
SUFFERED A SEVERE ELECTRICAL SHOCK WHILE WORKING ON THE ADDITION TO
THE BELL SYSTEM CENTRAL OFFICE.

    CITY POLICE REPORTED TIMOTHY WAS WORKING BESIDE A CRANE, HELPING
TO TIE ON SOME REINFORCING STEEL RODS WHEN THE ACCIDENT OCCURED.

    THIS MARKS THE SECOND ELECTRUCTION TO HAPPEN DURING CONSTRUCTION
JOBS ALONG STATE STREET IN FREMONT IN THE PAST FEW MONTHS.

#

Rob

Two men charged with market robberies were arraigned in city court
Friday and given a preliminary hearing date of May 17.

Also, after Deputy County Attorney Charles Wingate argued that
flelease of the pair from the city jail

"presents a grave risk" Judge Saul Feinstein

set a bond hearig for wednesday.

Mr. Wingate said Patrick McGillicudy and Paul Benjamin, both 19, are suspected of having committed at least eight robberies of super-markets involving more than $30,000.

They are charged with robbing wo Safeway stores, at 293 Center St. and 1440 Industry Boulevard, March 30 and Jan. 25. They are in jail on $10,000 bail.

#

Rapists

Spencer City—Two murder-rape suspects apprehended Spencer City at 5:30 pm Friday, were booked in the County Jail at 11 pm. Elk County Sheriff Sam Evans said the suspects were being held pending a warrant from the Aberdeen, Mississippi Sheriff.

Rodney Jones, deputy shefiff, said, Griff Smiley, 29, and David Powell Jr., 24, driving a stolen car with a white girl passenger, stoped at Ray's Service Station in Spencer City at 5:30 p.m.

Susan Jones, a nineteen year old girl, was hitchiking from L.A. to New York. When asked why she got into the car with two colored men, she replied that she had been "waiting all day for a ride" from Elm City.

She was raped in the rear seat somewhere between Elm City and Spencer City, said Officer Jones. At Riverview the two murder-rape suspects forced the girl to cash $199 in travelers checks at a bank. They robbed her of the money.

At the gas station the girl got out of the car to go to the rest room. Passing the station attendant, Lucas Smith, she said. "Is there a airport nearby, I don't want to go any further. There may be a hassle, they might have guns." Smith told the girl to hide in the rest room. "I (Smith) ran over to the sheriff's house (Deputy Jones). The girl was shaking and real scared."

Deputy Jones told Smith to go back to ghe station.

Jones radioed to Highway Patrol Trooper Bill Wolfe for assistance. While the trooper engaged the two suspects in routine questioning, Deputy Jones got a check on the vehicle. The car was stolen out of Florida. Jones then walked over to Wolfe and said: "The car is hot, let's take them." The two suspects were ordered out of the car, at gun point.

At the jail a teletype was sent to Aberdeen, Mississippi, and Florida's sheriffs.

A telephone cass from Aberdeen revealed the two were identified as raping and murdering a 20 year old colored girl, 6 miles south of that town. She was beaten to death by a heavy object, then dragged 100 feet off the highway into a ditch wher the police found her.

#

Succumbs

A five-year-old Wisconsin girl, who was struck by a car in front of her grandparents home Thursday, died unexpectedly Friday morning at Central hospital, according to Police Lt. Raymond Whistler.

The girl, Stephanie Joy Record, and her parents, Mr. and Mrs.

Harvey Record, from Battle Creek, Mich., were visiting her grandparents,
Mr. and Mrs. Leppert DePrey, 952 Ninth St., Thursday, according to Lt.
Whistler.

The girl stepped out from behind a parked car into the path a car
driven by Richard Bennett, 29, according to investigating officer
Raymond Heaps.

She was rushed to Central Hospital by her mother and grandfather,
where she was listed in critical condition Thursday evening. She had
a fractured skull and extensive head injuries, said Officer Heaps.

The girl was taken to Mercy Hospital for a brain scan and her
parents were told she did not need to have an operation, said Officer
Heaps.

She was in the Intensive Care Unit in Central Hospital at 2 a.m.
and died an hour later. The girl "seemed to die unexpectedly, according
to Lt. Whistler. Officer Heaps said the cause of death was unknown.

#

Pie

A 17-year-old female juvenile who flunked out of a class at Central
High School earlier this year, was charged with assault and referred to
Juvenile Court after enlisting her sister and a friend to throw pies in
her teacher's face.

The guilty parties had entered a math class one dressed in cape and
the other in a clown outfit, then hurled the pies at the teacher.

The female juvenile admitted full responsibility for the pie incident, saying she was retaliating for failing her class.

#

Probe

A series of recent burglaries occurring in large apartment complexes in the county may be the work of more than one man, accordikng to city police.

Sgt. Miles Gilmour, head of the burglarly detail, said recently-gathered evidence indicates that there may be two or more burglars committing similar crimes and employing similar te-chniques.

He said hs office is working with other law agencies in an attempt to solve at least 18 burglaries or attempted burglaries that have been reported since last March in the city and unincorporated parts of the county.

And although the crimes have keen committed during the early morning hours at large partment complexes, Sgt. Gilmour said lawmen now feel that there may be more than one suspect.

On Tuesday, city police reported that a woman living in a large apartment complex on the city's east side surprised a burglar who climed through a window and entered her kitchen at 4:30 a. m.

Sgt Gilmour said many of the recent burgalaries have been committed by a man who jimmies kitchen window.

He said, however, there are slight differences in the MO (motis operandi or motive of operation).

#

Jury

Since no one showed up to give se cret testimony to presiding and District Court Judge Robert J. Cooley Friday, the day he had sett aside for Residents to give such testimony, no grand jury will be called.

The court is required by law to allow citizeaens to testify in secret every two years as to whether a grand jury is necessary. Since no one arrived at the Connor County Courthouse to give such testimony, it was assumed there was no cause to convene the jury.

#

Collision

Two persons were killed and another critically injured Friday at 2:10 p.m. in a broadside collision at 27th Street and Main Boulevard.

Highway Patrol Trooper Horace Smathers identified the victims as Glen Grover, 21, 3241 Green Street, and Morris Martin, 70, 1521 Sest Roberts Lane.

Listed in critical condition late Friday at County Hospital was Mr. Martin's wife, Ruth, 66.

Trooper Smathers said that the vehicle driven by Mrs. Martin was southbound on Main   when it accelerated from a stop sign into the path of Mr. Grover's eastbound car and was struck broadside. Trooper Smathers said Mr. Grover's car was traveling well over the 55 mph speed limit at the time of impact.

Mr. Grover who was alone in his car, was thrown through the windshield and onto a dirt road as his car rolled into a the nearby canal.

Mr. Martin was thrown through the windshield of his car. His wife was trapped in the vehicle for about 20 minutes until sheriff's deputies and paramedics could free her.

Mr. Martin died shortly after arriving at County Hospital. Mr. Grover was dead on arrival at the hospital.

#

Cars

A five-car collision which caused nearly $2000 to three police cars and the West End police Substation occurred Monday.

Police said a collission occurred when a car driven by Max L. Gowans, age 75, of 2240 W. Benson Boulevard, collides with a car driven by Hal Soter, age 43, of Elm City as they both attempted to make right turns from West Ninth Street onto Evans Avenue.

The car driven by Mr. Foster msashed into three park squad cars at the substation. One of the cars parked there struck a sign which subsequently smashed a window of the substation at 525 W. 9th Street.

The 4:45 P.M. collission was under investigation, said Lieutenant joe Smithers, in charge of the substation.

#

Found

City Police are investigating the death of circumstances surrounding the death of a man found in a room at the Webster Hotel, 1121 6th St.

Lt. R. W. Throgmorton identified the fatality as Martin Sorensen, age unknown, a resident of the hotel.

Lt. Throgmorton said the man was discovered by a hotel attendant about 6 p.m. in his room. Police were summoned and they estimated the body to be dead three to five days.

The lieutenant said there were some markings found on the body that may be wounds of some type, but an autoposy will be conducted by the state medical examiner's office to determine the exact cause of the man's death.

The investigation is continuing, police said.

#

Train

A violent car-train crash Friday at 11:40 a.m. on 14th Street and the Southern Pacific Railroad crossing just east of thecity limits, left a well known County man in serious condition at County General Hospital.

Highway Patrol Trooper Ralph Wathen said a southbound car driven by Samuel J. Smithers, 42, 201 University Dr., skidded on snowpacked pavement into the first of two locomotives pulling a caboose.

The trooper said Newbold Lange, the conductor, estimated the speed of the train at 68 miles per hours.

The car was completely destroyed, and the one and a half inch steel plate of the first engine was cracked by the impact. Mr. Smithers, former Washington Junior High School track coach, is a physical education teacher at Clark school.

He was being treated for broken ribbs and hip, possible internal injuries, and numerous lacerations.

The patrol Friday identified a truck driver killed in an accident late Thursday on the interstate two miles north of Elm City.

Trooper John Larson said the driver was Brent B. Mathews, 32, 925 7th Street. He was driving a semi-trailer truck which collided with the rear of a car driven by Mrs. Victor J. Marx, 35, during a heavy fog Thursday at 6:55 p.m.

The truck then went out of control, overturning and trapping the driver. It took rescue crews until 10:15 p.m. to extricate Mr. Mathew's body from the wreckage.

Mrs. Marx and her daughter, 13, were treated at General Hospital and released.

While officers were still working on the wreck, a southbound pickup truck driven by Leroy Salmon was struck in the rear by a semi truck driven by Squires M. Staker, 51, 224 1sth Street. The pickup was knocked from the highway.

Mr. Salmon and a passenger, Verdian M. Wey, 53, of Jonesburgh,
were treated for lacerations and bruises. Mr. Staker was not injured.

#

Drown

One man drowned Sunday afternoon after aboat he and three other
persons were in capsized on Mackinaw Lake near Greenwood Boat Camp.

County Sheriff Elwood Harrison said Mr. James Remington, 41,
and his wife, Lucille, 41, both of 2432 River Road, and another couple,
Rulon and Kristen Markin, both 40 and of 2110 Fillmore Stree, were
fishing from an aluminum 12-foot boat when a brisk wind came up. While
they were attempting to pull in the anchor, the boat capsized, dumping
the four into the lake.

Sheriff Harrison said Mr. Remington was able to get his wife and
the Markins into back into the boat, but he disappeared under the
water before he could be rescued.

Twenty-five law enforcement officers from the Highway Partol and
the County sherrif's offices conducted the search.

Two skindivers, Britt Blumer and Austin Strong, County Sheriff's,
found the body about 6:00 p.m. in about 25 feet of water close to where
she went under.

The three were taken to General Hospital for treatment and were
later released.

#

21. OBITUARIES

One of the most mundane newspaper editing jobs is also one of importance: editing the obituary, or obit. The obituary is the single instance in which most lives are noted in print; for the survivors, the story becomes a family record clipped from the paper and pasted into Bibles and scrapbooks and used in genealogy. The obituary can more intimately shape the attitude of the deceased's friends and relatives toward the newspaper than anything else the paper carries. And it is a type of story the newspaper is uniquely able to carry in detail.

Obituary writing teaches the reporter the basics of style—since many vital statistics are used—and the importance of accuracy in using names, dates, and places and in checking these against standard reference works. For this reason, obituaries are often entrusted to the least experienced writers on the staff. Therefore, they require scrupulous care in editing. Editing obituaries calls for taste, restraint, compassion, and a high order of accuracy. The standards are basic, though practices vary widely by size of publication.

Major metropolitan newspapers do not have space for obits on all the deaths in their circulation areas, even when the smallest type is used. They run lists of deaths, but use stories only on prominent persons. A few have pages in which obituaries written as news stories are grouped. Deaths of especially prominent persons are judged by conventional news indicators. Smaller metropolitan papers use small-type obituaries run in obit columns, usually in an anchored position in the paper, whereas small dailies and weeklies memorialize all persons who die in stories in the circulation area.

Most papers keep a file of "advance obits" on prominent local figures, so that an appropriate story can be carried even if the death occurs close to deadline. These have to be updated periodically. The writing of these obits on major papers is entrusted to persons who are in effect mini-biographers and bring a high order of skill and craftsmanship to the job. A good story obit always plays up the person's impact on the times or on the community and subordinates the vital statistics.

More and more newspapers are imposing a charge for agate obituaries, through the funeral director. These obituaries may be handled by the classified advertising department, though on some papers the editorial department still bears final responsibility for editing them.

Guidelines for the Editor

Accuracy. Check all doubtful facts against standard reference works. Verify the statement of age with the birthdate. Question any anomalies in dates and place. (For instance, did the 35-year-old woman really have five grandchildren? Possible, but not likely.) The most useful reference works are the *United States Postal Guide* (which lists 40,000 towns that have first-class post offices) for spelling and usage of place names; the telephone book or city directory for spelling and usage of persons' names.

Some practical jokers think it's funny to call a newspaper with an erroneous report of a death, furnishing all the information needed for an obituary. Some states have statutes that make it a misdemeanor to knowingly give false information to a newspaper. The best protection, however, is to accept obituary matter only from a mortician or the family. Some papers require that the attending physician or medical examiner be contacted for information on the cause of death.

The obituary should be complete. The most basic obituary information, in addition to the name and date and cause of death, includes date and place of birth, names of parents, date of marriage and name of spouse, the list of survivors, and the funeral information.

Suicides. Policies on handling suicides vary widely. Some papers do not carry stories on suicides at all unless they involve prominent persons or where the circumstances are public or bizarre. One paper has a policy of printing a one-paragraph story as a first-day suicide account, stating only the cause of the death and circumstances of the investigation, but never in any detail. The following day an obituary is carried without stating a cause of death.

Taste. Dignity and restraint are needed. Obituary writing is impersonal in tone. Privacy should be respected unless there is what the American Society of Newspaper Editors code calls "a sure warrant of public interest." Even here the issues are rarely clear-cut. Some years ago a congressman was forced by his party and opinion leaders to withdraw from a reelection race because he had made false claims of having been a war hero. In his obituary the circumstances of his retirement from public life could hardly be omitted. Nationally, they were emphasized in the story. Locally, they were played down. The press is sometimes accused of being so wary of offending and so impersonal that stories become cryptic. There is some room for the occasional "color story" that illuminates a traffic fatality or a war death. In the exercises that follow, you will have an opportunity to judge between two versions of one such story to determine which is more appropriate.

Of course restraint never means facts are twisted. However, in obituary-column agate obits, the family's wishes with regard to eliminating touchy information such as divorces are usually respected. In story obits these facts will be used, however, if they are pertinent.

Nor does restraint mean retreating to euphemisms. Innumerable flowery phrases substitute for *died*, most often *passed away*. *Died* is simpler and more dignified. Phrases such as *beloved father* and such need be tolerated only when they appear in paid obituaries.

Headlines. Heads for story obits should include the name, even if it leads to a badly split head: Sara J.
     Jones
     Dies at 90
Writing the obituary head is usually not difficult, since only the name and the word *dies* or *succumbs* are essential. Often the age is expressed, and where space permits, the occupation or major point of identification.

EXERCISES

Jackson Obit

Robert Casey Jackson, 123 N. 5th St., former County Commissioner and prominent businessman, died Wednesday.

He was the first and only president of Second National Band and director of First National Bank for 50 years. He held these positions until the time of his death.

He was also on the County Commission from 1950 to 1956 and served on the County Planning Board.

A resident of this state all of his life, he was president of West Valley Irrigation Co., director of the Simon Distribution Co. and on the board of McLean Lumber Co. He was also the first chairman of the

County Soil and Conservation District, a position he held for 25 years.

An active member of the Methodist Church, he served in many leader-

ship positions.

He was a veteran of World War II.

He was born Dec. 28, 1920, in Elm City, to Harold and Matilda

Brown Jackson. He was married to Sarah Berman on Sept. 1, 1942. She

preceded him in death on June 5, 1975.

He was the beloved father of one son and one daughter, John J. and

Mrs. Jerry (Susan) Wilson, of San Bernadino, California. He is also

survived by six grandchildren.

Last sad rites will be Monday at 11 a.m. at the United Methodist

Church. Friends may call at the Sowerberry Funeral Home Sunday from

6 to 9 p.m. and Monday until 10:15 a.m. Burian will be in the city

cemetary.

(Jackson Obit)

(indicate age)

Robert Casey Jackson, 123 N. (5th) St., *banker and* former County Commissioner,

~~and prominent businessman~~, died Wednesday. (*Question where died – hospital, home?*)

He was the first and only president of Second National Ban*k* and

director of First National Bank for 50 years. ~~He held these positions~~

until ~~the time of~~ his death. (*question*)

served

He ~~was also~~ on the County Commission from 1950 to 1956 and served

on the County Planning Board.

Jackson was a lifelong

A resident of this state ~~all of his life~~, he was president of West

(*more*)

(2/ Jackson Obit)

Valley Irrigation Co., ~~and a~~ director of the Simon Distribution Co. and ~~on the board of~~ McLean Lumber Co. He was also the first chairman of the County Soil and Conservation District, a position he held for 25 years.

~~An active member of~~ the *United* Methodist Church, he served in many leadership positions *in*

He was a veteran of World War II.

He was born Dec. 28, 1920, in Elm City, to Harold and Matilda Brown Jackson. He ~~was~~ married ~~to~~ Sarah Berman ~~on~~ Sept. 1, 1942. She ~~preceded him in death on~~ *died* June 5, 1975.

~~He was the beloved father of one~~ *Surviving are a* son and ~~one~~ daughter, John J. *Jackson* and ~~Mrs. Jerry (Susan)~~ *(both?)* Wilson, of San Bernadino, (California), ~~He is also survived by~~ *and* six grandchildren.

~~Last sad rites~~ *(Funeral services* will be Monday at 11 a.m. at the United Methodist Church. Friends may call at the Sowerberry Funeral Home Sunday from 6 to 9 p.m. and Monday until 10:15 a.m. Burial will be in the city cemetery.

(#)

McGinnis Obit

Margaret "Maggie" McGinnis, 77 years young, of 3130 Porter Way, died of natural causes Friday at 11 a.m. in a local hospital.

Maggie was born May 31, 1903, in Evansville, Indiana, to Robert and Ruth Flint McGinnis. She married Terrence McGinnis in 1920 in

Evansville. He died in 1960. She was an employee of Walker Brothers Department Store for 42 years, where she loved her work as a saleswoman in the cosmetic department.

Surviving are two daughters, Roberta Richardson, and Pearl Moore, both of San Francisco, Calif., five granchikldren, six great-grand-children and a sister, June Moon, of Evansville.

Funeral services will be held Wednesday at 11 am at Sowerberry Funeral Home, where friends may call a half hour prior to services. Internment, City Cemetary.

Piper Obit

Walter Piper, known as the top newspaper editor in the state of New York, died Thursday night after a seizure which police attributed to excessive drinking. The exact cause has not been determined.

Mr. Piper, a lifelong resident of New York City, joined the Alternative Times as a reporter shortly after graduation from New York University in 1951. Born in Queens on Oct. 1, 1930, he often professed his love for the city. He moved up to chief copy editor of the weekly newspaper in 1957 and retained that role until his death.

In a column Friday, the Alternative Times said he was "the most oustanding journalist to come down the pike in this century and a man who had no peer in this state at the time of his death."

Hillary Obit

Donald Hillary, 51, died Friday evening.

Services will be held at the Parker Brothers Memorial Chapel at
5 p.m. Sunday evening.

Mr. Hillary was a physical education instructor at Hillside High
School. He served in that position for 29 years after graduation from
the University of Michigan.

He is survived by his widow, Jean; sons Tad, Ann Arbor; James,
Vermontville, Mich.; and daughter Jane, Brooklyn, New York.

Zanuck

LOS ANGELES -- Darryl F. Zanuck, co-founder of 20th Century-Fox
and last of the great movie moguls, died Saturday at 77.

He died at Desert Hospital in Palm Springs, where he was hospi-
talized Oct. 29 after suffering a heart attack. The hospital attributed
his death to stroke and complications from pneumonia.

Zanuck began as a writer but was primarily a man of ideas. He
retired in 1971, not long after he was dismissed as chief executive
officer of 20th Century-Fox after continuing losses at the studio
followed the big money-making decades.

A complex figure and the archtypical film tycoon, he liked to say
he created his own legend, exemplified by the title of his autobiography,
"Don't Say Yes Until I Finish Talking."

-- more --

222/Zanuck

Zanuck was the father of the screen musical. His early hits included "Forty-Second Street and "Gold Diggers of Broadway." Later he helped launch the semidocumentary and films based on current head-lines, such as "I Am a Fugitive From a Chain Gang."

He formed 20th Century Pictures with Joseph M. Schenck, then head of United Artists, and in 1935 became head of the company created by the merger of 20th Century and Fox Film Corp., a firm nine times the size of 20th Century.

Three times, in 1937, 1944 and 1950, he won the Academy of Motion Picture Arts and Sciences Irving G. Thalberg Award for the producer making the greatest contribution to the screen.

He was born in Wahoo, Neb., where his father owned a hotle. When he was 6, his family moved to Los Angeles. He got his first job in movies at 8, as an extra wearing the costume of an Indian girl. When his father discovered he had been playing hooky from Page Military Academy to watch the filming of movies at the old Esaanay lot in Glendale, he was shipped back to Nebraska.

At the age of 14 he managed to enlisted in the Nebraska National Guard, in a unit heading for service on the Mexican border. He also served in France as a private in the 163rd Infantry Division.

In France he began to write, and after the war, on the strength of a story sold to Phycial Culture Magazine, he set out for Hollywood to begin a writing career.

-- more --

3333/Zanuck

It didn't come easy. For four years he held an assortment of odd jobs efore breaking in with Warner Brothers as a writer to Rin-Tin-Tin, the great dog star. When he wa graduated to pictures with human stars he had 19 fil mcredits in a single year. In 1927 he became the studio's boss, with a jump in salary from $125 to $5,000 a week.

When sound pictures seemed inevitable, Warners gave him the job of making the first of these. The result was the first feature-length musical, "The Jazz Singer," starring Al Jolsen. This was followed by "The Singing Fool".

He helped to create such stars as Tyrone Power, James Cagney and Edward G. Robinson. He was the producer of two Academy Award-winning films, "All About Eve" and the first movie treatment of anti-semitism, "Gentleman's Agreement."

In World War II, Zanuck served as a lieutenant colonel in the Signal Corps, making training and documentary films for the Army. After the war he turned out such films as "Winged Victory," "Wilson," "The Razor's Edge," "David and Bathsheba," "Viva Zapata" and "The Man in the Gray Flannel Suit."

His wife, Virginia, and children, Darrylin Pineda, Susanne Savineau and Richard, a film producer, and 14 grandchildren survive. Funer services will be Thursday at Westwood United Methodist Church at a time to be announced.

-30-

Whitney

George William Whitney, 57, committed suicide Tuesday by shooting himself in the head with a .38-caliber revolver.

Police said Whitney was found in the study of his home, sitting in a chair and with the revolver in his hand.

A spokesman said the body was found by a relative, who entered the house through a back window after receiving no response to telephone calls and knocking on the door. Whitney apparently had been dead for about six hours, police said.

He was a salesman for Walters Brothers Inc., and had worked for the clothing company for 16 years. Survivors include his wife, Mary; sons Jason, 12, and Andrew, 10; and a duaghter, Marie, 8.

Private services will be held. The family asks that in lieu of flowers, donations be sent to the American Cancer Society.

Wadsworth

J. Wellington Wadsworth, 62, who served seven terms as Congressman from the 4th District until he lost a bitter election because of a sex scandal, died Thursday at his home in La Jolla, Calif.

Death was attributed to a heart attack. Wadsworth had lived in California since he retreated from public life following his defeat in 1976.

He was defeated because of his arrest on charges of soliciting

2/Wadsworth

sex acts from a police decoy prostitute in the seamy North Side on
July 21, 1976, at the height of the Congressional sex scandals.

Wadsworth protested his innocence to the electorate and in two
trials, in the city court and after appeal in district court, but was
convicted in both. He refused to bow to pressure from the Republican
party to withdraw from the election and lost in a landslide to Roscoe
Hayden, a Democrat.

Wadsworth was a broadcasting executive before he served in his
first elected office, as an Elk County commissioner. He served two
terms on the commission before making his successful bid for Congress.

After leaving Congress he worked as a disc jockey for a San Diego
radio station.

Until his defeat in 1976, Wadsworth was never seriously challenged
for re-election. He won an easy victory in taking the congressional
seat away from Ned Gumbleton, a Democrat who had held the seat in the
traditionally Democratic district for 12 terms.

As a freshman representative, Wadsworth served on two House-Senate
conference committees, an unusual distinction. He authored numerous
pieces of legislation, including the Heppenheim-Wadsworth Labor Act of
1970. He served on the Armed Forces Committee and in his last term was
on the Education and Labor Committee and Judiciary Committee.

_Wadsworth served in the United States Navy for four years in
World War II as a carrier pilot and won the Navy Cross in the Battle
of Iwo Jima. He rose the rank of lieutenant commander.

3/Wadsworth

He is a graduate of Fowler University, where he was student body president. He served one term on Fowler's Board of Trustees.

He married Rosemarie Whitman June 21, 1946. She survives, as do three children, J. Wellington Wadsworth Jr., Sarah W. Smith and Alicia Banner, all of La Jolla.

Funeral services will be Saturday in La Jolla. The family requests that in lieu of flowers contributions in his memory be made to the American Heart Association.

# # #

22. SPORTS

Every morning across the United States, millions of people unfold their newspaper, glance quickly at the front page, and then flip to the section that interests them most—sports. For countless men, and many women, that first cup of coffee just isn't the same without the sports page. Reading the sports page is part of preparing for the day, whether the destination is an assembly line or an executive suite. Sports have a universal appeal, cutting across social and economic boundaries. Saturday's college football game, Sunday's pro basketball game, or last night's major league baseball game are just as likely to open a dialogue between strangers as is a comment about the weather.

Editing sports copy poses a special challenge not only because of the nature of the games and the specialized rules involved, but also because of the sophistication of the audience. It is obvious that the percentage of avid sports-page readers at least matches—and probably exceeds—the percentage of avid readers of political, business, or other news.

The proliferation of entire pages of small-type box scores and statistical material in sports sections is testimony to that. Crowded for space, many papers carry box scores instead of stories on a number of games or limit the story portion to a paragraph or two. The avid follower of sports can scrutinize the statistical data and reconstruct the highlights without a story.

There was a time when sports pages were dominated by the major college and professional events—baseball, basketball, and football—with proper attention given to championship boxing matches and a few major horse races. Today the public's appetite encompasses a wide variety of other sports, largely participatory as well as spectator. A sports editor is now just as likely to hear a complaint about a missing Little League baseball score or Wednesday night bowling league result as to hear a complaint about a missing college football report.

Television, sensing a seemingly insatiable demand for sports entertainment in the United States, has popularized such once-unheard-of national and international competition as power lifting, superstars, skateboarding, hang gliding, wrist wrestling, tractor pulling, and darts, to name but a random few. Meanwhile, big money has found its way to pro golf, tennis, and bowling. Editors, knowing that fans like to read about what they've seen on television, are faced with ever-increasing demands for results, stories, and statistics. Americans have also immersed themselves in hunting, fishing, camping, hiking, and jogging. Newspapers, in addition to squeezing in everything else, are printing long lists of fishing conditions, features on the outdoors, and tips on staying in shape.

In such an atmosphere, and with advertising taking an ever-increasing portion of newspaper space, something has to give. Ultimately, it means ever tighter game stories and more statistics. Hence, the need for a sharp pencil.

Morning papers have the advantage in reporting results, since most competition concludes during their publication cycle, so editors on afternoon papers must use ingenuity to hold readers. It just isn't enough to repeat the scores. It is necessary to take a featurized approach, perhaps starting with an analytical comment about the contest and not even mentioning the score until the third paragraph or later. For instance, a morning story might read:

NEW YORK — Chester Williams lashed a two-run double down the left-field line with two out in the ninth inning Saturday to give the New York Bullets a 3-2 International League baseball victory over visiting Rochester.

The afternoon piece might take this approach:

NEW YORK — "It was that new aluminum bat, man. I knew I was gonna rip one."

Chester Williams flashed a wide grin as he said it, and the good-natured guffaws of his eavesdropping teammates added to the post-game merriment in the New York locker room Saturday night. Just minutes earlier, Williams' line-drive double to left with two out in the ninth inning had given the Bullets a come-from-behind 3-2 International League baseball victory over Rochester.

As an editor, you must be alert to the nuances of deadlines and follow-up stories. Sports pages help sell newspapers. A good editor will realize this, even if sports may seem intellectually trivial when placed against such subjects as world affairs, government, economics, crime, and energy.

Some critics place sports coverage in the general classification of entertainment and advertising, merely camouflaged as serious journalism. This is too harsh, because important issues involving rights, equality, and opportunity emerge in athletic competition as well as in business and politics. However, it also is true that the majority of sports copy is a byproduct of promotion, rather than response to real demand. In many communities, for instance, countless public meetings or performances that outdraw minor league sports are given scant notice, while sports have space guaranteed every day. It is safe to say that sports coverage has a hometown bias designed more to win support than to inform. Sportswriters and broadcasters quickly become friends of owners, managers, coaches, and players. Their own jobs may depend upon the success of the sport to which they've been assigned.

The ratio of soft to hard news is far greater in sports than in other areas of coverage. Traditionally, midweek sports pages have been filled with personality stories, pregame buildups, and other material regarded by critics as superfluous. The extension and overlapping of sports seasons, spurred by television coverage and promotion, has increased the number of "hard" stories appearing during the week, but midweek pages continue to be dominated more by what critics would call puffery than by serious journalism.

At the same time, new trends are obvious. In addition to reporting on a wide variety of leisure-time and recreation pursuits, writers are analyzing sports in the broad, social context. No longer are features limited to the narrow framework of Saturday's outcome and next week's buildup. Some editors, in their never-ending search for space, have shrunk midweek sports pages and granted extra columns or pages on heavy game days.

Sports coverage seems to be turning more and more in the direction of true journalism, but it still has a long way to go. There's a great need for editors who view sports as part of society in general and treat it as such, rather than as a sacred enclave for the participants and a few privileged press-box observers.

Sports is an area where the wire services fall short of their claim to report news objectively and not participate in events. The All-America teams, Outstanding Players, Comeback Player, Coach of the Year, and weekly team rankings—even on the high school level—are products of the wire services. This is boosterism at its most obvious and tarnishes the reputation the wire services otherwise have earned for detached, responsible coverage. Many newspapers have begun to turn away from such hoopla, giving All-America teams and weekly rankings only enough space for listings in small-size agate type—as opposed to front-of-the-section display complete with photos.

Still, it is possible to write almost any type of pregame, actual game, postgame, or game analysis story from a formula. In other areas of news coverage, words and phrases have become clichés. In sports, entire stories have become clichés: the coach of the undefeated team perpetually fearing the upcoming game with an underdog opponent; the player coming off the bench to run for "x" touchdowns and pass for "y" others; the winning coach describing how badly the team wanted to win; the losing coach decrying the team's "lack of intensity"; the midweek feature comparing the teams' supposed strengths on the basis of past statistics; the postmortem on the same statistical basis—one literally could write a book on such stories.

Some knowledgeable critics, in light-hearted fashion, have gone so far as to construct fill-in-the-blanks forms with word choices from which the writer may select, depending upon the situation. A baseball pitcher, for instance, may *handcuff* an opponent by allowing four hits. *Handcuff* is inappropriate, however, if the opponent should get a dozen hits—even if the final score of the game is the same in both cases. Instead of *handcuff*, the pitcher has *scattered* a dozen hits. This is but a modest example.

Baseball, the sport that probably has the most clichés merely because it has been popular—and promoted—longer than others, is especially fertile territory for cliché-hunters. A list of baseball clichés, with appropriate translations, appears at the end of this chapter, just before the exercises. You may find this section helpful if you are asked to edit sports copy.

There is no reason why sports cannot be reported in the same way as other events, using the necessary terminology without cloaking it in unintelligible gibberish that confuses the uninformed and merely amuses the knowledgeable. Some editors occasionally send general assignment reporters to sports events in an effort to generate copy that the casual follower can understand.

The wire services, although guilty of the promotion cited here, probably come as close to handling sports as news as anyone. For example, they urge their staffers not to use team nicknames, because stories usually are transmitted across state boundaries. When Oregon is playing Oregon State, the casual reader in New Jersey may be lost upon learning that "the Ducks moved to the Beaver 40-yard line." The wire services also urge staffers to avoid clichés. Still, the temptation remains strong to treat sports as an area deserving of special phraseology beyond the rules and equipment of the game, perhaps because many who are asked to cover sports regard it as trivial.

Three wire-service writers, for instance, once came upon a phrase none had seen before—a football player "tore a touchdown trail" through the opposing team. They were so taken by its alliteration and originality that they decided to promote it—by using it in every appropriate situation in the future. Throughout the season they used it time and again as game after game offered the opportunity to include it. However, on one occasion a member of the threesome covered a game in which all the points were scored on kicks or passes. The writer, not willing to break the string, imaginatively reported that late in the game the top runner of one team—upon being tackled—"threw up his hands at his inability to tear a touchdown trail."

There was a time when seemingly everyone wanted to be a sportswriter. In recent years, however, the popularity of sportswriting as a speciality has dwindled. Many young people say they cannot cover sports because they do not understand the rules. This is a mistake. To a prospective employer, this may be akin to saying you can't cover a business story because you don't know the intricacies of the stock market, or that you can't cover a city council meeting because you didn't major in government. A baseball game is no more difficult to cover than is a proposed bond issue. It simply requires a willingness to learn. The same is true of editors. A young editor must be willing to handle any story—including sports—because the editor's task is to reduce the complex to the simple.

And regardless of how you feel personally about sports, remember that it is part of the American social and recreational fabric. It is news. As an editor, you should approach it positively—not as critic or fan, but as a professional.

Some Baseball Cliché Terms (there are many more)
For a strikeout:
Whiff
Fan
"K"
For a walk:
Free pass
Base on balls
"Lost him"
For a home run:
Circuit clout
Fourmaster
Round-tripper
For a triple:
Three-bagger
For a double:
Two-bagger
For a single:
Safety
When a batter is up with men on base:
There are ducks on the pond.
When there are runners at first and third base:
There are men at the corners.
When a runner is on second or third base:
He's in scoring position.
When a batter gets a single, double, triple, and home run in one game:
He hit for the circuit.
When a batter is hitless:
He took the collar.

When a batter takes a third strike without swinging:
The pitcher caught him looking.
When a runner is tagged out at a base after a quick throw by the pitcher:
The pitcher caught him napping.
When a pitcher is having a good day:
He's throwing aspirin tablets.
He's giving them the dark one.
A high fly ball:
A can of corn.
When a fielder has plenty of time to catch a ball:
He camped under it.
When a batter fouls off a pitch:
He got a piece of it.
When a pitcher throws a slower than normal pitch:
He pulled the string.
He threw a change-up.
The nickname for a pitcher whose specialty is replacing other pitchers:
A fireman.
When a player is very fast:
He can fly.
When two men are out on a single play, an event commonly known as a double play:
It's a twin killing.
A left-handed pitcher:
A southpaw.
Lefty.
A portsider.
A right-handed pitcher:
He deals from the starboard side.
The equipment worn by the catcher:
Tools of ignorance.
When a team has failed to score:
There are goose eggs on the scoreboard.
They've been shut out.
When a pitcher has held a team to few hits:
He handcuffed them.
He twirled a (number of hits)-hitter.
When a pitcher allows a lot of hits but still wins:
He scattered (number of hits)
Other names for inning:
Stanza
Frame
When a pitcher intentionally throws a ball close to a batter:
He's keeping him loose.
Brushing him back.
Throwing a duster.
A curve ball:
A bender.
A hook.
The manager of a team:
The skipper.
Second base:
The keystone sack.

Third base:
The hot corner.
Umpires:
The men in blue.
The spot from where the pitcher throws the ball:
The mound.
The hill.
The rubber.
An outstanding catch of a fly ball:
A circus catch.
A stolen base:
A theft.

And, to cover a multitude of situations:

For a short fly ball that may fall in for a single, double, or triple, or be caught:
Texas Leaguer, blooper, humpback liner, or dying quail.

Master these and you will never be confused when you read a baseball story submitted by a reporter.

SELECTED READINGS

Gelfand, Louis, and Harry E. Heath, Jr. *Modern Sportswriting*. Ames, Iowa: Iowa State University Press, 1969. A comprehensive look behind the scenes in the specialized field of covering, writing, and editing sports. Chapters on the major sports. Includes the desk job and page design.

Isaacs, Neil D. *Jock Culture, U.S.A.: The Takeover of American Life by the Morality of Overemphasized Sports*. New York: W. W. Norton, 1978. The title says it all.

EXERCISES

Baseball

MT. ANGEL - After taking the collar in the first 8 stanzas, Joe Wilson stroked a fourmaster with men at the corners last night to give Mission a 3-2 win over front-running Mt. Angel in Western League diamond action.

Tim Heater, in a fireman's role, protected the win for the Beetdiggers starting twirler, Ron Fisher, by whiffing all three Bearcat batsmen in the bottom of the final frame.

Wilson had fanned twice and was robbed of a safety on a sparkling catch of a humpback liner before unloading his circuit clout with one man gone in Mission's last chance against Mt. Angel portsider Manuel Perez, who had shackled the Beetdiggers on five safeties.

(Baseball)

(MT.) ANGEL - ~~After taking the collar in the first 8 stanzas,~~ Joe Wilson ~~stroked a fourmaster with men at the corners last night~~ *hit a three-run home run in the top of the ninth inning* to give Mission a 3-2 ~~win over front-running~~ Mt. Angel *Western League baseball victory over first-place* *last night* ⊗ ~~in Western League diamond action.~~

Tim Heater, ~~in a fireman's role, protected the win for the~~ *replacing Mission starting pitcher* ~~Beetdiggers starting twirler,~~ Ron Fisher, ~~by whiffing~~ *struck out* all three ~~Bearcat batsmen~~ *Mount Angel batters* in the bottom of the ~~final frame~~ *ninth inning*.

Wilson ~~had fanned~~ *struck out* twice and ~~was robbed of a safety on a sparkling~~ *flied out once* ~~catch of a humpback liner~~ before ~~unloading his circuit clout with one~~ *hitting his home run with one* ~~man gone~~ *man out* in Mission's last chance against (Mt.) Angel ~~portsider~~ *lefthander* Manuel Perez, who had ~~shackled the Beetdiggers on~~ *allowed* five ~~safeties~~ *hits*.

Track

RIMROCK - Ed Norton, competing for Western Sprinters, overcame an early burst by John Alquisto of the High Steppers Track Club to take first place in the star-studded 100-meter dash at the Submurst Industries Superstar Invitational track and field meet Saturday at Rimrock University.

Norton, who was clocked in 10.49 seconds, leaned forward at the finish line to nudge Al Foster of the Beach Brigade by 0.8 seconds. Steve Walker of the Philadelphia Stevedores took third place, John Dames of Watsonville (Ca.) was fourth and Alquisto faded at the end to finish last.

James Beegers, competing before a home crowd, had a hot hand in the high jump and won the blue ribbon by clearing seven-feet-two. The Rimrock University star missed in three attempts at seven-three after the competition was over.

The powerful Rimrock women's team dominated its competition as Non Norton won the 1,500 meters and doubled back in the 800 for 20 of the Conquistadores' 33 points.

Meet

The State track team ended the season on a happy note over the weekend as they won their first duel meet of the season by downing the Air Force Academy, 78-76 in a meet held at Colorado Springs.

The State combined their track and field talent to capture 10 first places to scuttle the Falcon flying machine.

Weightman Ken Hoe took first placde in the shot put by tossing the ball 49-7 3/4. The big man also finished in third place in the discus.

State triple jumper Bud Anderson picked off a first place in his event by leaping 48-2 1/4. His brother Dave finished off a sweep of first placed by the family by winning the intermediate hurdles in a time of 54.6.

Bill Hyland was State's only tripple winner as he took first place in the 44 in 48.4 and anchored both of State's two winning relay teams, the 440 relay and the mile relay.

Mark Eden won the 880-yard run with a 1:59.8 clocking while Chick Crane did the same in his event, the three-mile run, with a time of 15:37.2.

State dominated the sprints, with Bimbo Bingham taking first in the 100-yard dash and Mercury Binks finishing first in the 220. Bingham's winning time in the 100 of 9.4 is the fastest the speedy little runner, who also doubles as a flankerback in football, has run.

Binks also had a good time in the 220 turning the distance in 22 seconds flat.

Besides Hyland, the winning 440-relay team was made up of Bingham, Binks and Bill McCarty, while the mile crew consisted of Smith, Trayner, Shields, and of course, Hyland.

#

Trim 1/3

Bowling

SAN JOSE, CALIF.--Mark Roth and Marshall Holman combined their outstanding bowling talents here Sunday to win the $80,000 Columbia PBA Doubles Classic, their second doubles victory in the last three years.

Two years ago, the duo triumphed here: they were third last year

Bowling -2-

in Seattle; and then Sunday they topped Californians Larry Lamb, Santa Rosa, and Palmer Fallgren, Sacramento, 406-374, while a national television audience (NBC-TV) looked on. The title was Roth's 19th and Holman's ninth.

The vistory represented another achievement for Roth as he became only the second player in PBA history to win three years in a row at the same bowling center. After teaming with Holman to win at Saratoga Lanes in 1977, he won the San Jose Open, a singles event, in 1978. Earl Anthony first won three straight in Waukegan, ILL., 1975-76-77.

After winning 11 of their 12 games of match play, Roth, North Arlington, N. J., and Holman, Medford, Ore., were top-seeded into the finals, with Laub and Fallgren, Jeff Mattingly, Tacoma, Wash. and Steve Martin, Kingsport, Tenn., and Dave Kappel, Chicago and Bob Handley, Fairway, Kan., rounding out the finals field.

Mattingly and Martin outlasted the Kappel-Handley duo in a 14-pin thriller, 413-399, and then the tables were turned on Mattingly and Martin, as Laub and Fallgren cameup with a spine-tingling one-pin victory, 378-377.

That set the stage for the title match, and although Holman opened in the first frame, Roth came up with a spare and a double and Holman responded with three strikes of his own to give them a lead they never relinquished.

Individually, Holman came up with a 213 and Roth a 193 in the title game, while Laub had a 171 and Fallgren a 203.

Bowling -3-

Roth's $8,000 share of the winner's check put him back in the PBA money lead, with $64,190. Earl Anthony, Kent, Wash., is second with $57,990, and Holman, with his $8,000, is third with $51,850.

Here are the leading money winners:

Pos.	Name City	Number Tournaments	Amount
1.	Mark Roth, North Arlington N.J.	14	$64,190
2.	Earl Anthony, Kent, Wash.	16	57,990
3.	Marshall Holman, Medford, Ore.	13	51,850
4.	Dick Ritger, River Falls, Wis.	15	49,670
5.	George Pappas, Charlotte, N. C.	17	47,015
6.	Johnny Petraglia, Staten Island, N.Y.	15	40,160

Fastpitch

The first set of statistics for the fastpitch travel league were released last week. In pitching statistics, the lowest earned run averages are Randy Beckstead with 0.55, Bob Mosteller 1.14 and Steve Leishman 2.25. In strikeouts, Leishman leads the league with 66 in 56 innings followed by Vaughn Alvey with 45 in 42 innings, Ron Nelson with 28 in 25 innings and Bob Mosteller with 42 in 42. Some of the pitching stats are mis-leading this early in the season due to the large discrepancy in the number of innings each pitcher has pitched.

In offensive categories, the leagues leading hitters are Bonner Warr with a .500 average followed by Cary Toone and Stan Buchanan both

at .464, Ken Hackmeister at .440 and Butch Latey and Steve Haycock both
at .417. Those are the only batters over the .400 mark with a minimum
of 24 at bats thus far. In home runs, there is a 3 way tie between
Cary Toone, Stan Buchanan and Bob Mosteller each having 3 round trippers.

Chicago

    Jerry Martin drove in three runs and Dennins Lamp and Dick Tidrow
combined to scatter eight hits Saturday to lead the Chicago Cubs to a
5-3 victory over the Los Angeles Dodgers.

    The Dodgers jumped to a 2-0 lead in the first inning when Davey
Lopes led off with his 16th homer and Steve Garvey stroked an RBI single.
The Cubs came back in their half of the first when Dave Kingman's single
scored Ted Sizemore, who walked and went to second on Bill Buckner's
single. Martin's two-run single to left put Chicago ahead 3-2.

    The Dodgers tied it in the second when Gary Thomasson drew a walk
from Lamp, 5-2, Joe Ferguson singled and losing pitcher Rick Sutcliffe,
6-4, singled in the tying run. The Cubs went ahead 4-3 in the sixth
when Kingman was safe on shortstop Bill Russill's error, stole second
and scored on Martin's double and added a run in the seventh when
Buckner's single scored Sizemore -- who had singled and stolen second.

    Tidrow gave up two hits over the final three innings to pick up his
second save with the Cubs.

                                   #

Miners   Trim 1/2

El Paso, TX -- For the second time in the last five years, the U. T. El Paso Miner track team has won the NCAA Outdoor Track and Field Championships.

And there was little doubt about it. After finishing second or tied for second the past three years, the Miners rose to the occasion and scored 50 points at the end of Friday's finals, enough to win the meet then. And on Saturday they added 14 more to compile a lofty 64 points to win the team competition going away. Villanova was a distant second with 48 points while UCLA was third with 36.

In all the Miners scored two firsts, four seconds and a third, a fourth and a fifth for the scoring, spread over nine individuals. A possible double by freshman Suleiman Nyambui and sophomore Michael Musyoki in the 5,000 and 10,000 never materialized since the Miners didn't need the points on Saturday and Coach Ted Banks scratched them from the 5,000. The two had taken first and second in the 10,000 on Friday.

The win was a sweet one for Banks and his crew, runner-ups for three years after winning the crown in Provo. For Banks, the NCAA gold was his tenth, including four indoor titles, four cross country titles and two out-door.

The two individual winners were Suleiman Nyambui who won the 10,000 in 28:01.38, unseating teammate and defending champ Michael Musyoki who was second in 28:03.25. Sophomore sprinting sensation

Miners - 2

Jerman Deal surprised the field by winning the 100 meters in a
blistering 10.19.

In addition to Musyoki's second in the 10,000, senior shot putter
Hans Almstrom was second with a toss of 64-10 3/4, senior discus thrower
Svein Walvik was second with a throw of 207-0 and freshman hammer
thrower was second at 218-2. Thommie Sjoholm, a sophomore, was third
in the hammer with a 214-1 effort, James Rotich picked up fourth place
points in the 5,000 in 13:42.24 and sophomore Peter Lemashon was fifth
in the 800 meters in 1:46.93. Six other Miner competitors failed to
score.

Only two of the nine scorers will be lost to graduation and all of
the underclassmen are sophomores or freshmen. And of those six who
participated and didn't socre, four are freshmen with the other two
juniors.

"This has to be the best group I've ever coached," said a proud
Banks following the meet. "We got some great leadership from our two
seniors (Almstrom and Walvik) who really wanted this one. They helped
fire the guys up and I think it really helped us on Friday. I"m so
very proud of these guys and the way they really came through for the
team. I was happy I didn't have to double Nyambui and Musyoki, since
I don't like to double them in the nationals if at all possible."

The Miners completed a fine year, winning the NCAA Cross Country
title in the fall and took second in the NCAA Indoor Championships in

Miners - 3

March and in that one, had it not been for a controversial disqualifica-
tion in the distance medley relay, the Miners would have won that title,
too.

"It was good win for us," Bank said. "And it's also nice to have
48 of those points coming back for next year along with some guys we
think will score next year, too."

#

Prep-Central League

Tom "Tornado" Thompson, Chesterfield's sensational sophomore
scatback, tore a 78-yard touchdown trail down the left sideline in the
fourth quarter Friday, sparking the Beetdiggers to a 14-7 gridiron
triumph over the Wallaceburg Warriors before 5,000 screaming fans at
Nathanson Stadium.

The win gave undefeated Chesterfield a 9-0 record on the season
while Wallaceburg dropped to 6-3.

Wallaceburg scored first when signal-caller Jeff Amundson took
the snap, turned the left corner, and scampered untouched into the end
zone, 29 yards away, with three ticks remaining in the first quarter.
Arvil Jones split the uprights with a perfect extra-point placement to
make it 7-0.

The Beetdiggers squared it 2:06 before intermission when Jerry Torbert, Chesterfield's all-conference linebacker, intercepted an Amundson aerial near the Warrior bench at the Warrior 45 and tiptoed down the sideline to score. Torbert also kicked the PAT.

Neither team crossed midfield in the second half until Thompson got loose on his game-winning sprint after taking a handoff from quarterback Ross White with 7:45 to go and breaking into the open over right tackle.

23. SCIENCE, MEDICINE, AND OTHER TECHNICAL SUBJECTS

In serving a mass audience, reporters and editors strive for simplicity in expression. Researchers in science, medicine, and other technical, highly specialized fields generally feel no such obligation. They write not for the general public, but for their peers. Reader understanding of complex terminology is assumed. To a person without such scientific training, reading a technical article is like trying to decipher hieroglyphics. Therein lies a conflict that has opened a wide gulf between journalists and other professionals.

Journalists want everyone to understand; consequently, they use commonly understood terms. Scientists or medical researchers are uncomfortable with attempts to reduce precise, specialized language to common phrases. Too often, it is claimed, journalists seek dramatic angles to enliven what might be dull copy otherwise. A doctor, for instance, may find evidence that a component of pickles is helpful in preventing heart attacks. The news article resulting from the research may give the impression that eating pickles is good for your heart. The truth may be that the component must be taken in such large doses that a person would have to eat two jars of pickles every day to get the required benefit. The same benefit may be available from a prescription drug.

Several years ago it was reported that cancer developed in rats given ingredients common to birth control pills. Following nationally distributed reports on this, prices of the shares of some firms dealing in these drugs declined on the stock market. Many people saw an immediate cause-and-effect relationship between the drugs and the development of cancer, without considering dosage levels or differences between rats and people. Because of the tendency of people to jump to conclusions, stories about research must be precise and complete, even if drama and liveliness must be sacrificed.

A good editor should have at least a nodding acquaintance with such subjects as biology, chemistry, and other scientific subjects as well as with politics, economics, and other areas. This is one reason that journalism departments generally require a comparatively small number of hours for a major and encourage students to obtain a board liberal arts education. Editors are forced to deal with all kinds of subjects. An editor who is supervising an in-depth report on a scientific project would do well to read about the subject before going over the copy. In one case, an editor concerned with a feature on world food problems spent a month reading the books and articles of a scientist who would be quoted extensively in the report.

People who deal in research often are wary of the news industry, fearing misinterpretation or misquotation that will cause them embarrassment among their colleagues. It is important to win the source's confidence, and there is nothing unprofessional about checking a story with such a source to make sure there have been no misstatements or misinterpretations. This is not the same as giving the source the right to edit the story.

At the other end of the spectrum are researchers who regard publicity as a means of attaining recognition that will enhance their careers and their opportunities to obtain additional support for their endeavors. In dealing with a reluctant or aggressive researcher, an editor always must consider caution as a byword.

Many cancer victims understandably grasp at so-called miracle cures. People concerned about world food problems read with great interest about ideas on turning deserts into gardens. Such stories, usually exciting, seldom reflect reality years after their publication. Too often they are mere items of the moment, products of inventive public relations people, or publicity-conscious researchers seeking support.

A wise editor will examine a technical story carefully to make certain negative aspects are explored as a balance to the ballyhoo. If "x" is such a great idea, why isn't it being implemented at this very moment? The editor must ask, "What are the problems and the shortcomings?" These answers are as important as the promises. An editor must be on guard against the bandwagon syndrome—the temptation to headline an interesting idea just because it is new, novel, promising, hopeful, and popular. Many reputable news organizations refuse to touch stories of a scientific, medical, or other specialized nature until reports first have appeared in scholarly journals of the professions involved—meaning that they have been examined by people with a recognized expertise among their peers. As with all guidelines, this criterion should not be taken as an absolute. There are times when articles about medicine or science should not await journal publication. That, however, is a matter for case-by-case judgment. Caution remains the best guideline.

Weather affects everyone, so weather is always of interest, although it's only "news" when extreme or unusual. Weather, like sports, can take on the appearance of a foreign language if a reporter chooses to use the technical terminology of the weather service. A good editor will strike references to *isobars*, *upper-level air charts*, and other matters of concern only to meteorologists. The bottom line in a weather story is its relationship to the reader—and nothing should be permitted to cloud it.

Here are some examples of how technical stories can be improved. In each of these cases, the editor would have to request a rewrite, instead of simply editing the copy as written.

Original

LOS ANGELES (NS) — Acute lymphocytic leukemia may be eradicated if the efforts of researchers are successful, an article in the *Moorhead Medical Journal* said Monday as it announced the development of a drug made from orange rinds.

"Tests on high-risk cases have given us hope that we can eventually achieve a 100 percent survival rate," said Dr. Joseph Tubmann, director of the Walters-Mather Research Center. "This is a very promising anti-carcinogen and our research staff is convinced its effectiveness can be increased."

He said the drug, known as Lukocite, has been more effective than others given in standard treatment.

Revision

LOS ANGELES (NS) — A drug made from orange rinds has been more successful in treating acute childhood-leukemia cases than have drugs used in standard treatment for the disease, says an article in the June issue of the *Moorhead Medical Journal.*

The survival rate for victims of acute lymphocytic leukemia, a cancer of the blood, has been 75 percent among 565 patients treated with the orange rind-based drug Lukocite over the past two years, the article said. It contrasted this with a survival rate of 20 percent for 800 patients treated with drugs commonly used against the disease for the past 15 years.

It said the tests have been limited to patients in advanced stages of the disease, but that the drug may be used soon on patients in early stages as well.

(Follow with additional explanation about the disease and its history, subordinating predictions.)

The importance of caution in handling medical reports cannot be overstressed. Researchers, being human, are prone to become excited about their work. It is important to play down highly optimistic claims and to concentrate instead on facts, even if the result is a story lacking liveliness. Also, it is essential to explain medical terms, paraphrasing them so people outside the profession will understand. Many know leukemia as a dread disease, but do not know its nature.

Original

WASHINGTON (NS) — A U.S. Nuclear Commission official said Tuesday he is "very optimistic" about the future of granite formations as disposal grounds for the nation's nuclear wastes.

"Critics of nuclear energy will have little to complain about if our experiments are as successful as we expect them to be," commission chairman R. Randolph Pinder said at a news conference called to outline the disposal program.

Pinder said that as he was speaking, technicians were lowering two-ton cannisters of nuclear reactor waste into 1,000-foot-deep holes burrowed into granite at three locations in two states.

Revision

WASHINGTON (NS) — Granite formations at two remote sites in Idaho and one in Wyoming are being tested as burial grounds for nuclear wastes, a spokesman for the U.S. Nuclear Commission announced Tuesday.

R. Randolph Pinder, commission chairman, said that as he spoke, two-ton cannisters of solid nuclear reactor waste were being lowered into 1,000-foot-deep holes burrowed into formations north of Idaho Falls, Idaho, and east of Laramie, Wyo. He said he would not disclose the precise locations until the holes were sealed Wednesday.

Pinder said granite formations may be ideal disposal sites because of their high density and remoteness from population centers.

As with medical stories, it is better to stress facts than to lead with optimistic claims. Opponents of nuclear energy would have cause to claim bias in the original version. The low-key approach in the revision does not take sides and it subordinates Pinder's optimism.

Original

CHICAGO (NS) — All the fish in Lake Michigan may die from a disease known as Roland's Syndrome unless industries stop using the lake as a dumping ground for wastes, a scientist said Tuesday.

"I'm not sure it will happen," Dr. Colin A. Norman of the Walters Marine Research Laboratory said in an interview. "But our figures show the syndrome is spreading beyond salmon to other fish."

He said the disease, which affects the gills, was found in 15 percent of the salmon tested last week as opposed to 9 percent in a similar test a year earlier. He added that 10 other species of fish were found to be affected this year, as opposed to seven last year.

Revision

CHICAGO (NS) — A fatal gill disease caused by industrial pollution is increasing among Lake Michigan salmon and is spreading to other fish, a scientist said Tuesday.

Dr. Colin A. Norman of the Walters Marine Research Laboratory said the disease, known as Roland's Syndrome, kills fish by clogging the gills with infection. He said scientists have not determined why salmon are more vulnerable than other fish, but that a waste chemical from the papermaking process was responsible for the disease.

(Follow with statistics and subordinate the doomsday prediction, on which Norman hedged in the second paragraph of the original.)

Black warnings fall into the same category as blue-sky optimism. Such statements should be relegated to secondary status so they can make way for facts. Diseases, and their causes, should be described—not merely mentioned as asides to dramatic statements.

Original

HOUSTON (NS) — The orbiting Futura II space laboratory has ceased sending data back to Earth and will have "no further role in our program," the Houston Space Center announced today.

Futura II's transmission system malfunctioned two days ago after beaming its 85th batch of information to scientists, a center spokesman said. He said Futura II would be destroyed.

Revision

HOUSTON (NS) — After two years of sending outer-space radioactivity readings to Earth, the orbiting Futura II laboratory has malfunctioned and will be destroyed, the Houston Space Center announced today.

"The lab did a good job for us," a spokesman said, "but two other space laboratories are giving us similar radioactivity readings and we'll just rely on them."

He said an orbit-altering mechanism in the 200-pound Futura II would be activated by a signal from the Houston center and that the space laboratory would burn up upon reentering Earth's atmosphere.

Perspective is important in stories about satellites and space laboratories. Stories often assume that readers are well informed about devices that have been used for any length of time. It is essential to give the reader an immediate grasp of the overall picture instead of focusing on fragmentary quotes and statistics.

Original

LAS VEGAS (NS) — A sleek, slender, death-dealing missile nicknamed "The Sword" was successfully fired from an underground base in the Nevada desert, the Pentagon announced Wednesday.

"This adds both to our first-strike and retaliatory capacities," a spokesman said.

He added that "The Sword," which carries a payload of nerve gas, will be produced under a $200 million contract with Defense Dynamics Co. if Congress gives approval.

Revision

LAS VEGAS (NS) -- A missile carrying enough poison gas to kill everyone within a 20-mile radius of its explosion has been successfully test-fired in the Nevada desert, the Pentagon announced Wednesday.

At a news conference in Las Vegas, a spokesman said the missile—10 feet long, 2 feet wide and resembling an arrow in appearance—was launched from an underground site and exploded on target 30 miles away. He said it can be guided accurately for more than 2,000 miles and has been nicknamed "The Sword."

Weaponry stories are frequently faulted by meaningless descriptions when they should emphasize the capacities and purposes of the devices. Nicknames and contracts are secondary to giving the reader a quick grasp.

In summary, stories of a technical nature must be handled with special precision because of the need to translate terms into common language and to avoid overdramatizing the world of science. As with other stories, it is tempting to seize on dramatic and unusual elements to capture the reader's attention. However, this is a mistake when dealing with the scientific community. Attention should be focused on giving the reader a soberly stated perspective as quickly as possible, subordinating the dramatic.

SELECTED READINGS

Burkett, David Warren. *Writing Science News for the Mass Media*. Houston: Gulf Publishing Co., 1965. The field of science; problems, ethics for the media.

Farago, Peter. *Science and the Media*. London: Oxford University Press, 1976. A Briton's essay on the difficulties of communicating science and technical facts and ideas to the nonscientist.

Krieghbaum, Hillier. *Science and the Mass Media*. New York: New York University Press, 1967. How and why science news is diffused.

Parr, Leslie, ed. *Science of the Times*. New York: Times Books, 1978. An anthology of some of the *Times*'s best scientific reportage by many of the nation's foremost science writers, together with a useful introduction by Walter Sullivan that describes the range of the science writer's beat.

EXERCISES

Buggy

A mobile intensive care nursery, designed to transport premature or critically ill infants to receive specialized care will go into operation at Valley hospital on August 9.

Nicknamed the "Baby Buggy," the unit is actually a 22-foot motor home equipped to "save time" in giving specific attention to the needs of the infant as it is being transferred from one hospital to another.

"It will be equipped with all facilities to work with the infant, short of surgery," said Nadine Helfrich, director of therapy at the hospital.

Sophisticated equipment to be found in the "Baby Buggy" includes an open isolette (open top incubator with to supply warmth according to the temperature of the baby); a vital signs monitor which electronically keeps tab on blood pressure, respiration and so on, a transcutaneous oxygen monitor to measure arterial oxygen to establish the oxygen needs of the baby and a blood pressure monitor which uses sound waves to calculate blood flow on small infants to measure their blood pressure.

There is also a ventilator to provide mechanical breath for infants who are unable to adequately breath for themselves, a blood gas machine to help technicians evaluate the acide-base, ventilatory and oxygen requirement of the baby; a device to measure lung capacity and other items.

Cost of the equipment will exceed $65,000, Ms. Helfrich said.

The unit will operate primarily within a 60-mile radius of the

hospital. It can handle two infants at a time, but "we usually pick

up just one," she said.

                                            #

(Buggy)

A mobile intensive care nursery, designed to transport premature or
                                    where they can
critically ill infants to~ receive specialized care ~will go into opera-

tion at Valley hospital on (August) 9.

Nicknamed the "Baby Buggy," the unit is ~~actually~~ a 22-foot motor

home equipped to ~save time~ in giving specific attention to the needs

of the infant as it is being transferred from one hospital to another.

"It will be equipped with all facilities to work with the infant,

short of surgery," said Nadine Helfrich, director of therapy at the

hospital.

~~Sophisticated~~ equipment ~~to be found~~ in the "Baby Buggy" includes an

~~open isolette~~ (open=top incubator, ~~with to supply warmth according to~~

~~the temperature of the baby);~~ a vital signs monitor, ~~which electronically~~
                                                        s
~~keeps tab on blood pressure, respiration and so on, a transcutaneous~~

~~oxygen monitor to measure arterial oxygen to establish the oxygen needs~~
                                    including one that
~~of the baby and a blood pressure monitor which~~ uses sound waves) ~~to~~

~~calculate blood flow on small infants~~ to measure ~~their~~ blood pressure, *a)*
                                        that   *s*   *ing*
~~There is also a~~ ventilator ~~to~~ provide~ mechanical breath~ ~~for infants~~
and a highly sophisticated blood-gas machine (x)
~~who are unable to adequately breath for themselves, a blood gas machine~~

                                (*more*)

2/ Buggy

~~to help technicians evaluate the acide-base, ventilatory and oxygen~~

~~requirement of the baby; a device to measure lung capacity and other~~

~~items.~~

Cost ~~of the equipment will~~ exceed $65,000, Ms. Helfrich said.

The unit will operate primarily within a 60-mile radius of the

hospital. It can handle two infants ~~at a time, but "we usually pick~~

~~up just one," she said~~.

#

Environment

The cancer-causing potency of crude shale oil is equivalent to many

crude petroleums and petroleum products, but hydrotreatment, upgrading

the shale oil, greatly reduces this carcinogenic potency and there are

no hazards associated with oil shale solids, according to Joseph Troy,

environmenthealth coordinator for Hiller Corp., Los Angeles.

He was one of the speakers at a four-day conference, concluding

Saturday, at the Convention Center, which has attracted 165 scientists

and health specialists, including more than 30 from foreign countries.

It is sponsored by the new Center for Occupational and Environmental

Health at University Medical School, the National Institute for Occupa-

tional Safety and Health, the Society for Occupational and Environmental

Health and the Health Division.

Based on extensive information available today, a commercial oil

shale facility would not present any unusual or hazardous occupational exposures when operated with industrial hygiene standards and practices currently used in energy industries," Dr. Troy said.

Commenting on the state of the industry, which could have a profound effect on Uintak if developed commercially, since the area holds large deposits of the shale, the scientists said the industry, "is still awaiting birth after more than 55 years of being in labor" and technology exists for commercial development, which is being held up by economics, uncertainties from the high rate of inflation and the impaired capital market, government policy on crude oil prices, changing environmental restrictions and the level of crude oil imports.

Hitting the economic high points, the scientist said a 50,000 barrel-per-day commercial project (the smallest economically feasible) would cost an estimated $1.05 billion (in 1977 dollars). The selling price to achieve a 10 percent profit after taxes would be $16.50 per barrel for hydrotreated shale oil and $12.40 per barrel for raw shale oil.

He said a major problem with environmental regulations is that, while oil shale developers have been trying to design commercial plants, the target emission levels have been constantly changing.

Abortions

An American Civil Liberties Union (ACLU) attorney was here Friday to emphasize on the local level theat persons should continue to fight for the right to secure "safe, legal abortions."

Diane McMullen, Washington, D.C., met with representatives from

Planned Parenthood, the National Organization of Women and local attornie to talk about the continuing legal battles over the abortion issue.

Courts and legislatures are creating too narrow of standard for women who want abortions. Why shouldn't therapeutic abortions be allowed? she asked. Also, some states are even seeking to ban abortions in the case of rape and inceist and that shouldn't be done.

Ms. McMullen said her group will continue to fight for the right to choice in abortions on both the state and federal levels.

She left the city Friday night to fly to Pheonix, Ariz. where she will continue her work.

The ACLU's main purpose goal at the present is to work for long run success with state legislatures.

National polls, Ms. McMullen said, show that the majority of the citizens across the nation favor abortion. She admitted, however, that such majority feelings may not be the case in our state.

On a national scale, theough, she said legislators tend to ignore the polls and listen only to the anti-abortion factions.

The attorney is visiting several states in her capacity as council to the Reproductive Freedom Project, sponsored by the ACLU.

Since the U.S. Supreme Court decision that said states do not have to finance abortions, Ms. McMullen said the ACLU has taken a more active role in preparing groundwork for changing that matter.

"It is clear that we are losing the battle to keep abortion safe and legal for all woeman. A major reason for this turn of events is that the so called pro-lifers I prefer to call them compulsory pregnancy

people have formed well organized nationwide political action network,"
she said.

Donor

The General Hospital Volunteer Blood Bank has reached a milestone:
it's 1,000th donor.

On Thursday Clementine Waxford became the 1,000th person to give
the "gift of life" since the blood bank opened its doors in
January. The striking 22-year old brunette has donated several times
before.

"I'm glad to help out -- it is the least I can do," she said.
"Giving blood is not hard at all. In fact, it's kinda fun."

She was visiting the hospital laboratory Thursday to obtain her
pre-marital testing as her wedding date in August drew nearer. At the
lab, she was advised that pre-marital testing is done free of charge
when the participants donate a pint of blood. She liked the idea, and
the milestone became history.

"The first six months of the blood bank's operation have been an
exciting time for us," Yodella Sanguine, laboratory manager, said.
"Every donor that has helped us deserves royal treatment. We want them
all to know thay are all special to us."

Clementine said she intends to visit the blood bank regularly. For
one thing, she said, "the graham crackers and juice are great."

# # #

Melanoma

Obtaining a deep tan this summer raises a greater than normal risk of contracting a form of cancer known as melanoma, warns Dr. Sigmund Hertzskein.

The reason: cyclic sunspot activity is expected to be at its high point this summer.

According to Dr. Hertzskein, of the University Hospital, the incidence of melanoma increases during certain three-to-five-year periods. Such periods occur every eight to eleven years -- the same period of sunspot activity.

Sunspots, or electromagnetic storms on the sun's surface, reduce the earth's protective ozone layer, thereby exposing sunbathers to increased radiation, including ultraviolet-B, which is blamed for triggering malignant melanoma.

# #

Israel

Israel faces a growing problem of alcoholism, particularly among younger persons, an Israeli physician said on a visit here yesterday.

"Jews have been reported to be moderate drinkers and infrequent drunkards. During the last two decades it has become evident that Israel, too, faces a steadily growing problem of alcohol addiction," said Marinel Sagiv, M.D., a pathologist at Kaplan Hospital, Rehovot, Israel.

Dr. Sagiv says that until the mid-60s, alcohol addicts were rather inconspicuous in the general population of Israel. They were middle-aged men or older, and most of them had been born abroad. Nearly all of them held jobs, had a steady income and a regular social life. he says.

"Reports in the last 13 years indicate a sharp change in this pattern," Dr. Sagiv said. In 1965 the lowest age of alcoholics admitted for the first time to psychiatric wards was 29 years. In 1973 women were admitted for the first time, along with other alcoholics under the age of 25.

Ethnic composition of the alcoholic patients is of special interest, he said. In one group of 29 alcoholics, 20 were Oriental Jews (12 from Yemen and 8 from Morocco). Most of the Israel alcoholics are Oriental Jews, and a high proportion are from Yemen. This despite the fact that Morocco and Yemen are Moslem countries where use of alcoholic beverage is forbidden.

"There is no satisfactory explanation to these findings," Dr. Savig expostulated.

"Although alcohol addiction is less serious in Israel than elsewhere, it should be realized that the problem exists and that, together with drug addiction, alcoholism is a formidable challenge to Israel's health and social systems," he declared.

# #

Downbursts

Deadly avalanches of descending air that burst as they hit the ground--sometimes at speeds reaching 50 miles an hour--and then spread out at speeds up to 120 miles an hour may have been the cause of some airplane crashes that now are attributed to "unknown causes," an atmospheric scientist has reported.

Waves of descending air, spawned by thunderstorms and called downbursts, are known to have caused fatal airplane crashes, leveled cornfields in Illinois, and damaged forests in Wisconsin.

Dr. T. Theodore Fujita, professor of meterology at the University of Chicago, who headed a study of the phenomenon, said there are many more downbursts in thunderstorm areas than expected. Ordinary weather radar, he said, can't detect most downbursts because most of the disturbances are small--less than five miles in diameter. Some downbursts last less than five minutes.

Because of the small size and short duration of downbursts, a network of radars, automatic surface observation stations and rain gages was established to gather data under a project named NIMROD, an acronym for Northern Illinois Meterological Research on Downburst. As part of NIMROD, the National Center for Atmospheric Research in Boulder, Colorado, funded by the National Science Foundation (NSF), operated 27 automated weather stations and two radars. In addition, the Illinois State Water Survey operated rain gages, hail sensors and weather radars.

Dr. Fujita's work was described in a report to the NSF which funded a major portion of the NIMROD study.

A principal objective of NIMROD was to determine what set of meteorological factors cause downbursts so that methods and equipment for detecting them in or near airports and major metropolitan areas can be devised. The prediction of downbursts far enough in advance could mean the difference between life and death for airplance passengers and near-by residents, Dr. Fujita said.

It was NIMROD data that revealed the large numbers of downbursts in thunderstorn areas--many more than scientists thought they'd find. For example, a downburst on May 29, 1978, that occurred eight miles from Chicago's O'Hare Airport could not have been detected if there had been no NIMROD network, according to Dr. Fujita.

The term downburst was given to the phenomenon by the Chicago researcher after he determined that a fatal airplane crash at John F. Kennedy International Airpost on June 24, 1975, was caused by an avalanche of air that descended from a thunderstorn just north of the airport. One hundred and twenty-two persons were killed and 12 injured in the crash which occurred as the airplane attempted to land.

Using aerial photography and surveys, it also was determined that a forest of pine trees was flattened in eastern Sawyer County in Wisconsin by a downburst on July 4, 1977, and a cornfield was demolished in Illinois on September 30, the same year.

"Damage from downbursts is often highly localized, resembling that of tornadoes," Dr. Fujita said. "Very often there is close interaction between tornadoes and downbursts and a downburst can even change the path of a tornado. It's even possible for a strong downburst to wipe out a tornado or to add intensity to one. depending on the direction of the twist and the location of the downburst."

# #

Parabolic

VALLEY FORGE, Pa. -- A prototype of a new solar collector being designed by General Electric for this country's largest industrial solar energy application has produced high efficiencies in initial tests at Sandia Laboratories in Albuquerque, New Mexico.

Created to collect engineering data, the 16 1/2-foot (5-meter) diameter prototype of the parabolic dish collector demonstrated efficiencies of over 60% at 600°F. The collector is under development for the Solar Total Energy - Large Scale Experiment in Shenandoah, Georgia, a project sponsored by the U. S. Department of Energy (DOE). The full-scale version will measure 23-feet (7 meters) in diameter.

The Shenandoah Project is one of a series of Solar Total Energy experiments being implemented by DOE to provide engineering and application data for future industrial, commercial, institutional and residential installations. The system currently under development is expected to produce at least 60 percent of the annual energy requirements for the 42,000 square foot knitwear factory including electric power for lights, motors, sewing machines; process steam for the presses, and hot and chilled water for space heating and cooling.

Data collection on the high temperature receiver and the two-axis tracking control were the primary objectives of the recently completed Sandia tests. Testing of the two-axis tracking control also showed that the parabolic dish can be pointed at the sun extremely accurately by using computer-calculated data. That means that additional sun sensing may be unnecessary.

Designed for small as well as large energy users, the parabolic dish has the potential to collect about 1.7 times as much of available sun energy as a parabolic trough of equal size. Sun is focused onto stainless steel coils within a cup-like receiver. Oik flowing through the receiver coils removes the absorbed heat and transports it to a steam generator.

The concentration ratio of the prototype collector is 150 to 1. The concentration ratio of the full-scale collector for Shenandoah will be 235 to 1, producing an even higher operating temperature, 750°F, and improved efficiency.

The system design envisions a total of 192 parabolic dish collectors installed in a solar collecting "field" adjacent to the Bleyle America, Inc. knitwear plant. In addition to this field of parabolic collectors, the Solar Total Energy System for the Large Scale Experiment at Shenandoah will include an extraction steam turbine, a trickle oil thermal energy storage system, and an absorption-type air conditioning unit. The system is scheduled to begin operating in 1981, and will be interconnected with the Georgia Power Company public utility system.

According to Jud Poche, program manager from General Electric's Space Division, Valley Forge, Pa., "Results from these initial tests confirmed our high expectations for the parabolic dish collector. The excellent measured performance together with reduced collector costs achieved by fabricating the reflector from die-stamped aluminum petal ultimately mean a lower total cost."

# # #

Cancer

Two researchers announced today that a chemical extracted from the bark of pine trees is effective in arresting the growth of cancer cells.

"This is the breakthrough the medical profession has been looking for," Drs. Walter O"Hanlon and Avery Thorpe of Riverton said in a news release issued through their office. Both practice internal medicine.

The release said they had developed an elixir based on the bark chemical and combined with vitamin supplements.

"The supplements are an aid to nutrition," the news release said. "It is essential that cancer patients develop health new tissue once the carcinoma has been stopped."

The researchers said that through various tests, they had isolated the bark chemical as the agent which arrested the growth of cancer cells in patients with both mild and terminal forms of the illness.

"Medical ethics prohibit us from disclosing any further details," the release said. "The doctor-patient relationship is a sacred one. However, we expect to be marketing the elixir soon under the brand name 'NewLife.'"

# # #

Heart Defect

For a fetus to survive within the uterus of the mother, its blood bypasses the lungs and circulates directly to the head and body. This

is accomplished through a channel (ductus arteriosus) which connects
two main arteries. At birth, as blood begins to circulate through the
lungs, the normal process is for this channel to close. However, in
some babies that are born prematurely, the ductus arteriosus remains
open, resulting in a serious heart defect called patent ductus
arteriosus.

Children's Hospital Medical Center (CHMC) has recently been awarded
a $2.5 million grant from the National Institutes of Health to administer
a 3 year national cooperative study which will evaluate the two modes
of therapy currently being used to treat this condition, and determine
under what circumstances each would be beneficial. Dr. Alexander Nadas,
Professor of Pediatrics at Harvard Medical School (HMS) and Chief of
Cardiology at CHMC will be the principal investigator of the study.

Surgery, according to Dr. Nadas, has been the traditional treatment
when infants fail to respond to medical therapy. Recently, several
small studies have shown that the use of the drug indomethacin (used
in treating adult arthritis) is effective in closing the patent ductus
arteriosus, making surgery unnecessary. This treatment is still regarded as experimental by the Food and Drug Administration.

"Ther is no sure evidence that all babies born with patent ductus
arteriosus would be better off having the du-tus closes," Dr. Nadas
said. "It has been proposed that the blood vessel should be closed
only if it causes serious problems, such as heart failure or breathing
trouble (hyaline membrane disease)," he said. An estimated 20% of
small premature babies -- weighing 1750 grams or less -- run into these
difficulties (about 20,000 per year in the U. S.).

Eleven major U. S. medical centers will participate in the study, in order to obtain a large enough population sampling. Dr. Nadas and his colleagues will investigate the conditions under which it is worth-while to close the patent ductus arteriosus, and if so, the best time and most effective method. Observations of the babies' responses to the treatments will be made during their hospital stay, and through the months following discharge. After the children are seen at one year of age, the data from all the hospitals will be compiled in the Department of Epidemiology at the Harvard School of Public Health (HSPH).

Also participating in the study is Dr. R. Curtis Ellison, Associate Professor of Pediatrics at HMS and Senior Associate in Cardiology at CHMC, who will be the director of the data-coordinating center at HSPH. Dr. H. William Tauesch, Jr., Associate Professor of Pediatrics at Boston Hospital for Women and Chief of the Joint Program in Neonatology will be the neonatologist in charge at Children's.

Nelson

Though fake medicines actually relieve pain one third of the time, doctors and nurses use them more to punish difficult patients than to help them. They also use placebos to try to prove a patient is imagining or exaggerating pain.

These findings emerged from an unusual survey reported today. Sixty doctors-in-training and 39 nurses in two hospitals

responded to a questionnaire sent by Dr. Robert Bram, assistant professor
of medicine at University Hospital.

Dr. Bram found that both doctors and nurses were generally ignorant
of a placebo's ability to alleviate pain physically. Studies have
shown the psychological stimulus of receiving what is thought to be a
real drug or therapy stimulates the release of a pain-relieving brain
hormone. Only 16% of the doctors and 40% of the nurses said they ever
were taught about placebo response, and most greatly understimated the
number of patients who might benefit from placebos.

The survey showed most of the young doctors misuse sham medications.
They said they used them mainly to verify authenticity of pain or to
deal with overdemanding and unpopular patients.

                                   # # #

Hospitals

WASHINGTON -- Five Catholic hospitals and one health project
received "Achievement Citations" at the annual awards dinner of the
Catholic Hospital Association (CHA) held here Friday.

The hospitals were Calvary Hospital, Bronx, N.Y.; Good Samaritan
Hospital & Health Center, Dayton, Ohio; Holy Cross Hospital, Salt Lake
City, Utah; Holy Cross Hospital, San Fernando, Calif.; and St. Margaret's
Hospital, Boston, Mass. The East Coast Migrant Health Project also
received an award.

The CHA citations are given to individuals, groups and/or institutions who have made an impact in the delivery of health services over and above ordinary community service programs and projects.

##

24. DISASTER AND FIRE

Disasters like airplane crashes, explosions, and floods are difficult to cover. An editor must be doubly wary of speculation and generalization when dealing with these events.

Plane Crashes. Most plane crashes aren't witnessed. An editor must be careful to qualify statements, because information frequently comes from a variety of sources with conflicting information. One may say the plane had a single engine. Another may say it was a twin-engine aircraft. Attribution is essential.

Explosions. Explosions must be qualified carefully. Too often papers rush to announce an explosion when perhaps only a sonic boom was involved. It is no error to quote an authority as saying an explosion apparently occurred. It is a sin to write on your own that there was an explosion in the absence of solid, attributable information.

Floods. Whenever there is a flood, it is axiomatic that erroneous information will flow right along with the water. A few years ago, when a dam burst in Idaho, some reports quoted the possibility of 150 deaths and later the danger of rattlesnake bites. As it turned out, fewer than a dozen persons died in the flood and there were no reported instances of rattlesnake bites. Rumors are rampant following disasters. An editor must insist on precise, responsible reporting, even at the risk of producing a story that is dull by comparison with those of competitors.

Fires. By tradition, some events are automatic news. Fires fall into that category. Where there's smoke, people talk. Where there's fire, they gather. Flames will draw crowds, including reporters, faster than will any news conference or public meeting. Why? Because fires fascinate people. Equally important, however, is another truism: Journalists are attracted by easy, spectacular stories. Fires aren't hard to cover. Locations are established, scenes are described, and authorities are quoted.

As an editor, your task is to cut through the trivia and tell the reader the essentials. It isn't easy. Reporters are fond of phrases like *five-alarm*, *contained*, and *damage estimated at* (pick a dollar figure). What does any of that mean to readers? If you stop 100 people on a street corner, few will be able to tell you what a five-alarm fire is. Almost none will relate to damage estimates.

Readers ought to be told about fires in terms they can understand. It is better to say how many firefighters and pieces of equipment were sent to a scene than to describe the situation in terms of "alarms." It is better to describe the nature, size, and contents of damaged buildings than to give dollar-loss estimates, which are meaningful only to people involved in insurance settlements. The same advice applies to shorthand like *contained*, *controlled*, and *mopped up*. As an editor, seek to inform the public—don't burden it with labels that you've come to understand simply by sitting in a newsroom.

You don't know the difference between a five-alarm fire and a three-alarm fire? You aren't sure about the distinction between *contained* and *controlled*? Call your local fire department. Now try your hand at the following disaster stories.

EXERCISES

Plant Fire

A fire of undetermined cause origin caused at least $30,000 in damages to equipment and injured one employe Friday night at the City Power Plant.

No power outages were reported as a result of the fire, police reported.

Power department employe Farrell P. Donnell, 46, suffered wnd-degree burns on forearm and his face. He was treated and released.

City Fire Department received the fire alarm at 6:48 p.m. and brought the blaze under control wih within about 45 minutes, said Capt. Bob Isherwood of the fire department. He said damage was contained to equipment and no structural loss was incurred.

The fire apparently started in relay switching equipment. Capt. Isherwood said. He said it was uncertain whether the blaze was caused by equipment failure or human error.

A deisel engine which drives on generator ran out of control as a result of the fire and sustained heavy damage. Capt. Isherwood added. He added that damage to the engine and the generator which it powers was not included in the $30,000 damage estimate figure.

Power within the building was turned off Friday night, however, electrical service to customers was not interrupted because officials were able re-route a power from other sources.

Power officials could not be reached for comment Friday night because radio and other communications at the power plant were disrupted by the fire, Police said.

#

(Plant Fire)

A |fire ~~of undetermined cause origin~~ caused at least $30,000 in damages to equipment and injured one employe*e* Friday night at the City Power Plant.

No power outages were reported as a result of the fire. ~~police reported.~~

Power department employe*e* Farrell P. Donnell, 46, suffered ~~wnd~~-*second* degree burns on *his* forearm and ~~his~~ face. He was treated *(at a hospital ?)* and released.

City Fire Department received the ~~fire~~ alarm at 6:48 p.m. and brought the blaze under control ~~wih~~ within about 45 minutes, said *Fire* Capt. Bob Isherwood. ~~of the fire department.~~ He said damage was ~~contained~~ *limited* to equipment. ~~and no structural loss was incurred~~.

The fire apparently started in relay switching equipment. Capt. Isherwood said. He said it was uncertain whether the blaze was caused by equipment failure or human error.

A d(e)isel engine which drives ~~on~~ *a* generator ran out of control as a result of the fire and sustained heavy damage. Capt. Isherwood added.

(more)

(2/Plant Fire)

~~He added that~~ damage to the engine and the generator which it powers was not included in the $30,000 ~~damage~~ estimate ~~figure~~.

Power ~~with~~in the building was turned off Friday night however, electrical service to customers was not interrupted because officials were able ʌre~~f~~route ǝ power from other sources.

Power officials could not be reached for comment Friday night because radio and other communications at the power plant were disrupted by the fire, Police said.   (#)

Propane

Propane gas fumes exploded at a house under construction Saturday, seriously burning a 20-year-old man.

The victim, identified by Deputy. Sheriff Ray McIntyre is Clarence Gray, who was in seriously condition late Saturday at General Hospital.

Deputy Mac Intyre said the victim had crawled under a plastic cover which wha which covered recently poured concrete, when the blast occurred. The deputy said a propane heater had been un used to heat the foundation and apparently some of the gas had escaped.

#

Chief

ELM CITY -- (CHARLES JACK HANSEN, A 16-YEAR VETERAN OF THE DEPARTMENT, WAS NAMED FIRE CHIEF BY THE CITY COUNCIL THURSDAY NIGHT.

HANSEN, AN ELM CITY NATIVE WHO ROSE TO CAPTAIN IN 10 YEARS, WILL

SUCCEED RETIRING CHIEF LEONARD BOSWELL JAN. 1.

BOSWELL SERVED AS CHIEF 25 OF HIS 40 YEARS IN THE FIRE DEPARTMENT,

DURING WHICH TIME HE SUCCEEDED IN IMPROVING THE CITY'S FIRE RATING UP

SEVERAL GRADES.

Canyon Fire

HOPKINS -- Fire, started from an incenerator, threatened two trailer
homes and two homes as it burned over more than 100 acres of grass and
brush at the mouth of Ponderosa Canyon Thursday at 1:55 p.m.

Firemen reportedthat a piece of burning cardboard box fell out of an
incinerater to ignite the dry grass. A brisk breeze quickly spread the
flames into oakbrush and to within feet of the homes.

Scores of men and women from Hopkins mannd manned shovels to fight
the fire until the first county fire trucks arrived.

An additional truck was dispatched from Union along with a large
tanker to refill the smaller trucks, said Fire Chief Calvin Woodward.

The flames were whipped into a private game preserve threatening
pheasants and other wildlife, Chief Woodward said.

Smoke billowed several hundred feet into the air.

Brush

The County Fire Department fought a brush and grass blaze for more
than seven hours Friday before contain after 10:30 p.m.

A volunteer fireman, John Peters, 22, of No. 2 station, was overcome by smoke in a gully. He was carried to safety by John Douglas, a
full-time fireman at the same station. Mr. Peters was treated for smoke
inhalation at General Hospital and released.

Battalion Chief Bill Petrowski said between 40 and 50 acres of brush
land here burned just west of the new shopping center being built nearby.

He said the fire was difficult to put out because of the thinkness
of the tumbleweeds, grass and brush that packed down three to four feet
deep and had smoldered for hours, then broke into flame again.

Several trucks and 16 men fought the blaze, along with crews from
the nearby Toland Construction Co.

#

Temple Fire

A spectacular fire causing caused $350,000 damage to the LaborTemple,
229 2nd Street, late Thursday and early Friday morning, gutting the
offices of the United Steel Makers of America; Painters Local; Muscians'
Union; Day, Bill and Jones, attorneys; Circuit Electronics, and Salon of
Beauty. Asst. Fire Chief M. B. "Sandy" Springer said the alarm was
turned in Thursday at 11:15 p.m. and by the time fire trucks arrived
the structure was almost completely involved.

He said the main floor, including Circuit Electronics and Salon of
Beauty, was was a total loss as was the third floor of the structure.
The second floor was almost a total loss after the wooden -- tar paper
foof caved in at the heighth of the blaze.

The soaring flames -- even at that late hour -- attracted a large crowd of spectators.

Five members of the City Fire Department sustained injuries. Lt. suffered a cheeck laceration requiring 10 stitches; Larry Mabel suffered a severed wrist tendon when an explosion caused flying glass; Jack Pulley had lacerations on his arm requiring five stitches; and Orville Brooks and Jack Koiter had minor cuts.

Chief Springer said Circuit Electronics estimated their loss at $150,000; loss in the building wah $122,000 and $30,000 loss to the union offices and "beauty" salon.

The basement suffered considerable water damage. It was designated as a Civil Defence Fallout Shelter, and some equipment suffered damage, but the amount of damager was unknowns.

Action

A quick thinking woman motorist saved a young man from extensive burns when he was sprayed with buring gasoline while trying to start a truck with jumper cables at 2453 15th Street.

Rodney White, 18, of Elm City, is listed in serious but stable condition at General Hospital with burns over 20 per cent of his body.

Highway patrol troopers credited Mrs. Mildred Fox, 23, of 1933 Fuller Way, with preventing more serious injuries when she grabbed a smock and wrapped it around him to put out the flames.

Mrs. Fox said she was driving past with her mother and two small

children when she saw him drop to the ground and roll trying to put out
the flames.

"I grabbed my mother's smock and jumped out of the car as he started
rolling on the ground. I wrapped it around him to smother the flames,"
Mrs. Fox said.

Troopers said White was apparently pouring some gasoline into the
truck's carburator when fumes were ignited by sparks from the jumper
cable.

Twister

A tornado struck a ranch house in rural Heunessey County near
Riverview wednesday evening killing five persons and injuring three
others.

"The bodies were strung out from the farmhouse southwest, anywhere
from 10 yards to 15 yards," said highway patrolman Roger Patten. "We
got ambulances out there as soon as possible."

The four victims were pronounced dead on arrival at Riverview
municipal hospital.

Names were withheld pending notification of relatives.

"The house was completely destroyed," the trooper said.
"Shortly before it was raining extremely hard and hailing, visibility
was real bad out here."

Three occupants of the house were found injured but not seriously.
Ranch house was destroyed. Dead animals were found strewn across the
adjacent barnyard.

Two more persons were injured in a tornado near Pike City, and a twister destroyed a church, a 60-foot long trailer house damaged three other trailers and eight houses in the same area.

#

Plane

GROVE JUNCTION -- The disintegrated wrecka e of a twin-engine Piper-Seneca aircraft, with the body of a passenger still strapped in, was found Saturday at 9 a.m. three miles north of here -- but it took searchers another seven hours to find the body of the pilot.

The pilot, John Peter Christian, 50 , was finally located 150 years from the wreckage Federal Aviation Administration officials said that they plan to ask for an autoposy on the cause of death to see if Mr. Christian had been alive long enoughto walk or crawl that far from the wreck.

They said Mr. Christian's seat belt in the plane was unbuckled and the reason his body was not found for so long was that it had been covered with six to eight inches of snow from Friday night's snow storm, which might have been a contributing factor to the plane crash.

The passenger was identified as Benjamin J. Throckmorton, Capital City, an employe of High Valley Electric Co., who was doing electrical consulting work for Jonesville Construction Co., who employed Mr. Christian.

Prince William County Sheriff A. Pierce Marmaduke said the search

for th plane was started shortly after it took off from the Aspine City
Airport Friday at 6:00 P.M.

But it wasn't until early Saturday that a search plan from McClelland
Air Force Base, Sacremento, California, picked up a radio signal from
the downed plane's emergency location transmitter and guided ground crews
to the location of the tragic crash.

The plane was finally located by the ground crew about a quarter of
a mile from State Highway 15.

####

U3021

Floods, 350

NEW BRAUNFELS, TEX. (NS) -- A FOOT OF RAIN IN A DAY BULGED THE
GUADALUPE RIV R OUT OF ITS BANKS FRIDAY, TEARING AWAY HOMES AND CARS
AND THE PEOPLE IN THEM AND FLOODING THE TEXAS COUNT YSIDE WITH WATR
HOUSETOP HIGH.

AT LEAST EIGHT PERSONS DROWNED -- SIX IN NEW BRAUNFELS AND TWO AT
SEGUIN, 15 MILES DOWNSTREAM.

MORE T AN 4,500 RESIDENTS WERE EVACUATED FROM A RIVERFRONT HOMES
ALONG 25 MILES OF THE MUDDY RIVER, WHICH HEAVED AN 18-FOOT WALL OF WATER
OVER THE LAND. ENTIRE FAMILIES WERE MISSING.

"SEVERAL HOUSES FLOATED AWAY," SAID PATROLMAN THOMAS CLAXTON.
"AT LEAST 10 CARS WITH PEOPLE IN THEM WERE WASHED AWAY. WE WERE
SWAMPED WITH CALLS -- PEOPLE SAYING, "HELP ME, PLEASE! MY HOUSE IS
FLOATING AWAY."

POLICE SAID THE DEATH TOLL WOULD RISE WITH THE FLOODWATERS.

"SO MANY PEOPLE WERE WASHED AWAY. WE FEAR THE TOTAL WILL GO MUCH HIGHER," SAID NEW BRAUNFELS POLICE CHIEF ROYCE COUCH.

GOV. PRESTON SMITH CALLED OUT THE TEXAS NATIONAL GUARD TO HELP EVACUATION AND CLEAN-UP WORK AROUND NEW FRAUNFELS, AND OLD GERMAN SETTLEMEN OF 18,000 POPULATION. THEY USED HELICOPTERS, BOATS AND TRUCKS.

THE NATIONAL WEATHER SERVICE SAID TEXAS WOULD BE FLOODED BY THE GUADALUPE ALL THE WAY TO VICTORIA, 125 MILES SOUTHEAST NEAR THE GULF COAST, FOR THE NEXT WEEK.

ONE OF THE DEAD AT NEW BRAUNFELS WAS CLARENCE R. E. KENTSCH, 51, SECRET SERVICE AGENT IN CHARGE AT THE LYNDON B. JOHNSON RANCH DURING HIS YEARS AS PRESIDENT. KENTSCH, WHO DROWNED WHILE HE TRIED TO PULL FLOOD VICTIMS FROM THE RIVER, HAD BEEN IN CHARGE OF THE SAN ANTONIO SECRET SERVICE FOR THE PAST TWO YEARS.

IN OTHER PARTS OF TEXAS TORNADOES AND OTHER VIOLENT WEATHER WAS REPORTED. SEVEN TWISTERS STRUCK NEAR WINNIE, DANBURY, MANVILLE, BROOKSIDE VILLAGE, THE HOUSTON SUBURBS OF PEARLAND AND ROSEMONT AND NEAR SEGUIN. NO SERIOUS INJURIES WERE REPORTED.

814 CST

Part V

Headlines

25. WRITING MEANINGFUL HEADLINES

Headlines are at once a great strength and a shortcoming of newspapers. They are sound when they convey information accurately and quickly and stimulate readership. They fail when they aren't clear and correct on first reading, and they should be condemned when they distort. "They're killing us in the headlines," is a common complaint from people in business, science, and other occupations that deal in complex problems. A newspaper story may be accurate but a headline may tell another story. One complaint goes so far as to suggest that a headline writer for the *New York Daily News* cost Gerald Ford the 1976 presidential election with a famous Page One double banner: "Ford to City: Drop Dead." By oversimplifying the issue of federal loan guarantees to the city, the head writer, so the complaint went, cost Ford the city's vote and with it the state's electoral vote and the nation's. Farfetched? Perhaps. But a major reason for credibility problems of newspapers is the fuzzy, incomplete, inaccurate, or misleading headline.

Yet while the headline is an imperfect means for communicating complex information, it serves the newspaper's need to provide information quickly and to structure the voluminous contents of the typical publication coherently. The headline advertises the story and tells the reader the essential news. It also grades the copy, because headline size and placement indicate how important the editor considers the story to be. Headlines offer a variety of ways of captioning a story in sizes of type and styles, so they determine how the

275

newspaper page looks. The headline, more than any other quickly perceived part of the newspaper package, reflects the newspaper's personality: "8,000 See Man Chewed to Death," says one headline on a story of a snowmobiler's death—no question here that the paper is pulling out all the plugs for readership. "Snowmobiler Is Dragged to Death," says another in a more restrained way.

Headline writing is the copy editor's second major function, after the story copy has been edited. The copy editor's success depends greatly on the ability to tell the story in a few words. Writing headlines requires talent and discipline. The best headline writers are really poets. They find the right words to express the thought economically.

As the newspaper headline writer, you'll face obstacles. Your headline will have to fit the paper's headline style (see next chapter). You will also have to produce headlines that fit designated numbers of columns in specific type sizes. On all metropolitan dailies the headline is ordered by the editor of a department (sports, business, etc.) or a makeup editor after he or she assigns a story to a position on a page. The headline writer, usually a copy editor, may not improvise on the number of columns, lines, or type size specified by the page makeup person. On much smaller papers, such as weeklies, the headline often is written by the person who designs the page.

Compressing the details of a three-hour city council meeting into a 20-word lead is tough enough; putting it into, say, three lines of 11 letters each is formidable. In addition, you'll usually work under considerable time pressure, often writing dozens of heads against the deadlines for several editions. Sometimes any headline that fits the designated space and form and is a reasonable clue to the story will simply have to do. But as in all good writing, writing the headline means seeking the best way—not merely the quickest and most obvious way—to tell the story. Good headline writers are zealous self-critics.

Many newspapers have become more permissive in recent years. Today the editor has fewer artificial headline patterns to cope with. The trend is toward naturalness—the fresh, lively, conversational headline that talks to the read—and toward lively, inventive appearance. The label head with no verb was once scorned. Now it is permissible in almost all papers if it is the most effective way of telling the essence of the story. The headline "Journey of a Joint" over a story on how marijuana comes into the United States has no verb but is bright and descriptive. (Some novices are asked to produce a "title headline" rather than a sentence headline.) Label heads should not be written when they simply circumvent the verb: not "Drop in Book Circulation" but "Book Circulation Drops." Later in this chapter we'll talk about the strength of the verb approach, but it's better to have a bright label or title head than a dull verb head.

Writing the Headline

Most headlines are simple declarative sentences distilling the major idea of a story and expressing it straightforwardly. After a little practice, the head writer gets the feel of writing this sentence, on the first attempt, to the dimensions specified. Until then it is best to begin with what is sometimes called a full news point sentence and improvise on it until it fits the space and pattern requirements. This often means substituting words, usually by finding shorter ones to express the same idea. Try starting with a one-idea sentence that captures the essence of the story.

Headline Fundamentals

Minor words may be omitted. The articles *a* and *the* usually are not used, although they should be inserted if meaning is improved and space permits. Sometimes they are needed to make the headline correct. They should not be eliminated merely to make the headline sound urgent, though this sometimes is a happy byproduct.

The comma may be substituted for *and* and sometimes for *but* ("Smith, Jones Report to Nation") when the usage is clear. Parts of the verb *to be* may usually be omitted. The words *are* and *is* often merely clutter the headline. (The major exception is when the direct object is itself the subject of a clause, as in "Jones Says Smith Is Unfit." However, "Jones Calls Smith Unfit" is correct usage.) Key words are not repeated in the head or between the head and banks. But do not avoid key words just for elegant variation, as in *cold stuff* for *snow*.

Headline writers soon develop a knack for finding short words. Much of the news deals with proposals, for which the words *seek* and *ask* are appropriate. Conventional thesauruses are collections of words referring to concepts. They are based on word associations and are not much help to headline writers. They usually slow the work. Books of synonyms and headline glossaries are useful. One of the best is *The Synonym Finder*, published by Rodale Books, Emmaus, Pa. When you're stuck for a word, rework the thought—rather than sift through dictionaries and other crutches, which often will at best give you only a close approximation of the word you really want.

Voice. Active voice is preferred. It is the most normal and vibrant way of expression. The subject is expressed and is both the logical and grammatical doer: "President Orders Carrier to Gulf." In the passive voice, the direct object becomes the grammatical doer, with the logical doer unexpressed but usually understood: "Carrier Ordered to Gulf." It is permissible to write the headline in passive voice when what is done is more important than who did it. In heads of more than one line it also often permits the essence of the idea to be stated in the top line, a desirable construction:

> Carrier Ordered
> To Gulf Station
> By President

A headline in the active voice in which the subject is understood may form an unintentional imperative or seem to give a command to the reader, such as "Find Mugger in Bowery." This is a lazy tabloid device logically indefensible. In general, any headline that begins with a verb, singular or plural, should be avoided. If necessary, use the passive: "Mugger Found in Bowery."

Passive voice also may allow considerably more to be said. In a two-line head active voice may be able, because of the limited space, to accommodate only

> Court Decrees
> Life in Prison

rather than

> Life in Prison
> Decreed in Slaying

Tense. Present tense is used in headlines to convey the *past:* "President Reports to Congress." It also may be used to convey the *future* when a definite time element is used: "President Reports to Congress Monday." The simple past is used where the past perfect would be used in the story: "President Reported to Congress" (not *had reported*). The infinitive *to* also may be used for future tense: "President to Report to Congress" (next Monday). *Will* may be used for the future, but generally when the action is definite: "President Will Report to Congress."

Punctuation. Keep it to a minimum.

The *comma* is used where it would be in normal text construction, in addition to its special use in substitution for *and* or *but*.

The *semicolon* is used as periods would be, for a full stop, usually at the end of a line. *Periods* are not used.

The *dash* may be used for abrupt stops and occasionally for attribution: "President— Inflation Worsens."

The *colon* is used as it normally would be but also serves the same purpose as the dash. Both the colon and dash can be handy devices for compressing by taking the place of a verb or even a clause and also for enlivening the head. "Autonomy—Israel Settler's View"; "Grand Hotel: Service and Discretion."

Both the dash and colon can become gimmicky and also can encourage lazy habits. Don't resort to them frequently.

Quotation marks are used as the style dictates and for direct quotations. They also are used to cast doubt, reservation, or irony: "'Lost' Boy Arrives Home." Single quotation marks are used exclusively in headlines to save space.

Exclamation marks should not be used. The size and position of the headline should convey all the astonishment needed.

Tone. The tone of the headline should be consistent with the story's. A funny story needs a humorous head, a suspended interest story one that doesn't give away the ending. Teaser headlines are discussed in the section on writing the bright head.

Guidelines in Headline Writing

Make the Headline a True Index to the Story. All other considerations are secondary. The headline should never go beyond the story. It may not assume facts not explicitly conveyed in the story. It may not editorialize. Numbers are especially troublesome—make sure numbers expressed in the head agree with those in the story. One newspaper headline, for instance, reported that an organization had collected $245 in a sale, including $50 for a special contest. However, the story itself said only that "more than $200" was raised and never mentioned the $50.

Most cases of factual inaccuracy can be avoided by simply referring the headline facts to the story after the head is written. Here's a case in point:

> Lance Asked Favor of IRS,
> Memorandum Discloses
>
> *The lead:* Bert Lance allegedly told a *federal banking regulator* last year he "just wondered if you could see your way clear" to lift restrictions on a Georgia bank that Lance headed, according to an IRS memorandum disclosed Tuesday. The conversation was reported secondhand in a memo released by the Senate Governmental Affairs Committee. The committee said it received the summary Tuesday, from the Internal Revenue Service, of an interview conducted by IRS investigators with an *attorney* in the Office of the Comptroller of the Currency.

The italics are added, but twice, early in the story, it's clear even in this fairly tortuous proceeding that it wasn't the IRS from whom the favor was allegedly asked. A further fault of the headline is in using a full line for *memorandum discloses*, rather than using it for attribution and qualification expressed in the story.

A better head (same count) would be

> Lift Restrictions on Bank,
> Lance Reportedly Asked

Headlines shouldn't go beyond the story. Here again is Lance, an ousted director of the Bureau of the Budget (who complained, with some justification, that he was ill used by the press):

> Lance 'Explains' Flights
> In Bank's Private Plane

The quotes are used to cast doubt, but the story was a straightforward account of Lance's denial. The use of quotes here was plainly editorial.

In this headline the copy editor made a quantum leap from the facts to an over-generalization:

> Portuguese
> In Disarray

The headline suggests far more than the story: "The downfall of Portugal's minority Socialist government today provoked *fears of* political instability and a deepening economic crisis" (italics added).

Make the Headline as Complete as Possible. Tell as much of the story as you can in the limited space available. Sometimes even obvious elements of the news story are left out of the headline:

> Hijacked Airliner Raided
> By Germans in Somalia

The story, the climax of a days-long drama, could have been expressed adequately as

> Hijacked Airliner Raided:
> 86 Safe, 3 Terrorists Die

Here's another:

> Judge Rules Bank
> Not Guilty of
> Discrimination

What kind of discrimination? This point could easily be included with a bit of recasting to eliminate the long word *discrimination:*

> Judge Rules Bank
> Is Innocent of
> Sex, Racial Bias

When the attempt to add detail leads to confusion, it should be abandoned:

President Threatens to Veto Oil Bill for People

The phrase "for people" is at best ambiguous and possibly even double-faced, since it could be interpreted as the people's oil bill. Making the essentials as specific and meaningful as possible produces:

President Threatens to Veto Gas-Pricing Bill

It's particularly hard to write a complete head on a complex story with two or more major points which sometimes take coordinate importance in the lead of the story: a record snowfall that snarls traffic, closes schools and downs power lines, for instance; a first-day story in which it is important to get reaction as well. Typically, in the restricted number of words with which you will work, you will find it necessary to make a judgment as to which of these elements is most important to feature in the headline.

Obviously, you can't tell the whole story in the headline. If you have difficulty writing the head, it may well be that you're trying to say too much. A famous head in a New York tabloid said:

> Jug Ump Hitter
> On Rolling Rap

Totally incomprehensible. The story was about the arrest on a robbery charge of a man who had once been jailed for hitting an umpire. Besides assuming readers were hep to police jargon, the headline tried to say too much.

Be Specific. This goes hand-in-hand with the "Be Complete" guideline. Don't write:

> U. S. Envoys Arrive
> For NATO Meeting

if you can just as easily particularize:

> Vance, Haig Arrive
> For NATO Meeting

Nonspecific heads often result from focusing on superficial angles which are not the real point of a story. "Power Company Releases Annual Report" should be the headline only if the release of the report is the story; usually it's what the report said that makes news. Similarly "Police Investigate Burglary" usually is a poor head; the point almost always is the burglary itself, not the investigation: "$60,000 in Goods Gone in Store Burglary."

A common kind of generalization fault is the "meeting was held" headline:

> Psychological Factors Discussed
> During Arthritis Public Forum

It is not that psychological factors were discussed but rather what was said about them that is of interest to readers. Hence:

> Arthritics Often Suffer
> Depression, Forum Hears

Avoid headlines that generalize about rulings, decisions, statements:

> Narcotics Officers
> Hail Top Court's
> Drug Case Ruling

What kind of ruling? Unless this headline covered a related subordinate story at the side of a main story (a *sidebar*), the writer could not make the presumption the ruling is understood, even in a second-day story. With a little effort the head could read:

> Narcotics Officers
> Applaud Court OK
> On Using Informers

Identify Clearly. A troublesome headline question is how to identify persons who are not well known. A good general rule is to use in headlines only those names that are instantly recognizable. Still, there's scant excuse for these expedients:

> Bank Scribe Predicts Good Quarter

The "scribe" was the bank vice president and economist, who edited a newsletter. When names are household words, they should be used. Not:

> U. N. Executive Voices
> World Unrest Dismay

Apart from the tortured syntax of the last line, and the fact that the story did not say he was dismayed, the head can be faulted for failing to name the executive, Secretary-General Kurt Waldheim, one of the world's best-known statesmen.

The lead: "Secretary-General Kurt Waldheim, in his annual report on the state of the World, predicted Thursday that conditions in 1978 will be 'serious and unsettled.' " Try:

> Waldheim Predicts
> Unsettled Year

How about this one?

> Russian Monk's
> Daughter Dies

The Russian monk was Rasputin.

> Late President's
> Daughter Dies

said a headline over a story on the death of Ethel Carow Roosevelt at Oyster Bay. She was the daughter of Teddy Roosevelt.

And this one?

> Representative, 77,
> Blasts Image of Old

The blaster was Rep. Claude Pepper, one of the best-known members of Congress. Why not:

> Pepper Assails
> Image of the Aged

In addition, the original could be easily be read to mean he blasts his own old (that is, former) image.

Identification in headlines can be heavy-handed:

> Legendary Crooner,
> Bing Crosby, 73,
> Dies of Heart Attack

Belaboring the identification merely kills the opportunity to use the extra line for additional information:

> Bing Crosby Dies
> In Spain at 73
> Of Heart Attack

Fortunately, American newspapers have not gone as far as the British in using short-hand designations for people in the news. A common British device is to write such a head-line as "M-1 Girl Recovering" in reference to a girl hurt on the M-1 Highway, or "Bear Man" for a story on a man mauled by a bear. Don't resort to such expedients. And avoid *man* or *woman* if a way can be found to make the identification more specific: don't use "Man Hurt in Fall" if he was a "Climber Hurt in Fall."

Be Literal. Don't write: "Woman Hurt in Crash With Truck." It's asking quite a lot of the reader to provide the missing "Auto." Similarly, "Man Hurt Hitting Train" is laugh-able. It's just as easy to write: "Train-Car Crash Hurts Driver."

Double check the head to make sure that on first reading it makes the sense you intend to convey and does so literally. This will help you to avoid the "two-faced head." Usually this occurs when a verb or adjective can be read two ways: "Germans Fine Scien-tists" on a story about two scientists fined in a German court. Sometimes it involves a noun that can be read in two senses: "Oil Strike to Involve 350 Workers"—a labor dispute or an oil find? By now you know that you don't approach head writing by trying to produce some-thing that "sounds like a headline." Heads are written in normal English.

First, make it grammatically correct. This seems elementary, yet headline writers resort to grammar outrages that they'd quickly pencil in a story:

> Hungarian Jet Crashes
> In Romania, Kills 29

The subject of the verb *kills* is not *jet* but the unexpressed *crash*. It's a simple matter to recast it thus:

> Hungarian Jet Crash
> In Romania Kills 29

Another head with the same grammatical problem:

> Trade Deficit Decreases,
> Buoys Economic Outlook

The subject of the verb *buoys* logically is not *deficit* but *decrease*. Hence:

> Trade Deficit Decrease
> Buoys Economic Outlook

There's no excuse for:

Village Faces Power Loss
Unless They Conserve Now

The pronoun *they* is out of agreement with its referent word, *village*. It should, of course, be "Village . . . It" or "Villagers . . . They."

In addition, the headline should avoid twisted syntax, even that seemingly required by space limitations:

Benefits
Noted
Of Health
Groups

The misrelated modifier could easily be eliminated under the same count:

Health
Group
Benefits
Noted

And why:

New Plan
Unveiled
On Cities

When it could just as easily have been written:

New Plan
On Cities
Unveiled

Avoid Headlinese. A major caution when you search for short words: Headline writing tends to become cliché-ridden, usually built around handy short words scarcely seen outside headlines. The words *hike* for *increase*, *panel* for *commission*, *pact* for almost any agreement, *probe* for any investigation or inquiry are headline words that have migrated into the general language because of their prevalence in newspapers.

Lazy headline writers do not schedule meetings; they *list*, *chart*, *map*, *set*, or perhaps *date* and *slate* them. They do not ponder problems, but *mull* them. They see *looming* events against which people must *brace*. To them all legislators are *solons* and all teachers *savants*. They have a handy glossary of punitive verbs to indicate disapproval: *hit*, *rap*, *rake*, and even *flay*, which literally means to whip off the hide. They hand nicknames to even distinguished personages—"Rocky" was a short headline name that the late Nelson Rockefeller accepted in good humor for himself. Presidents with even moderately long names became FDR, HST, Ike, JFK, and LBJ, while Nixon, Ford, Carter all have compact names that do not require headline condensation. The late Russian leader Nikita Khrushchev was *K.* or *Mr. K.* Israel's late Golda Meir was *Golda* because *Meir* with *Mrs.* was often formidably long.

Headline craftsmen avoid these expedients, called *headlinese*, as much as possible. Some papers have absolute prohibitions against the use of some of the more offensive headline words. The *Los Angeles Times*, for example, banned the following headline words:

mom, *dad*, *grandma*, *tot*, *kids*, *cops* (except in certain feature heads—some papers ban it altogether on grounds of taste, too), *bare* in the sense of disclose, *eyes* used as a verb, *meet* and *win* as nouns except on sports pages, *nabbed*, and *probe* where it is possible to write *inquiry*.

Silly expedients used to get around headline rules also can be classed as headlinese. On one paper where *is* is banned outright as headline padding, the headline writers work around it with a contraction:

> Auditor's Optimistic
> On County Budget

producing a headline almost impossible to grasp on first reading when the reader has to make the adjustment from possessive to contraction.

Avoid Split Heads. Don't split the thought between lines illogically. In a split head, clauses spill from one line to the next. Usually this occurs when a word or two necessary to complete the clause on a top line begins the second line. It also occurs when a top line ends with a word modifying the succeeding line, such as an adjective or adverb. These splits should be avoided when they confuse the reader, as when a false picture is provided, however momentarily:

> Battle Lines Form in Milk
> Price War in Sacramento
>
> President Sees Lincoln
> Ideal Nearing Reality

Another type of split is caused by ending a top line with a preposition, article, conjunction, or infinitive. Most papers will not tolerate this construction. A few don't care. Adherence to this rule seems to be mere formalism.

Avoid Tentative Heads. The tentative head says something *may* happen. It should be written only if the story itself focuses on the tentativeness. If something may happen, it also may not, and a stronger way usually can be found to express the action: Don't write "University May Get Federal Funds" if it's "University Applies for Federal Funds."

Keep Figures to a Minimum. Where possible round figures out. Keep use of figures consistent; don't write it "Four Killed in 3 Accidents."

Shun Confusing Abbreviations or Acronyms. LPGA is fine for the sports page, where readers will recognize it as Ladies Professional Golf Association, but don't use it anywhere else in the paper. Many agencies have the same or very similar letter designations (ICA and CIA). A few years ago the OAS (Organization of American States) and OAS (Algerian Secret Army) were in the news simultaneously, and great care had to be taken that the context made clear which body was involved.

Strive for a Strong Verb. Verbs convey action and help make headlines direct, forceful and lively: "Tornados Tease South."

Don't Write Nonheads. Heads that say nothing, like "College Unit Sets Meeting," are called *wooden* heads. Any key-word label head is better if nothing else comes to mind: "Sorority Meeting."

Avoid Question Marks. It's lazy to resort to the question mark just to avoid a preposition:

> Sewer Bond Vote?
> City Replies No

Rather than

City Replies No
On Sewer Bond Vote

As a rule, use question heads only when a legitimate question is posed as a paramount consideration of the story. Your job is to tell—not quiz—the reader.

EXERCISES

At the top of each of the following stories, write a headline of four to six words. For the moment don't worry about counting the number of letters or about casting the headline in any particular form. One reminder: Although you will have a headline in mind before you go very far into the story, do not write it until you have thoroughly edited the story from every standpoint. Facts, emphasis, or organization of the story may have to be changed.

Reservist

Ft. WASHINGTON--Rivlets of perspiration traced an erratic stream through the dust that coated her face in the intense 103° heat as Specialist Four Victoria Helmschmidt beamed her pleasure at a job well done during Annual Training for the Sixth Battalion, 83rd Field Artillery at Ft. Washington, which began August 1st.

Specialist Helmschmidt, who prefers being called "Vickie," works as a secretary for the State department of transportation most of the time, but on weekends and for 2 weeks each year she is an army TAMMS clerk. She explains that TAMMS means The Army Maintenance Management System and her job is to keep track of maintenance and dispatch of vehicles. This unit is going through the paces of an Army Training Test and everyone seems to be doing his or her best to see they pass the test.

Viki is one of four ladies attached to the 6/83rd for annual training. Because the Artillery unit is a combat arms unit, subject to deployment in the event of conflict, girls may not be assigned.

She says she likes to work hard and enjoys a challenge. Viki likes
to, "go different places and do different things." She says, "girls in
the Army Reserve are like girls anywhere. We aren't looking for guys and
just want to do a good job."

"The guys I work with are just like big brothers," she said. "They
tease me a little, but respect the fact that I have a job to do and know
how to do it." She says they occasionally play tricks on her because she
hasn't been in the Army too long and sometimes ask her to go after a
"bucket of steam" to clean something or ask her to go to the dining hall
and bring back a "piece of chow line," but do so in a way not to make her
mad.

The attractive 21-year-old lady reservist likes her job with the
6/83rd well enough that she and the other women attached to the unit are
considering asking the commander, Lieutenant Colonel Roger McDaniel, to
make the arrangement permanent.

#

Reservist

Woman Reservist Enjoys Summer Training

Ft. WASHINGTON--Rivulets of perspiration traced an erratic stream
through the dust that coated her face in the ~~intense~~ 103° degree heat as
Specialist-Four 4 Victoria Helmschmidt beamed her pleasure at a job well
done, ~~during~~ If she was in Annual Training ~~for~~ with the Sixth Battalion, 83rd Field Artillery,
at Ft. Washington, which began August 1st.

Specialist Ms. Helmschmidt, who prefers being called "Vickie," ~~works as~~ is

More

(2/ Reservist)

a secretary for the State department of transportation ~~most of the time,~~ but on weekends and for 2 weeks each year she is an ~~army~~ (TAMMS) clerk. ~~She explains that TAMMS means The~~ (Army Maintenance Management System) ~~and her job is to~~ *She* keep *s* track of maintenance and dispatch of vehicles. This unit is going through ~~the paces of~~ an Army Training Test ~~and everyone seems to be doing his or her best to see they pass the test.~~

Viki is one of four ~~ladies~~ *women* attached to the ~~6/83rd~~ *unit* for annual training. Because ~~the Artillery unit~~ *it* is a combat arms unit, subject to deployment in the event of conflict, ~~girls~~ *women* may not be assigned *permanently.*

She says she likes to work hard and enjoys a challenge. Viki likes to "go different places and do different things." She says, "girls in the Army Reserve are like girls anywhere. We aren't looking for guys and just want to do a good job."

"The guys I work with are just like big brothers," she said. "They tease me a little, but respect the fact that I have a job to do and know how to do it." She says they occasionally play tricks on her because she hasn't been in the Army ~~too~~ long and sometimes ask her to go after a "bucket of steam" to clean something or ask her to go to the dining hall and bring back a "piece of chow line," but ~~do so~~ in a way not to make her *angry* ~~mad.~~

The ~~attractive~~ 21-year-old ~~lady~~ reservist likes her job ~~with the 6/83rd~~ well ~~enough~~ that she *like the other* ~~and the other~~ women attached to the unit, *is* ~~are~~ considering asking the commander, (Lieutenant) (Colonel) Roger McDaniel, to make the arrangement permanent. (#)

Aliens

A study of the Nation's immigration policy by Abba Schwartz has been approved by the Trustees of the Twentieth Century Fund, it was announced today.

Schwartz, former Assistant Secretary of State for Security and Consular Affairs, was instrumental in the passage of the immigration act of 1965. He plans to review the history of the act and recent amendments to it in order to propose new measures to improve and strengthen its provisions. He will be assisted by Marion F. Houstoun, formerly with the Department of Labor Immigration and Naturalization Service, who will be co-author of the study.

His project is one of a series of analytical studies sponsored and supervised by the Fund, an independent research foundation that conducts studies on major economic, political, and social issues.

Schwartz will focus particular attention on illegal immigration. Citing recent Justice Department figures indicating that between one and ten million illegal aliens are now living in the United States, Schwartz suggests a grant of "amnesty" to those who have resided in the country since 1968, when the act's quota system took effect, as a possible means of reducing the dimensions of the problem.

#

Derail

ELM CITY -- Nineteen cars of a 79-car Union Pacific freight train derailed near here early Saturday, blocking both east and west-bound rail traffic.

The 4:35 a.m. derailment of the westbound cars caused no injuries, a spokesman for the Union Pacific said, but crews said traffic would be blocked for an indefinite period of time.

The spokesman said the cars contained General Motors auto parts, however many of the cars would be rail cars would be salvaged and loss to the auto pasrts was minimal.

He said the cause of the accident was till still under investigation but he speculated that a brokem wheel on one of the cars had caused it.

The accident accident damaged 1,000 feet of track. About 60 crewmen were on the scene late Saturday, attempting to clear the tracks.

The Up UP official said the accident shut off all east-west tr rail transportation, which includes about 20 trains.

He said workers were to continue repairs but he expected at least one track to be cleared up by midnight Saturday.

Cleanup work will continue.

#

Botulism

FREMONT -- A general botulism seminar encompassing all types of the disease will begin here April 17 for a three-day session in the Frontier Room of the International Hotel withspecialists from across the United States presenting papers on their particular research and findings.

Dr. Horace Isom, microbiologist at the Elk Valley birg refuge research station, reported the seminar is sponsored by the Inter-Agency Botulism Research Coordinating Committee.

Dr. Isom said officials of the Food and Drug Administration from Washington, D. C., and a research team from the Center for Disease Control, Atlanta, Georgia, will attend and present facts and figures on the mortality rate due to certain types of botulism.

Physicians, specialists and microbiologiest from California universities, the University of Wisconsin and the University of M Michigan will also present their papers during the seminar sessions.

Frat

Gamma Gamma Fraternity members of the University chose their new sweetheart for the year Saturday night during the annual Sweetheart Banquet at Marina Lodge on Lake Wahapeto.

Martha Martin, Pi Beta Phi Sororoty, was picked from six fina lists at the dinner and dance. She was ushered in with a bouqu of roses while out going weetheart Clara Button was honored likewise as outgoing sweetheart.
Other Finalists was Dadie Glutz, Connie Switzer, Pamela Westley, Mitzi Broman, Cindy Mathers and LIz Jones.
Approximtely 65 couples attended the social affair. The fraternity with St. Constanine as it patron founder traditionally pays for the dinner and overnight lodging.

Budget

ELM CITY -- An ordinance revising the budget and appropriating funds to govern expenditures of Elm City for the Fiscal year ending

June 30 has been ordained by the City Council, according to Frank W. Evans, city recorder.

The amended budget for the current fiscal year brings the budgeted amounts in line with expenditures which have been necessary because of various changes throughout the year.

The budgeted amount for the administrative department for the fiscal year was changed to $113,299.86 from $87,571.90 to cover the city's expenditures for the industrial park, an item which came up during the fiscal year.

The fire department budget was lowered by approximately $35,000, reflecting an amoung budgeted for a new fire station which was not during the year.

Buedgeted funds for the electrical department were also changed. The electrical production department budget was increased by $7,0000 to cover the increase costs of electricity purchased and the budget for the electrical department's physical system was increased from $94,825.88 to $170,488.28 to cover the increased costs of rebuilding the electrical distribution.

26. HEADLINE TYPOGRAPHY

The headline came into use about the time of the Civil War, in the late Penny Press era, when newspapers began dealing in urgent news. In the late nineteenth century, bold spread heads covering many columns were introduced, partly in response to the popular journalism of the day, partly because new printing techniques permitted the rotary press to accommodate them. Shortly after the turn of the century, headlines in most American newspapers had standardized to a *dropline* or *stepped* headline pattern that was to dominate head styles for more than half a century. In this form the top line was set flush to the left margin and each succeeding line was indented under it until the last line fit flush right. Headlines set in all-capital letters also were common:

BEWARE OF MAN WITH SNEEZE, IS WARNING

Rapid Spread of Disease in the State Causes Public Officials to Renew Their Efforts.

From the *Salt Lake Tribune*, 1919, by permission.

More often than not the headline was set in several banks, that is, in the major unit of several lines, followed by one or sometimes several units of subordinate headlines, each describing a part of the story in one or more lines, as in the example above.

These decks or banks also followed formal patterns. In the example above the auxiliary deck follows the form called a *hanging indention*. The top line is set flush left and sometimes flush right with subsequent lines indented an equal measure underneath. Sometimes the deck or bank under a top head was set as an *inverted pyramid*, with the top line flush left and right and each subsequent line of shorter length centered underneath.

Today you would look almost in vain for these kinds of patterns, so they are mostly of historical interest. *The New York Times* still uses the stepped, all-cap pattern on Page One; however, the inside pages are made up chiefly of single-line multiple-column heads. The major section pages are truly artist's pages in which new, highly inventive headlines defy rigid stylizing.

The *Chicago Tribune's* unusual "Feminique" section departs from standard headline formats entirely. Headlines are the lead of the story. A succession of the three or four first lines of the story lead, each set in progressively smaller type, forms the headline and reads directly into the body type.

Five years ago she was working at the Museum of Modern Art and writing for Art in America. Today, the name Joan Vass

on a sweater automatically makes it a hot fashion item.

She claims the transition from art and a byline to fashion designer with a status label was not planned or a lifelong ambition but merely a matter of "altruism."

"I just wanted to help women who had marketable skills," Vass says. "I wanted to give some talented women an outlet for their creativity."

Vass, who started designing clothes that women could make in their homes, now heads what amounts to a cottage industry right in New York City.

"All our things are made within a 100-mile radius of Manhattan, and everything is handmade, one at a time, and we never ask anyone to make anything she doesn't like," Vass says.

From the *Chicago Tribune*, December 10, 1979, by permission.

The flush-left headline is the prevailing pattern in America. The lines (one to four, rarely more) are set evenly flush to the left margin (or slightly indented) and are allowed to run more or less ragged to the right, provided they are reasonably symmetrical:

Energy Czar Sees Potential In Shale

From the *Salt Lake Tribune*, 1980, by permission.

Headlines in which each line is centered in the column sometimes are used, but mostly for accent:

Here's Glance
At Latest
Developments
In Mideast

From the *Salt Lake Tribune,* 1980, by permission.

The subordinate headlines, nowadays usually referred to simply as decks and less commonly as banks, are, when used at all, usually set flush left, often indented under the top head:

Hundreds Displaced
by Wyoming Floods
Parts of Colorado Get 1½ Feet
of Snow, Causing Schools to Close

From the *Los Angeles Times,* April 25, 1980, by permission.

In this example the deck is indented about a sixth of an inch (one pica) from the left side. This spacing is quite standard, although a few papers indent more deeply, whereas some others do not indent at all. The theory in indenting is to improve balance between the two headline units, the top and the deck. The white space left by the deck indentation balances the white space left by the ragged flush-left lines of the top head. Indentation also sets off and emphasizes the deck.

The term *deck* is sometimes incorrectly used to mean each line of the headline. The term is more properly applied to the headline *unit* consisting of one or more lines.

For a discussion of how the deck is written, see p. 314.

The kicker headline—a line set in smaller type, usually centered or flush left above the main headline—has also become widely used. It performs much the same function as the deck without having to conform to a rigid pattern. Kickers usually are set at least two type sizes smaller than the main headline and in headlines of more than one column width are rarely more than half as long as the main head. In addition to providing an opportunity to give the reader more information, they help dress the page and accent the headline by providing more open or white space around it.

In Idaho, Texas

Air crashes kill 5

DEAR ABBY

Husband Wants Wife to Drop Her Best Friend

From the *Salt Lake City Deseret News*, 1980, by permission.

A reverse kicker form also is used by some newspapers, but only for special effect. The kicker line is only a single dramatic word or two, set in large type, with the main headline running underneath or alongside in substantially smaller or contrasting type. The term *hammer headline* is sometimes applied to this form.

Oil prices
OPEC doves plan $6-per-barrel boost

MX Deseret News takes look at missile, effects on Utah

From the *Salt Lake City Deseret News*, 1980, by permission.

Thus, headlines are becoming more and more inventive in appearance and much less tied to formal patterns. In addition, page columns have become wider, decidedly so on major display pages. The six-column front page has largely superseded the eight-column page. While the pages are mostly smaller than the broadsheets of a few years ago, in order to save costly newsprint, the columns themselves are from a quarter to a half inch wider, allowing more to be said in the headline.

Headline Schedules and Charts

The headline schedule lists the head patterns used by a newspaper, showing style, count, and usages. Some papers have abandoned formal schedules and rely on patterns known to be acceptable to those putting the paper together. Radical daily departures from typical appearance would do violence to the day-to-day look of the paper. Each publication cultivates a pattern its readers recognize. So just as the style guide arbitrates standards for text writers, there are pattern regulators for head writers and makeup editors.

A headline schedule included at the end of this chapter offers a wide variety of headline choices. Our schedule specifies capital and lower-case letters. Every word is capitalized. In some other schedules conjunctions and prepositions of fewer than four letters are in small letters, sometimes even at the beginning of lines. Either form is acceptable as long as it is followed consistently. Some papers have gone to all lower case except for the first word and proper nouns. Almost all use the less legible all-cap headline sparingly, and only for accent.

Designations

The headline schedule uses the four-digit method of designating headline sizes that has become fairly standard in American papers. A 1-30-3 headline designation tells the compositor:

1 (1 column width)
30 (30-point type)
3 (3 lines of type)

Sometimes this designation is listed with dashes separating the elements: 1-30-3. Usually the dashes are not used: 1303. In our headline schedule, the number of lines is set off by a dash: 130-3.

The schedule includes the abbreviations specifying the name and style of the type used: TH for Tempo heavy, TB for Tempo bold, MM for Metro medium, and MB for Metro black. Some schedules use a number of suffixes and affixes to the four-digit designation to explain special headline distinctions: The letter W before the number means a wide-measure column (often 14.9 picas wide instead of the standard 11): W 2242. The pica is a printer's measure: there are 12 points to the pica and six picas to the inch. The letter K means the head must include a kicker: K 2241. J designates a jump head, a headline over the portion of a story that is continued to another page. An X after the designation means the head is to be set in italics. B means the head must be counted slightly shorter so that it can be in a box, that is, so a line may be ruled around it. Thus it is possible to quickly and simply designate a wide-column boxed headline in italics with a kicker for a jump story as WBKJ 2302X.

Heads for variant column sizes drop the first digit and use instead the width designation in picas: 15.9 picas-24-2. The headline *chart* lists unit counts for the complete assortment of head sizes and lengths possible in eight columns, or far more than are *illustrated* in the headline schedule itself. A chart listing per-column count of headline type follows the headline schedule at the end of this chapter.

Counting the Headline

You will need to know how to write headlines to fit a predetermined space. This is the system called *counting in.* In using the videoscreen to edit copy, you will have the distinct advantage of composing the headline on the tube and knowing instantly whether it will fit the designated space you have coded for it according to the instruction of the layout editor. Otherwise, you will need to count the headline. In either case, some knowledge of why and how a combination of letters does or doesn't fit a designated space is essential.

Type is variable in width. Every letter of any type face and size differs from the shape and width of every other letter in the same grouping (or "font"). This is different from the typewriter, where each character and space is of the same width (except for the few variable spacing typewriters like some IBM Executive models in which each letter has a unit value). Point charts do exist that tell the precise width in points of every type character in a given point size and style. They aren't used on copy desks. To add up all point values of the individual characters to determine whether the words would fit the designated space would require a calculator. And it's not necessary. This is because *unit values* can be assigned to groups of letters for easy counting.

The unit value of a letter depends to some extent on the type design itself. Generally, however, the following unit counts are used, and they are the ones expressed in our headline schedule.

Count as follows:

1 unit: all lower case letters except i, l, f, j, t, m, and w.
$\frac{1}{2}$ unit: i, l, f, j, t.
$\frac{1}{2}$ unit: punctuation marks except the question mark, which is 1.
$\frac{1}{2}$ unit: space between words.
$1\frac{1}{2}$ unit: m, w.
$1\frac{1}{2}$ unit: all numerals except 1 ($\frac{1}{2}$ unit) and the dollar sign (1).
$1\frac{1}{2}$ unit: capital letters except M, W (2 units), I, and J (1).

Experience tells the headline writer how to improvise on these counts. For example, in the commonly used headline type called Bodoni, several small letters counted as a full unit are on the thin side: c, e, s, r, in lower case. If many of these appear in the line, the copy editor generally compensates by adding a unit or so of count. The Bodoni upper-case K, H, and R are very wide. One paper that uses the Bodoni face has gone to a different counting system that takes these variations into account. The basic unit for lower-case letters in that system is 2, with the smallish letters counting $1\frac{1}{2}$. On some papers spaces are counted a full unit. This is desirable where all lower case or all caps are used in headlines so that words would tend to read together.

Let's count a headline, using our unit system, to see if it would fit as a 3302 M-Black headline:

2	$\frac{1}{2}$	1	1	$\frac{1}{2}$	1	$\frac{1}{2}$	1	1	1	$1\frac{1}{2}$	1	$\frac{1}{2}$	$1\frac{1}{2}$	1	$1\frac{1}{2}$	$\frac{1}{2}$	$\frac{1}{2}$	$\frac{1}{2}$	1	1
M	i	d	d	l	e		I	n	c	o	m	e		F	a	m	i	l	i	e	s

$1\frac{1}{2}$	1	$\frac{1}{2}$	$1\frac{1}{2}$	1	1	1	$\frac{1}{2}$	$1\frac{1}{2}$	1	1	1	$\frac{1}{2}$	1	1	$1\frac{1}{2}$	2	1	1	1
T	o		F	a	c	e		H	o	u	s	i	n	g		W	o	e	s

The first line adds up to 21 units, the second to $20\frac{1}{2}$. Both lines will fit, because our headline-counting chart shows a maximum count of $23\frac{1}{2}$ for each line. The lines fill the allotted space well and are approximately the same count, so they will appear symmetrical, rather than ragged, when set in type. If either line were even half a count over the maximum, it would have to be rewritten. Do not confuse the headline size designation in points with a unit count for each head size. There is no correlation.

Head counting comes quickly with a little practice. You won't have to list and add up these figures once you count by teaming up two half units to make a full unit:

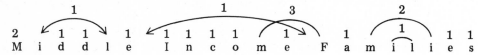

Type Measurement

As an editor you will be working with type faces. Some knowledge of type faces and how type is measured is essential, though you no longer will be burdened with the old print-shop nomenclatures that were in use with hot metal type and letterpress printing processes.

Type is measured in points. A point is approximately 1/72nd of an inch. The size of type is its height. This means from the top of the highest letter to the bottom of the lowest letter. (In typography language, from the top of the highest ascender—the stroke above the center body—to the bottom of the lowest descender—the stroke below the center body.) The width of any character of type is not its size; widths vary considerably within sizes according to the design of the individual letters and whether they are expanded or condensed, light or bold.

If you measured with a printer's line gauge (which is marked in picas) from the top of the letter h to the bottom of the letter g in Bodoni, you would get its size in printer's measure. If you measured with a standard ruler and the type were half an inch high, it would be 36-point type, a quarter inch high would be 18-point type, and so on.

In most type faces, a variety of standard sizes is offered. The smallest type used in newspapers is 5 ½ point, called *agate*. It is used for box scores, market reports, long lists of names and other statistical or tabular matter. Other point sizes often used for text or body of the story are 6, 7, 8, 9, 10, 11, and 12. One reason for knowing the term *agate* is that newspaper advertising rates are quoted in agate lines, 14 to the inch. The most commonly used size in newspaper stories is 8 point.

Standard point sizes for headline faces are 14, 18, 24, 30, 36, 42, 48, 60, and 72. These larger sizes also are used for advertising titles and other major display printing. Some faces include 84-, 96-, 120-, and even 144-point sizes, which are used only for banners— headlines that go all the way across the top of the page. Our headline schedule provides 72-, 96-, and 120-point faces for banners but does not include an 84.

Type sizes once were designated by names. A depth of 6 points is a *nonpareil*, and 6-point type was known as nonpareil type. A depth of 12 points was a *pica*, and 12-point type was known as pica type. Brevier was the name given to 8-point type, English to 14-point, Long Primer to 10-point.

In addition to the term *agate*, the only survivor in general usage among the old names is the term *pica*, denoting 12-point type. The term *em*, which is a horizontal space of the same number of points as the size of type in use, is used nowadays in newspaper work only to refer to the pica em—hence the terms *pica* and *em* are used interchangeably by editors to refer to 12 points. Six picas or ems equal an inch, 72 picas equal a foot. The term *en*, or half an *em*, is hardly used any more on newspapers except in crossword puzzles. It is used, however, in book production.

The selection of type faces that go into the headline schedule, and the combining of these with a legible and harmonious text type, is largely the province of the typographer and artist who design the paper. The serious journalism student will want to know more about type selection and display, although this knowledge is not essential to the headline writing craft. The references at the end of this unit will be of considerable help.

Headline Schedule

114-1 M-Black (count 16)

Only A Dummy

114-1 M-Blk Ital (cnt 16)

So Long, Friends

118-2 MM (count 15)

**Tory Chief Bows
Out As Leader**

1182-MM Ital (count 15)

***Plymouth Street
Up For Auction***

1182-M-Black (Count 13)

**A Chart To Aid
The Job Count**

124-2 MM (count 11)

**'Clear Track'
To Freedom**

124-3 M-Black (count 10)

**Wide Hunt
Continues
In Robbery**

K-124-3 MM (count 9½)

MISS UNIVERSE

**If Charms
Don't Help,
Charm Will**

K-124-3 MM Ital (cnt 9½)

FIVE INCHES

***Santa Rosa
Cleans Up
After Rain***

124-2 MM ital (count 11)

***Home Rule
Too Much***

124-2 M-Black (count 10)

**Color Film
On Wildlife**

124-2 M-Black ital (cnt 10)

***Go On And
Get Sick***

342-2 T-Bold Ital (count 16½)

FBI Agents Called In Baker Probe

348-2 T-bold Ital. (count 15)

Crowd Watched As He Drowned

348-3 T-H (count 14)

Anchor Dropped On House Economy Cruise

348-3 T-H Ital. (count 14)

Producing Less, Earning More At The Factory

230-2 M-Black (count 15½)

Tipster Cashes In With Speedy Call

K-230-2 MM (count 16)

SENATE ACTION

Forward Step For Voting Rights Bill

K-242-2 T-B Ital cent. (count 12)

'SO LONG!'

Old Grey Fox Heads North

342-3 T-H Ital (count 16)

Trapped Child, 3, Obeys Orders, Helps Rescuers

360-2 T-B ital (count 13½)

Let's All Play Musical Chairs

360-3 T-H (count 11½)

Hopefuls See Oregon As Ultimate Test

360-3 T-B (count 13½)

Disaster Lurks In Race To 'Instant' Riches

872-1 T-M Ital. (count 32)

Bandits Grab $38

896-1 T-H caps (count 21)

YANK FLIER

8-120-1 Franklin Gothic caps (count 20)

PLANE WIPE

PER-COLUMN COUNT OF HEADLINE TYPES

TYPE	MAXIMUM COUNT BY COLUMNS							
	1	2	3	4	5	6	7	8
14 pt.								
Metro Black*	16	32	48					
18 pt.								
Metro Med.*	15	30	45	60				
Metro Black*	13	26	39	52				
24 pt.								
Metro Med.*	11	22	33	44	55			
Metro Black*	10	20	30	40	50	60		
30 pt.								
Metro Med.†	9	18	27	36	45	54		
Tempo Bold Ital.	8	17	27	34	42	51		
Metro Black†	7¾	15½	23½	31	38¾	46½		
Metro Med. CAPS	7	14	21	28	35	42		
Tempo Heavy Ital.	7¾	15½	23½	31	38¾	46½		
36 pt.								
Tempo Heavy*	6	12	18	24	30	36	42	
Metro Med.†	7½	15	22½	30	37½	45	52½	
Tempo Bold*	6½	13	22	28	34	45	52	
42 pt.								
Tempo Heavy*	5½	11	15¾	22	27	33	38½	47
Tempo Bold*	6	12	18	24	30	36	42	50
48 pt.								
Tempo Heavy*	4½	9	14	19	23½	28	32½	38
Tempo Bold	5	10	15½	20½	26	31	36¼	41
Tempo Bold Ital.	5¼	10½	15¾	21	26¼	31¼	36¾	42
60 pt.								
Tempo Heavy†			11½	15	19½	24	27	
Tempo Bold*			13½	18	22½	28	32½	37
72 pt.								
Tempo Heavy†			10½	13½	16½	20	23½	27
Tempo Bold*				14½	18	21½	25	29
Tempo Med.†				16	20	24	28	32
96 pt.								
Tempo Heavy†				13½	16½	20	23	27

*Denotes italic available, count same.
†Denotes no italics available
(48 pt. tempo bold exception).

EXERCISES

On the following stories, write the headline designated. Refer to the headline schedule for
the appearance and the schedule or count chart for the unit count maximum. You may not
exceed the maximum count, nor should the head be too short. Use the space effectively.
This means your headline should not be more than two counts short of the maximum.

The headline should be written at the top of the page just as it is to appear. (A two-
line head is written in two lines.) Edit the story completely first. The headline designation
code remains on the story and is circled, as are all instructions to the printer.

Philanderer   (230-2 *M Black*)

Much has been said and written about sexual harassment of women on

the job. The boss who fondles his unwilling secretary, the executive who

demands sex in return for a job or promotion--many such cases have been

documented. However, such pressures are by no means focused exclusively

on working women.

It happens at the University.

One former student claimed she had such an experience with a profes-

sor in the Communications Department. Her problem was twofold because he

was both her instructor and faculty adviser.

Three years ago, she said, she was attending a meeting with fellow

classmates to discuss a large class project. Her professor, who is now

tenured and still with the University, called her out of the meeting.

"He had flirted with me before and made comments about my body, but I

didn't think much of it. I really didn't take him seriously," she said.

"This day he told me that we had some things to discuss privately so I

followed him into an office. When I got there I leaned against the wall.

He put his arms aroung me and started telling me how nice I looked, then started unbuttoning my blouse."

The student said she didn't know how to respond. She wanted to get out of the situation but feared negative repercussions if she got angry. She finally decided to make light of the situation and escape gracefully.

"I slipped out of the hold but felt damned uncomfortable about it for some time later. Even today it still bothers me," she said.

This professor was aggressive and did not let her denial in that one instance stop him from continuing to harass her for sexual favors. She said he offered her a prestigious position, which most of her classmates sought, if she would "come around."

"He never came out and said, 'Have sex with me and I'll give you the position,' but it was strongly implied," she said. "He told me to make my quarterly review appointments with him last so 'we won't be disturbed.' Sometimes he was even so bold to say, 'Let's get this affair rolling.'"

Every quarter she had to visit him for her quarterly review. She said the thought of being alone with him became so unbearable that she had to change advisers. When asked by department officials why she changed she would say, "We had personality conflicts."

According to the student, part of the problem may have been because she was divorced. He was still married.

#

Philanderer

Sex Harassment:
It Happens Here
(230-2 M Black)

~~Much has been said and written about~~ sexual harassment of women on the job: The boss who fondles his unwilling secretary, the executive who demands sex in return for a job or promotion. ~~Many such cases have been documented. However, such pressures are by no means focused exclusively on working women.~~

It happens at the University.

One former student claimed she had such an experience with a professor ~~in the Communications Department~~. Her problem was twofold because he was both her instructor and faculty adviser.

Three years ago, ~~she said,~~ she was attending a meeting with fellow classmates to discuss a large class project. Her professor, who is now tenured and still with the University, called her out of the meeting, *she said.*

"He had flirted with me before and made comments about my body, but I didn't think much of it. I really didn't take him seriously," she said. "This day he told me that we had some things to discuss privately so I followed him into an office. When I got there I leaned against the wall. He put his arms around me and started telling me how nice I looked, then started unbuttoning my blouse."

The student said she didn't know how to respond. She wanted to get out of the situation but feared negative repercussions if she got angry. She finally decided to make light of the situation and escape gracefully.

"I slipped out of the hold but felt damned uncomfortable about it for some time later. Even today it still bothers me," she said.

This professor was aggressive and did not let her denial in that one

(more)

2/Philanderer

instance stop him from continuing to harass her for sexual favors. She said he offered her a prestigious position, which most of her classmates sought, if she would "come around."

"He never came out and said, 'Have sex with me and I'll give you the position,' but it was strongly implied," she said. "He told me to make my quarterly review appointments with him last so 'we won't be disturbed.' Sometimes he was even so bold to say, 'Let's get this affair rolling.'"

Every quarter she had to visit him for her quarterly review. She said the thought of being alone with him became so unbearable that she had to change advisers. When asked by department officials why she changed she would say, "We had personality conflicts."

According to the student, part of the problem may have been because she was divorced. He was still married.

(#)

Strike

118-2 M Black

A strike continued Friday at Refreshment, Inc. Bottling Co.'s bottlin plant but how many workers were off the job was not clear.

A company spokesman said "14 to 16," but the employees' representative with the United Steelworkers of America said the figure was closer to 40. He said the union represents about 90 of the firm's 220 employes.

At stake are union demands for 45 cents an hour across the
board and many items in fringe package.

The bottling plant was operating "normally," the company
spokesman said.

Daycare   （330-1 *Metro Med*）

Proposed cuts in statewide day-care funding and programs will be
among items discussed during a meeting of Parents for Good Day Care
Monday, September 25, at 7:30 p.m. at the Central City Center, 243
Industry Boulevard.

According to Olga Jenson, splkeswoman for the organization, this
year's State Family Services budget includes little money for day care.
Yet additional money is needed if center are to be improved and made
available to more people.

Ms. Jenson also said that will not assist families needing day care
aid for more than four children. "So it's crucial that more funding be
allocated. It's the large family that has the fewest resources to go
to paying for day care," she said.

Steessing that the meetings are open to all parents, citizens and
day care center operators interested in improving day care facilities and
programs, Ms. Jenson said the members will also focus on a Congressional
Bill which has earmarked $500 for day care programs.

The organization is also in the process of distributing brochures on
the availability of state aid to assist low income working families with
rising day care costs.

#

Conserve

(742-1 *Tempo Heavy*)

The State Public Service Commission and the State Energy Office
jointly announced the launching of a public service campaign to persuade
people to conserve energy during peak usage times.

The program is called "Energy Alert Day" will be comprised of
30-second spot announcements telling the people to use as little energy
during the daytime as possible on days when the temperature reaches 95
degrees.

The announcement will tell people to avoid using their electric
dishwasher clothes washers and drier appliances until after 9 p.m., and
to eliminate all other unnecessary energy consumption.

The reasons, according to PSC and Energy Office officials, is that
electrical energy facilities are designed to accommodate a certain peak
usage, and when usage goes above that designated pek, more expensive and
less efficient backup systems are needed.

If energy usage is spread more during the daytime to make energy
usage more even throughout the day, it places a less demand on the system
and may, in the long run delay need for building costly new power plants.

PSC Chairman Sally G. Carter said that because energy consumption
has declined a bit recently -- she credits the energy crisis and higher
utility rates -- the construction of a plant in Elk County has been
delayed by a year.

She said that one-year delay will save ratepayers $10 million.

Reed Searle, director of the State Energy Office, said the National
Weather Service has agreed to include "Energy Alerts" on all their for-

-more-

Conserve 1st add /

casts for temperatures of 95 degrees and over. He said also that the announcements are being distributed to all radio stations in the state.

"Electrical energy use is highest in summer months and reaches its peak generally on the hottest days of the year when air conditioners put their greatest load on the electrical power system," he said. "If annual and daily peaks of energy usage can be reduced, we not only save energy, we save money. That's why Energy Alert Day was instituted," he said.

#

Dance   (324-1 Metro Med)

A program sponsored by the State Division of Fine Arts introduce grade of Fine Arts introduced a grade school children to modern dance and at the same time provide exercise and stimulate creativity was held at Valley Elementary School.

According to Marsha Termilliger, public information director for the division, the program is unique because it stimulates creativity in children and at the same time provides a medium with which they can express themselves.

The program consists of professional dancers coming into the school and working with students helping them learn how to explore the possibilities of using movement as a form of expression.

The program is part of the division's Arts in the schools program, was started this year as part, and is funded in part by the National Endowment for the Arts. Ms. Termilliger said that, thus far, the program has been "very successful," and the fine arts division intends to continue the in school dance program next year in schools throughout the state.

She said that one of the reasons the program has been successful is that young children, unlike adults, don't tend to look on modern dance as a complicated art form.

"The kids look on dance as something different -- it's not complex or difficult to them. It's unstructured and they can appreciate it -- and it's fun," she said.

Termilliger added that the dancers in the schools is a "special" program, because it teachers the children one a different form of self-expression, and this adds to their experience and helps make them more well-rounded individuals.

Dancers from several local professional dance troups have participated in the program in the school district, and Tuesday's final performance program was taught by Modine Walker of the Walker Dance Troupe. Walker has been dancing for about 10 years, and has worked in other troupes.

Walker said the program, usually offered to each class three or four times, serves as a medium to incorporate helps younger students be more appreciative of dance by incorporating it into their curriculum. Also, it satisfies the need of physical exercise for the students in many cases.

"We're here because the program gets the students to work creatively

through dance, and helps make them aware that they can use their bodies

as a form of expression," she said.

#

27. OTHER HEADLINE FORMS

Decks

Remember, a *deck* is a subordinate part of the headline (but not a *subhead*, a term explained here). Forms of decks were discussed earlier in this section. The content of the deck should both amplify the information given in the top and add new information:

> Prisoners Hold 2 Guards   (Top)
>   Take Over   (Deck)
>   Cell House
>   In Indiana

The deck is particularly valuable in complex stories but is of some help to the reader even in the relatively simple hard news piece:

> Three Inmates Flee
> Over Prison Walls
>   None Hurt Despite
>   Hail of Gunfire

Note that in the first example above the deck does not have its own subject. This is permissible. Often decks begin with verbs which have as their subject the subject of the top portion, but the verb should always be in agreement with the subject in number.

Few papers use more than one deck. When more than one is used, the first deck is the most important. In *The New York Times*, the first deck is sometimes followed by a single crossline pointing up some important or dramatic fact succinctly; the last deck rounds up whatever is of most compelling value that has not been stated.

Decks are usually set in type at least two sizes smaller than the top (18-point decks under 30-point tops, for instance), to provide contrast. Since deck sizes for particular heads are standardized, on most papers, it is necessary in the headline designation typically to order only a "with 1 col deck" or even a "plus 1." One-line decks under multiple-column heads are fairly common today. Decks under smaller headlines in subordinate positions on the page have been all but abandoned.

Kickers

Kickers also go by the names *whiplash*, *eyebrow*, and *flash*, but *kicker* is understood among all American newspaper journalists. It is a single line, usually half the length of the main headline or even shorter. Its function is similar to that of the deck: It amplifies, usually by pointing up a salient point not included in the main head. Kicker line are also used for standing head titles for columns, names of columnists, and roundup columns such as "People in the News." Although the kicker is positioned above the main head, it is set in smaller type and the presumption is that it is read after the main line. Kickers usually are set in the same type face as the main head. Sometimes an italic kicker is used with a Roman headline, and vice versa. As with decks, the kicker lines should not contain key words found in the main head.

The kicker's function in adding information is particularly welcome to the head writer when an idea or word or words that must be used to make the head complete and accurate is too long for the body of the head, e.g., "reapportionment," "constitutional convention," or when the idea that should be conveyed by the headlines is especially complex. Study the headlines in newspapers available to you, with attention to the question of whether kickers add something or are used merely as adornment or as a makeup expedient.

As in the case of decks, the kicker must be in grammatical and logical agreement with the main head. In the following head, the kicker at the top left is incongruous:

Struck by Lightning
Charred Body Found on Ship

The kicker should of course read: "Sailor Struck by Lightning."

Jump Heads

A *jump head* is an additional headline ordered to cover the "jump" or continuation portion of the story on another page. Jumps are used less frequently today under the impact of streamlined makeup, since relatively few stories are carried over even from Page One to inside pages. But virtually all newspapers jump at least some stories. Jump heads are of many kinds. Some papers simply reset the original headline for use on the inside pages. Others use only a key word from the original headline or one that is central to the story, so that "President Confers on Energy Crisis" may be set as "Energy" for the jump story. Others rewrite the headline, often to different size specifications, to meet inside page-make-up requirements, and still others use all three of these forms.

The jump head should be a close paraphrase of the original, so the reader can find the continuation of the story quickly and easily. It is *not* a headline only for the continuation portion of the story.

Subheads

Subheads function almost solely to break up long stretches of type and thereby to make reading material more inviting. They are rapidly becoming rare because of changes to horizontal makeup: Stories are now often packaged in multiple columns rather than allowed to run in long vertical rivers of type. New ways of breaking up vast forbidding areas of gray type are being introduced, including the use of boldface or italicized inserts, often in large type and ruled top and bottom, which in effect become headlines in themselves.

Magazines long have used devices to break up type every few paragraphs, often with a large, boldface initial letter (for example, a 24-point initial letter followed by the balance of the initial word in all capital or small capital letters in the same size as the text). Some news magazines use several bold cap and lower-case heads spaced at intervals in the story and set on the same line as the regular body type. Some papers have used dashes or stars to give the reader places at which to pause. Others abandoned subheads and now merely insert a white space of about a line's depth (8 points) at intervals in the story. Some use a boldface capitalized word or two at the beginning of every three or four paragraphs to give the paper dress. In some papers, subheads are set in larger and more contrasting type than the body, sometimes up to 14 points, especially when type is set in two columns rather than one. Sometimes the subhead is set flush left on the column, sometimes centered, sometimes flush right. The centered cap-and-lower-case boldface subhead is most commonly used.

A subhead is inserted every three or four paragraphs at approximately equal intervals in long stories. Some papers decree that subheads be used for all stories of more than six inches or six paragraphs in length; others, like *The New York Times*, use them in stories that run at least half a column, or about 10 inches. The subhead is written between the lines on the copy at the place it appears in the story and usually is designated merely as SH, which is circled. If you are working with a printer unfamiliar with your subhead style, be sure to specify the typography, however; (for example, "bfclc centered," meaning boldface cap and lower case).

Subheads should be informative. Where possible, they should be inserted at natural breaks in the story, in effect as a headline for the paragraphs that follow, generally the paragraph immediately following. They follow all the rules for headlines, including typographical rules (for example, single quotes are used). The space is short, typically only about 30 spaces at a maximum—and subheads should be counted short to provide white space for emphasis. So the subhead more often than not must be a label headline.

Most papers insist that there be at least two subheads or none, but whatever logic there was in this seems lost. As a commonsense proposition, if you follow the rule of placement every three or four paragraphs in a story of 10 inches or more, you will be writing two or more subheads.

EXERCISES

On the following stories, write the headline designated. Remember, a K prefix means write a kicker. Refer to the headline schedule and counter for appearance and unit count.

Jazz

Shaw University's synt synthesis Jazz Ensamble has just returned from a three week concert tour of Romania and Hungary behind the Iron Curtain.

The 15-member troupe, directed by J. Robert Morton, played 11 concerts. Vocals were given by Sarah Ringer and Norma Ballard, he said

The tour was sponsored by Friendship Ambassadors, Inc., a New York cultural exchange organization which has sent numerous American musical groups to Rumania. This is the f first year Hungary has been included, the maestro said.

He said jazz is expecially popular in Eastern Europe and audiences
consistently clapped in unison -- demanding encores.

(#)

*Jazz Group Back
From E. Europe*

(Jazz)

(118-2 MM)

(Shaw University's ~~synt~~ synthesis Jazz Ensãmble has ~~just~~ returned
from a three/week concert tour of Romania and Hungar~~y behind the Iron
Curtain.~~

(The 15-member troupe, directed by J. Robert Morton, *performed in* ~~played~~ 11
concerts. Vocals were given by Sarah Ringer and Norma Ballard ~~he said~~

(The tour was sponsored by Friendship Ambassadors, Inc., a New York
cultural exchange organization ~~which~~ *that* has sent ~~numerous~~ *other* American musical
groups to Rumania. This is the ~~#~~ first year Hungary *was* ~~has been~~ included,
Morton
~~the maestro~~ said.

(He said jazz is expecially popular in Eastern Europe ~~and~~ audiences
consistently clapped in unison, demanding encores.

(#)

Burglary

(118-2 MM)

Police investigated the burglary of an auto repair shop at 442 E.
7th Street in which property valued at $5,129.25 was stolen.

The victims said the thieves broke a window to enter the business

and then they left with a bank bag contining change from a vending
machine and a large amount of tools.

#

Cows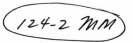

David O. Hinkley, Elm City, told sheriff's deputies that someone
attacked one of his cows in a field at 2575 W. 3300 North, shot it full
of arrows and took off with parts of the animal.

Vandals   124-2 MM

Ladd Hartmann, 625 Bluff View Avenue, told police that while he
was out vandals emtered his home and did extensive damage to the premises.

Apparently a hammer was used to smash a bed, television set, dresser
mirrors, bathroom fixtures, out. A wooden sword had been struck in the
middle of the bed, a painted American flag had been left on the floow
and on the wall were painted the words "De "Die you pig."

Approximate damage to the property was set at $2,000.

Smith. New
Hills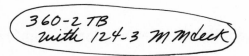

Full cooperation of residents in the Arlington Hills area to help
the City Police Department cope with the problem of keeping motor bikes

and off-road vehicles from scarring the mountain slopes was promised Wednesday when three persons interested in the area and its picturesque setting appeared before the City Commission and explained their interests and produced maps showing the areas where vegetation has diminished because of off-road vehiculer traffic.

Public Safety Commissioner Arnoldo J. Cortesi, Jr., said the police department is set up to patrol the various areas and has the trail bikes to do it with.

He explained the department did it last year but there was problems of prosecution. Maps of the area and the promise of residents they will testify in court cases will be of great benefit.

"Under this new proceedure it can be determine what private properties are being used by unwanted vehicles," he asserted. "The police will be patrolling these sections of trial bikes when the weather entices the motor bike riders to head for the hills."

Allen H. Tibbals, who lives at 1286 Windsor Drive, in high Arlington Hills, reminded commissioners off-road vehicles traveling the hillsides are a menace to drainage and cause erosion problems. He specifically cited the Holy Moses "motorcycle gang" as offenders. Although he did not amplify these remarks in the meeting he told reporters afterward the gang was composed of "wanton despoilers" who used the hills for reckless "joyriding" every Sunday during the summer.

Presenting a map showing areas needing protection, full cooperation of residents in combatting the problem was promised.

Mr. Tibbals recalled that two years ago this problem was serious and an ordinance was adopted providing that no one could ride on private property unless they had written notice from the owner.

A former State University professor of botnay recalled that 27 years ago the area above the City Cemetaryw as flooded and settlement along the steep front north of the city had previously been impared by past grazing abuse and cheatgrass fires.

Doctor Parley P. Seruggs, Professor Emeritus at the University, said the ravaging flood 27 years ago courses through the cemetary exposing graves and continued through residential areas causing $345,000,000 in property damage.

"We are ripe for such another catastrophe if we should get similar downpoors of rain in the areas," he warned. "This time the beginning channel's of these steep hills is not the result of too many hooves of sheep and cows, but to swarms of motor bikes or other off-road vehicles."

H. F. Eagle, who lives at 239 Aerie Street, property owner in the area, said there would be planting projects by the property owners. He said plans are to plant several thousand shrubs.

"There is no point in starting such a project until we can get the motor vehicle problem definately answered," he asserted.

Mr. Cortesi said the city would cooperate. He added that city officials were happy the residents were so willing to help solve the problem.

"Of course such a problem would not have arisen if this was a city watershed," he explained.

#

Bond

Elm City--Sale of three parcels of surplus property within the Elm City School District has been approved for sale by members of the District Board of Education.

The property to be disposed of includes land fronting the new Junior High School on 9200 North; the major portion of the old Junior High School and land located avross the road south of the Jefferson Elementary School.

The action was taken at the regular meeting of the board held at the district offices.

Two appraisers--one from the community in which the property is to be sold is located and one from outside the immediate community--will be employed to appraise the property. After studying the appraisals submitted, the bids will be called for each parcel of land from interested firms.

The board reserved the right to accept or reject bids that are not in line with the value placed on the property by the board.

Property for home sites will be sold near the new Junior High School. This fronts the school on 9200 North. It was noted that the City has asked the board to reserve two ten foot walk strips from the subdivision immediately south of the school board property. This leaves 1,238 frontage feet for sale. Depth of the property varies from 106 ft on the extreme west to 113 feet.

The shop and adjacent classrooms at the old Junior High School will be retained for warehouse purposes and for sheltered workshop teaching, officials said, with the main building of the building facility offered for sale.

A first right of refusal on property located back of the business

district has been granted to the City.

At the Jefferson School a small strip of property described as being

about ten feet deep is being offered.

                                            #

Fires   *118-2 MM*

     SPENCER CITY--SPENCER FIRE OFFICIALS SAID FIRE LOSSES IN

MAY WERE THE LOWEST TOTAL FOR THAT MONTH IN THREE YEARS.

OFFICIALS SAID THE LARGEST FIRE LOSS RESULTED FROM A LUMBER

YARD WIRING FIRE. OFFICIALS SAID DAMAGES WERE PUT AT $1,700.

OFFICIALS SAID THE MONTHLY TOTAL LOSS TO PROPERTY WAS $15,280.

OFFICIALS SAID THE YEAR'S TOTAL ENDING IN MAY WAS $158,675.

Water   *K124-3 MM*

     New water rates which will limit the amount of water used by

city residents to 43,000 gallons per month and an increase in the

costs of water used in excess of 23,000 gallons per month have

been adopted by the City Councio.

     The new rates are a manditory way of enforcing water restrictions

in the city and will remain in affect only while the drought conditions

exist.

Under the ordinance the rates for 10,000 gallon minimum each month and the overage use up to 23,000 gallons per month will remain the same as now.

Treatment

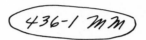

ELM CITY -- Elm City saturday will dedicate a surface water treatment plant, the biggest even for the 600 citizens of this area since pioneer times.

The ceremonies will beging at 10 a.m. at the treatment plant, with Mayor Emery MacIver acting as -master of ceremonies. The public is invited to the ceremony and to participate in tours that will be conducted until 4 P. M.

Mayor MacIver said the plan is of interest to all residents of the area as it is the first treatment plant of its kind in the state.

The $500,000 project culminates a five-year effort to provide the city with an adequate culinary water supply system that has the approval of the state board of health.

The plant is automated and will require only a part-time operator.

Built at a cost of half a million dollars, the plant serves 168 hookups, 10 of which are located outside city limits. The minimum rate is $8 per month per connection.

Rescue

(118-2 M Black)

A seven-year-old boy was uninjured Friday when he was buried by dirt that fell on him while playing in a house construction site at 423 Rosemont Ave. at about 11:30 a.m.

A spokesman for the City Fire Department said Blair Murphy, son of Mr. and Mrs. B. Alton Murphy, 497 Rosemont Ave., was uncovered by construction workers who witnessed the small landslide that covered the youth while he was playing in an area excavated for construction of a home.

The youth suffered a small bump on the head when inadvertently struck by a shovel weilded by one of his rescuers. He was treated and released at General Hospital.

                                    #

unanswered questions: _____

Parade

(124-3 M Black)

Oak City--High-stepping bands, colorful floats and pretty girls greeted the thousands of persons who Friday night watched the Pioneer Days parade here.

The parade, one of the state's largest, recalls the pioneer heritage. It highlights a weekend of activities sponsored by groups in the County area.

Running along Main Street from 10th South to 4th North, an estimated 30,000 spectators viewed the parade.

Leading this year's parade were two grand marshalls -- Rock star
Larry Fisher and Mrs. Rhoda Reilley, the state's Mother of the Year.

#

Media Center

While some few people still associate the idea of a church library
with eight, dusty, paperback volumes lying in the corner of a church
secretary's office, the media center at Baptist Conference Center shows
church workers that their libraries can be more than this.

"We are trying to enlarge the concept of library ministry through
our media center," explained Ernest Snyder, consultant with the church
library department of the Southern Baptist Sunday School Board and
director of the media center. "We're showing that a good library
shouldn't only have books, but also audio-visuals, tracts, maps and
clippings.

"Our center demonstrates what individual churches can do in their
own libraries. Every church, no matter what size, can have at least
some of what we have here."

The media center's 3000 square feet of space is filled with dis-
plays, study carols, a listening area, an audio-visuals preview room
and reading areas.

In addition to serving as a demonstration library, the media
center offers a number of other services to conferees, according to
Snyder. One of these services is the taping and duplication of the

2/2/2/Media Center

various weeks' worship services and conferences onto cassette tapes.
Last summer 6,640 of these tapes were sold to conference participants.

The media center also offers a large amount of reading and study
materials. These include free materials from many of the Southern
Baptist Convention boards and agencies, a display of the various church
literature published by the Sunday School Board, daily newspapers from
across the nation, state Baptist newspapers and over 4,000 books. All
of these materials are available for leisure-time reading, examination,
personal study or sermon preparation.

Another service offered by the media center is its materials preparation area. Here program leaders can find supplies and equipment to
use in preparing posters and teaching aids.

Special program helps are also sold in the media center. These
helps undergird the programs of the Sunday School Board.

Although the media center, which is in it fourth year of operation,
is available year round, it is fully staffed only during the summer
months. Last year more than 48,000 persons visited the media center,
according to Snyder.

Fashion

8301 Metro Med Caps

"You can look like a million bucks without spending it," says a
University fashion expert, but only if you're willing to make the
investment of time and planning.

Fashion - 2

"It's not how much you spend on your clothes that makes the difference," says Greta Peterssen, graduate assistant in the Department of Family and Consumer Studies. "It's the time, thought and artistry which you use to make the best choices."

The former assistant buyer for Goldwater's in Phoenix says the consumer can be trained to recognize fabrics, design lines and styles of major reputable clothing manufacturers, and that knowledge will make bargain hunting easier.

"I look for clothes that I recognize were made by a nationally known designer but that are being sold under a private label or no label at all--and at a savings," says Peterssen. "And many of the chain stores carry merchandise from these same manufacturers with no label."

Often bargains are waiting for the professional shopper who's not afraid to look in lesser-known outlets.

"Discount stores and thrift shops offer great bargains," says Peterssen. "Bargain basements are another gold mine."

Peterssen explains that major department stores located in larger cities are often organized with the designer shop on the top floor, the better dresses on the next floor down with the bargain shop located in the basement. If a dress does not sell in the designer shop, says it may be moved to better dresses and so on, until it's been marked down and ends up in the bargain basement.

"it's possible to find a Halston in the basement if you're really lucky," she adds.

Fashion - 3

  She warns that shopping in discount stores will test the imagination
of the shopper, since little effort is made to showcase merchandise. For
the creative shopper who's willing to sacrifice atmosphere and fancy
dressing rooms, there are great bargains in the discount stores, says
Peterssen.

  The former fashion buyer advises it's wise to set up an on-going
relationship with professional sales people. These are individuals who
maintain a personal file of customers which include size, taste and
specific garments desired. She also says it's wise to establish charge
accounts, since credit customers often receive advance notice of sales.

  Sales are a good way of saving money, says Peterssen, but the
shopper must be alert to some common pitfalls.

  "Shop very carefully, being sure to double check for flaws, good
construction, matching plaids and other design problems," says Peterssen.
"And be on the lookout for ship-ins, merchandise that has been brought in
just for a sale."

  "The easiest way to spot a ship-in is to notice a lack of quality or
construction, an off-brand or a tag that has obviously been forged to make
it look like legitimate markdowns have been made."

  Take time in shopping, she adds, to make sure you're getting the best
buy.

  "The malls make it easy to check several shope to make sure you're
getting the best garment for your money," says Peterssen. "And don't be
tempted to buy something at a store where you have a credit card when you
could buy it for less somewhere else if you had the cash."

Fashion - 4

Never impulse buy "for something to wear tonight," she advises. "Always look past tonight to determine if the dress you're considering can be adapted for office use and wear for other occasions.

Finally, Peterssen stresses the importance of cleaning and care after purchase to maximize a clothing budget.

"Always buy garments with care labels and fiber content clearly marked. A cheaper buy that must be dry cleaned may turn out to be more expensive than the higher priced washable item.

"And don't assume your dry cleaner will be able to tell the fiber content of an unmarked garment," she warns. "There are too many blends of synthetics and natural fibers to be sure."

# # #

28. HEADLINES THAT SING: WRITING SPRIGHTLY, OFFBEAT, AND HUMOROUS HEADLINES

As a result of the abandonment of rigid headline rules in most papers, you'll have an opportunity to write a sprightly head that might be difficult or impossible to bring off in the face of rigid rules. The label head, remember, is a perfectly permissible form, especially if the story warrants a title with zip that teases the reader into the story.

Most head writers agree that while some have a special flair for picturesque expression, almost any good writer can develop the knack. It takes encouragement, thought, and willingness to experiment. It has even been argued that the bright head is the easiest to write because it is free from conventional rules. Tortured headlines often result from juggling words to fit the rules as well as space.

A few cautions, here, however. There's a fine line between a catchy headline and a banal one. If it doesn't come off well after you've experimented with it, back off and write a straight head. Then, too, some stories are intrinsically funny, so a mere recital of the facts in the headline without any embellishment is sufficient. Others are intrinsically dramatic. Who can improve on "Man Walks on the Moon" or on "Israel, Egypt Make Peace"?

The personality of your paper may dictate to what extent you should strive for the bright head. Two great newspapers of record have quite different personalities as projected by their headlines and major news page makeup. *The New York Times* still is built dominantly on the traditional news headline, whereas the *Los Angeles Times* is more willing to strive for the bright phrase. The tabloid *New York Daily News*, until recently the nation's largest-circulation daily paper, is brash and uses lots of bright and even zany headlines. But not even the *News* tries to make every headline sing.

In every case the most fundamental considerations in writing any headline remain: Does the head give the reader the central idea of the story and lead the reader into the story; and is it accurate in substance and tone? A tricky turn of phrase mustn't trick your reader. Sprightliness does not necessarily mean humor. There's a place for a humorous head; on a humorous story.

As newspapers become more magazine-like in their formats, so also are they becoming more like magazines in their use of title headlines. Typical types of magazine titles in addition to the summary include:

Striking Statement: "Lesbian Mothers"
Direct Address or "You" Statements: "It's a Free Country, Jose"
Question: "Can the Army Hold?" (But remember to use these sparingly.)
Label: "Initiative for Peace"

Similarly, many of the rhetorical devices that play on words are fair game for the headline writer:

Alliteration: "Balance the Budget Boom"
Allusions: "Settling the Star Wars" (on a story about strife at the *Washington Star*)
Puns: "Statistician's Life Dull: It Figures"
Rhymes: "Going Free in Tennessee"
Plays on Familiar Expressions: "There's a Ring, By Jupiter"; "Bearbaiting" (on a story of China's diatribes against the Soviet Union); " 'Don Giovanni' on Film: a Loss in Translation"
Homonyms: "Grisly Fare for Grizzly Bear"
New Uses for Old Words: "Fresh Baked Bread: The New Money-Making Books"

Usually it is unnecessary to use quotation marks around the words you play with. If you find yourself having to do so, the pun or homonym or whatever probably isn't appropriate.

The best puns are those that come naturally and appropriately but still convey the clout of unexpectedness: "All Electric Homes Got Jolt When Rates Rose." All puns are acceptable only when both meanings of the pun word are appropriate. "Market Opens, Poles Vault In," would be acceptable if the people of Poland did indeed rush into the market and the story clearly conveyed that they did.

A touch of alliteration is often helpful: "Ingrid Bergman: A Triumph in Time." Heavy-handed alliteration that merely calls attention to itself should be avoided. It's often a good idea to recast a highly alliterative straight headline lest it be mistaken for an ill-conceived attempt at humor.

Again, the key is your own taste and feeling for appropriateness. This strongly alliterative head was perfectly appropriate for a story on a new automated pepper picker—a little obvious, perhaps, but certainly not clumsy or unsuitable:

Peppier Pepper Picker
Sure Beats Peter Piper

Similarly, self-conscious rhymed headlines rarely are called for unless the subject has a relationship to verse. You may question the propriety of the following headline on an obituary, but Ogden Nash himself might have liked it:

> Laughter Bows to Sighs:
> Verser Ogden Nash Dies

SELECTED READINGS

Arnold, Edmund C. *Modern Newspaper Design.* New York: Harper & Row, 1969. The most widely accepted book on this subject.

Garst, Robert E., and Theodore M. Bernstein. *Headlines and Deadlines.* New York: Columbia University Press, 1961. Though dated, this book is an excellent discussion of editing and headline writing skills by two master teachers and former *New York Times* editors.

Hamilton, Edward A. *Graphic Design for the Computer Age.* New York: Van Nostrand, 1970.

Hurlburt, Allen. *Layout: The Design of the Printed Page.* New York: Watson-Guptill, 1977.

Hutt, Allen. *The Changing Newspaper, 1622–1972.* Montclair, N.J.: Abner-Schram, 1974.

Riblet, Carl Jr. *The Solid Gold Copy Editor.* Chicago: Aldine, 1974. A particularly valuable book on headline writing by a longtime copy editor and teacher of professional copy editors.

Turnbull, Arthur T., and Russel N. Baird. *The Graphics of Communication*, 3rd ed. New York: Holt, Rinehart and Winston, 1975. A thorough discussion of basic typographic principles with which the editor should be acquainted. Includes typography, layout, and design.

EXERCISES

In the following exercises, try writing a nonroutine, bright head to the specifications. If the story does not warrant a bright head, explain why in a marginal note.

Garden

114-1 M Black

Young Republicans are going to pick the posies and meet their candidates Friday at a garden party at Symphony Park.

Perry Jones, a spokesman, said the party which starts at 5:30 p. m. will offer Republicans a chance to meet the candidates, determine who to support and let voters express their wants.

Clean

Patrolman Melvin Whitney was eating his lunch at a drive-in, keeping his eye on a group of teenagers as they watched him and whispered to themselves.

When he left the restaurant, he found about 20 youngsters surrounding his patrol car and braced himself for trouble. However, the teenagers stepped back to reveal that they had washed, waxed and polished the vehicle.

"Now, you've got the cleanest police car in town," one of the grinning youngsters said. All Officer Whitney could say was "thanks."

Garden   *Reject humorous head. Edit facetious matter.*   114-1 M Black

Young Republicans ~~are going to pick the posies and~~ will meet their candidates Friday at 5:30 p.m. at a garden party at Symphony Park.

~~Perry Jones, a spokesman, said~~ the party ~~which starts at 5:30 p. m.~~ will offer Republicans a chance to meet the candidates, determine whom to support and let voters express their wants.

324-1 Metro Black

Clean   *Teen-agers Set Shining Example*

Patrolman Melvin Whitney was eating his lunch at a drive-in, keeping his eye on a group of teenagers as they watched him and whispered to themselves.

When he left the restaurant, he found about 20 youngsters

more

(2/*Clean*)

surrounding his patrol car and braced himself for trouble. However,
the teenagers stepped back to reveal that they had washed, waxed and
polished the vehicle.

"Now, you've got the cleanest police car in town," one of the
grinning youngsters said. All Officer Whitney could say was "thanks."

Jackpot   (118-2 *m Black*)

LAS VEGAS, Nev. -- More than half the big jackpot won in Las Vegas
Saturday will go to the federal government in taxes, according to the
Internal Revenue Service.

A spokesman said IRS will take up to $180,000 of the $280,000 slot
machine jackpot won by a California woman.

Roberta Wheatley took home a check for the full $280,000.

# # #

UFO   (124-2 *m m*)

Arabia has its mythical flying carpet. But we can lay claim to
a genuine flying waterbed.

A queen-size waterbed floated high above the city Friday aftern oon
when a publicity minded store, store balloon waterbeds, 252 Lois Lane,
got more than it bargained for. Lori Christensen, store owner, said

employees had filled the bed with helium and tied it to the roof as
an advertising gimmick.

The wind tore the bed loose. The bed cli-mbed more than 1,000
feet and disappaered over Mt. Majestic. It was still missing late
Friday.

The airport was notified of the flying object.

# # #

Dog Story

(K 124-3 *mm*)

A dog that has no home can be sure of one thing -- it's next owner
will be able to write well.

The dog, a purebred year-old male Springer Spaniel, was found
several weeks ago and the Animal Shelter has searched in vein for
the owner.

Rather than have the valuable dog destroyed, the shelter officials
have decided to award it to the child who writes the best essay.
Children must tell why they want the dog and how they would take care
of it. The contest is open to all residents under the age of 18 but
parental consent is required.

Contact Rodney Fairweather, animal control director, at the
shelter, 2924 Industry Boulevard.

Nest

224-2 𝑚𝑚

If it's good enought for a skyscraper, it's good enough for a nest.

So with her mind made up, a pigeon who'd kept a close eye on the nes Security Office Building decided the "neighborhood" was fine.

A masonry worker, Wilford Fitzgerald, noticed the bird's interest in the small scraps of heavy gague meshing scattered across the one of the upper floors. He gathered a small pile of scraps.

Sure enought, the pigeon built a metal-mesh nest on one of the building's ledges. But when workers moved too close, she left the nest -- and an egg. She built a second nest, a but again construction inched closer.

The persistent bird Friday was working on a third -- again in the "unstable" high-rise neighborhood.

#

INDEX

★★★★★★★★★★★★★★★★★